OVERCOMING INTOLERANCE IN
SOUTH AFRICA

Analyzing South Africa's political culture during the initial years of the country's experiment with democracy, *Overcoming Intolerance in South Africa* provides the first comprehensive study of intolerance ever conducted outside the developed world (and the first outside the United States in nearly twenty years). In a field so heavily dominated by research on stable democracies, this book is a refreshing reminder that political tolerance is crucial to successful democratic politics in every corner of the globe. The research of Gibson and Gouws creates a new agenda for the study of political tolerance by going far beyond simply reconsidering the questions normally investigated by scholars in the West. Instead, the overwhelming focus of this research is on *change*: how the tolerance and intolerance of South Africans respond to both short-term and long-term political, economic, and social forces. Thus, the emphasis of this book is not merely on *what is* in South Africa, but *what might be* as well.

Employing a variety of innovative research techniques – including using actual experiments incorporated within a representative survey of more than three thousand South Africans – *Overcoming Intolerance in South Africa* certainly reports some pessimistic findings. Most important, tolerance and intolerance may not be cut from the same cloth. Intolerance is a "strong" attitude, keenly felt, resistant of change, directive of actual political behavior, whereas tolerance is anemic and more susceptible to change, in part because tolerance holds an uneasy and often unsupported position within the broader constellation of democratic attitudes and values. But the research also points to means by which South African intolerance can be constrained and perhaps neutralized. Gibson and Gouws discover that those who are intolerant can sometimes be convinced – by arguments and deliberations, by the intervention of institutions, and so forth – to put their intolerance aside and let a democratic outcome emerge from political disputes. Intolerance is strongly driven by perceptions of intergroup threat, which are in turn connected to certain aspects of social identities. Anything that reduces threat perceptions and group identities will therefore undermine intolerance. *Overcoming Intolerance in South Africa* is not just groundbreaking social science; it is a thoughtful and nuanced prescription for how South Africa can become more tolerant and thereby consolidate its democratic transition.

James L. Gibson is Sidney W. Souers Professor of Government at Washington University in St. Louis. He has published four books and numerous articles on mass attitudes and behavior and democratization in the United States, Europe, and Africa. He has recently held visiting research and teaching positions at the University of Stellenbosch (South Africa), the Institute for Justice and Reconciliation (South Africa), and the Russell Sage Foundation.

Amanda Gouws is professor of political science at the University of Stellenbosch. She has been involved in numerous survey research projects in South Africa and has published academic articles on political tolerance, the electoral system, and gender politics in South Africa.

Cambridge Studies in Political Psychology
and Public Opinion

Editors

James H. Kuklinski, *University of Illinois, Urbana-Champaign*
Dennis Chong, *Northwestern University*

This series has been established in recognition of the growing sophistication in the resurgence of interest in political psychology and the study of public opinion. Its focus will range from the kinds of mental processes that people employ when they think about democratic processes and make political choices to the nature and consequences of macro-level public opinion.

We expect that some of the works will draw on developments in cognitive and social psychology and relevant areas of philosophy. Appropriate subjects would include the use of heuristics, the roles of core values and moral principles in political reasoning, the effects of expertise and sophistication, the roles of affect and emotion, and the nature of cognition and information processing. The emphasis will be on systematic and rigorous empirical analysis and a wide range of methodologies will be appropriate: traditional surveys, experimental surveys, laboratory experiments, focus groups, in-depth interviews, as well as others. We intend that these empirically oriented studies will also consider normative implications for democratic politics generally.

Politics, not psychology, will be the primary focus, and it is expected that most works will deal with mass publics and democratic politics, although work on nondemocratic publics will not be excluded. Other works will examine traditional topics in public opinion research, as well as contribute to the growing literature on aggregate opinion and its role in democratic societies.

Books in the series are listed on the page following the Index.

We dedicate this book to Nelson Mandela
and all South Africans who have died as a result of
political intolerance.

OVERCOMING INTOLERANCE IN SOUTH AFRICA

Experiments in Democratic Persuasion

JAMES L. GIBSON

*Washington University
in St. Louis
United States*

AMANDA GOUWS

*University of Stellenbosch
South Africa*

CAMBRIDGE
UNIVERSITY PRESS

CAMBRIDGE UNIVERSITY PRESS
Cambridge, New York, Melbourne, Madrid, CapeTown, Singapore, São Paulo

Cambridge University Press
40 West 20th Street, New York, NY 10011-4211, USA
www.cambridge.org
Information on this title: www.cambridge.org/9780521813907

First published 2003
First paperback edition 2005

Printed in the United States of America

A catalog record for this book is available from the British Library.

Library of Congress Cataloging in Publication Data
Gibson, James L., 1951–
    Overcoming intolerance in South Africa : experiments in democratic
persuasion / James L. Gibson, Amanda Gouws.
        p.   cm. – (Cambridge studies in political psychology and public opinion)
    Includes bibliographical references and index.
    ISBN 0-521-81390-5
    1. Political culture – South Africa.   2. Democracy – South Africa.
    3. Toleration – South Africa.   I. Gouws, Amanda, 1959–   II. Title.
III. Series.
JQ1981 .G53   2002
306.2'0968–dc21   2002017416

ISBN 13 978-0-521-81390-7   hardback
ISBN 10 0-521-81390-5   hardback

ISBN 13 978-0-521-67515-4   paperback
ISBN 10 0-521-67515-4   paperback

Contents

Contents

Contents

Tables and Figures

TABLES

Tables and Figures

xi

Tables and Figures

Preface

Regimes attempting to overthrow authoritarianism and replace it with democracy face a host of daunting problems. Citizens may have little experience with or regard for democratic values and practices; elites may be waiting in the wings, ready to steal the state's assets, reimpose dictatorial rule, or both; and the struggle itself may have contributed to a cultural infrastructure very much at odds with peaceful and democratic political competition. It is not surprising that consolidating democratic change is perhaps more difficult than initiating such change.

The problem of political intolerance is one of the most vexing issues for regimes in transition. How does one come to tolerate those who have been responsible for the worst oppression? How is reconciliation possible between those who were masters and slaves under the previous regime? Democracy requires that people with vastly different ideologies "put up with" one another – how do people learn to tolerate ideas they have been taught to regard as evil and criminal? The transition from armed struggle to democracy is never an easy one.

The problem of intolerance plagues all transitional regimes. But nowhere is this democratic deficit more urgent and more real than in South Africa. Apartheid was perhaps one of the world's most strident and insistent ideologies of intolerance. Although apartheid was defeated in South Africa, its legacy persists in many important ways. In the New South Africa, Boers must cooperate with blacks, the African National Congress (ANC) must coexist with the Inkatha Freedom Party (IFP), and whites must somehow come to terms with their minority status and newly found political impotence. These circumstances provide strong challenges to tolerance – indeed, the challenges are among the most intense found anywhere in the world.

This book is about political intolerance in South Africa. We started this project with the assumption that intolerance was widespread in South Africa (and our findings have not undermined that basic intuition). But we came to this research from the objective of studying both *what is* in South Africa and also what *might be*. That is, we sought to take advantage of a number of advances in political psychology and the theory and methods of survey research to assess whether means can be found to induce South Africans to put aside their intolerance and accept their political opponents. Thus, the most important aspects of this book have to do with the dynamics of intolerance, the ways in which people can be converted or changed to accept more democratic positions and practices.

In focusing on change, we (like everyone else in the world) have been inspired by the New South Africa's first democratically elected president – Nelson Mandela. Mandela is an icon of tolerance; his dream of a multiracial, democratic, and tolerant South Africa inspired us throughout our work. Mandela reminds us that tolerance is not the same thing as lack of conviction, that one can believe strongly in the rightness of one's cause, and the wrongness of one's enemies, while at the same time rejecting demands for repression and intolerance. Tolerance requires forbearance, it requires controlling one's natural desire to strike out at one's enemies. Mandela's strength of conviction – both in his view of what constitutes a just society and his willingness to debate openly those holding a contrary view – is a role model that all South Africans must emulate if democracy is to succeed. It is for this reason that we dedicate the book to the former president.

Thousands have died in South Africa as a direct result of political intolerance, and we also dedicate this book to them. The apartheid system was responsible not only for denying political rights and liberties to the vast majority of its citizens, but also for instigating and promoting intolerance within the black communities in South Africa. Apartheid left a horrible legacy for the country, one not easily overcome. No ideas are more in conflict with the ideology of apartheid than that all people are equal before the eyes of the state, that all have the right to political expression, and that the marketplace of ideas is the only legitimate means of identifying more and less useful political philosophies. Many died due to apartheid's intolerance, and we seek to honor those victims in our dedication of this book.

This book is about the possibility for a more tolerant South Africa. Unfortunately, the results of our various efforts to manipulate and change South African intolerance are not particularly pleasing. Though we contribute important empirical findings for theories of political psychology, in the end, our techniques are better at inducing intolerance than tolerance. This has been an extremely discouraging aspect of this project.

It seems that tolerance and intolerance are not cut from the same cloth. Indeed, this is perhaps our most important finding. Intolerance is a "strong" attitude – it is salient to people, is resistant to change, and it has strong implications for action. Tolerance is a "weak" attitude, as seen in the numerous ways in which it can be undermined and neutralized. We did not expect these findings, and we regret them.

Still, our commitments to scientific research on the nature of political cultures and individual political psychology have not wavered. Knowledge is always preferable to ignorance. We only hope that those who read the reports of our various experiments will be motivated to solve the problem at which we failed – how to create more political tolerance.

Many institutions and people have contributed to this research. Most important – the *sine qua non* – is the National Science Foundation. Without the generous support of the Law and Social Science Program of the (U.S.) National Science Foundation (SBR 9424287 and SBR 9710214), this research would not have been possible. We are especially indebted to C. Neal Tate, Susan White, and Patricia White for their enthusiastic support of this research. We also acknowledge support from the Limited-Grant-in-Aid program at the University of Houston.

It is always challenging to try to explain to South Africans why an agency of the United States government would be willing to spend considerable sums of money on an investigation of the attitudes and values of ordinary people in South Africa. The motivation of NSF is our motivation – the belief that the indispensable basis of a better world is knowledge. Few agencies are motivated by such noble purposes. The contribution of the United States to social science is unparalleled in the world; other governments should come to accept some of the responsibility for advancing efforts to understand important social and political phenomena throughout the world, as the Americans have.

Two people have made particularly important contributions to the intellectual foundations of our work: George Marcus and Paul Sniderman. Marcus – with his colleagues John Sullivan and Jim Piereson – essentially created the modern study of political tolerance in their pathbreaking book published in 1982. But more than this, George has been an insightful and generous critic of our work on tolerance, over a twenty-year period. Honest, informed, and tough criticism is the most valuable gift one colleague can give another. George will surely not be entirely pleased to see that we have not always followed his advice. But certainly there is no one whose counsel is more valuable to us, and we are deeply indebted to him for his many contributions to our research program.

Paul Sniderman has long been a dear friend and true inspiration to all of those (including us) who seek to understand something about why people think and act as they do. Few people we know have more useful insights and intuitions than Paul, and few are as generous in sharing their views with others. Paul Sniderman is the consummate scholar. Paul too will not be entirely happy with our stubbornness in resisting some of his recommendations on this manuscript, but our appreciation for his work and counsel – and friendship – is unbounded.

Several colleagues read all or parts of this book and have made most helpful comments. We are especially indebted to Jeremy Seekings, Mr. Justice Albie Sachs, Mr. Justice Richard Goldstone, Jan Leighley, Jim Kuklinski, Greg Caldeira, Valerie Hoekstra, and Andrew Martin. We are grateful for the invaluable research assistance Marika Litras, Vanessa Baird, Kris Guffey, Ingrid Anderson, Marthane Swart, and Grisalda Steward provided on this project. Gibson is also most grateful for the friendship of Chris Willemse, who is responsible for a substantial portion of Gibson's understanding of South African history and politics.

As we note in Appendix A, the fieldwork for this project was conducted by Decision Surveys International (DSI), located in Johannesburg. DSI did an exemplary job on the survey, for which we are grateful. Two individuals, however, contributed beyond the call of duty to both the operational and logistical portions of the work: Carrol Moore and Danny Manuel. Without the thoughtfulness, diligence, and competence (and, we might add, patience) of these two individuals, we are certain the survey would not have been concluded so successfully.

This project soon became a labor of love (at least for Gibson) as the beauty of South Africa and its people became so gloriously apparent (even if South Africa is at once among the most beautiful and ugliest countries in the world). Coming to understand the country and its people has been a true delight.

ACKNOWLEDGMENTS

Chapter 4 is based largely on "Social Identities and Political Intolerance: Linkages Within the South African Mass Public" by James L. Gibson and Amanda Gouws (*American Journal of Political Science* 44 (2), April 2000, pp. 278–92). Chapter 5 is based largely on "Making Tolerance Judgments: The Effects of Context, Local and National" by James L. Gibson and Amanda Gouws (*The Journal of Politics* 63 (4), November 2001, pp. 1067–90).

Cape Town, South Africa
June 2001

Part I Introduction

I

Political Tolerance in the New South Africa

In April 1994, South Africans of every race streamed to the polls to register their choices in the first all-race election ever conducted in the country. The voting in South Africa's first democratic election was the culmination of a long and brutal struggle by the majority of South Africans to share in their own governance. The opening of the political process to all the citizens of the country marked the end of authoritarian rule in South Africa by the white minority.

The implementation of institutions of majority rule should not be understood as the culmination of the country's transition to democracy. Instead, the election marked the *beginning of a process* of democratization. Democracy requires far more than political institutions through which the majority can express its preferences. At a minimum, democracy also requires institutionalized protections for the opportunity of political minorities to compete for political power, to attempt to become political majorities. Moreover, successful democracy most likely requires a host of supportive nongovernmental institutions, often referred to as a "civil society." Without strong institutions capable of checking the power of the state, democracies often slip back into authoritarianism (or "illiberal democracy"); without strong institutions to recruit and nurture citizen participation and to develop a sense of competence at self-government, citizens in democracy often abdicate their crucial roles. Parliaments and presidents are important for democracy, but so too are strong courts, businesses, interest groups, and perhaps even a middle class.

Even beyond institutions, flourishing democracies profit from (if not require) a particular set of cultural values. Democracies experience difficulty in encouraging widespread political competition if citizens are too deferential to authority, for instance. Certainly, the willingness of citizens to put up with their political opponents, to allow – indeed, to encourage – unfettered political competition among all who seek

3

political power through peaceful means is essential if democracy is to prevail. Without widespread cultural beliefs and values that are compatible with the institutions and processes of democracy, it is difficult for self-government to take deep and effective root in a polity. As the distinguished American jurist Learned Hand (1952, 190) observed:

I often wonder whether we do not rest our hopes too much upon constitutions, upon laws and upon courts. These are false hopes. . . . Liberty lies in the hearts of men and women; when it dies there, no constitution, no law, no court can save it; no constitution, no law, no court can even do much to help it.

These are all challenges for South African democratization. Institutions of majority rule have already been established, and a new constitution enshrines the right to compete for political power. But have nongovernmental institutions sufficiently changed their role from before the transition to serve as vital checks on the new South African leaders? Are the South Africans themselves ready for self-government? If ready, are they, or can they become, competent at self-government? Most basic, to what degree does the political culture of South Africa – the beliefs, values, and attitudes toward politics held by ordinary people – impede or promote the development of democratic institutions and processes and the consolidation of democratic reform? At present, the answers to these crucial questions are unknown.

Frankly, we begin this inquiry into South African political culture with a considerable degree of pessimism about the prospects that the country will successfully consolidate its democratic transition. South Africa has many characteristics typically associated with the *failure* of democratization. Democracies do not typically profit from widespread illiteracy among the mass public. Democracies require a certain amount of wealth in society, and at least some minimal degree of equality in the distribution of that wealth. Democracies often fail when confronted with rigid, historical cleavages in society, and racial and ethnic cleavages are some of the most difficult to put aside and overcome. The prognosis for successful democratization in South Africa generated from existing theoretical and empirical models is guarded at best, and, more realistically, is poor. If South Africa succeeds in establishing a thoroughly democratic political system, it will do so against all odds, and its success will be virtually unprecedented in the history of the development of democratic government throughout the world.

Moreover, there is little reason to suspect that the ordinary people of South Africa are particularly well versed in the requirements of democratic self-government in an integrated institutional democracy. Great proportions of South Africans have never had any direct experience with self-government (even if many South Africans are quite experienced at protest). Few democracies in the world have suffered from more political violence than South Africa, and the violence has *not* been confined to the violence of the state against its citizens. Hatred and distrust are in no short supply in South Africa. Some segments of the South African population seem too passive to be effective at self-government; other segments seem too aggressive to tolerate and compromise. The lawless activities of the regime under apartheid (now widely reported through the truth and reconciliation process) have done much to undermine respect for the rule of law. Communalism is often at odds with the liberal individualism that facilitates so many democratic institutions and processes. Most South Africans are poorly educated and desperately poor. The average South African has few attributes that political scientists associate with effective democratic citizenship.

We recognize that contemporary South African political culture most likely has few of the characteristics that contribute to successful democratization (and an important part of our objective here is to document this assertion). But our analysis of democratization in South Africa is as much about *what can be* as it is about *what is*. Thus, this research considers the possibilities for *change* in the beliefs, values, and attitudes of ordinary South Africans. We are certainly interested in thoroughly describing South African political culture, and in analyzing the etiology of political beliefs and values, and a considerable portion of this book is devoted to those tasks. But we also pay a great deal of attention to strategies for changing the political views of ordinary South Africans, exploring several theories of persuasion, and testing a variety of hypotheses about short-term attitude change. In the final analysis, this book is as much about the future of the South African political culture as it is about the state of contemporary South African culture.

We have noted here that our interest is in the beliefs, values, and attitudes of South Africans, under the general rubric of political culture. In fact, one set of values in particular dominates this research: political tolerance. We contend that political tolerance is a crucial element of democratic political cultures in general, but that in the South African case, political tolerance is perhaps more important than any of the other democratic values. South Africa is one of the most polyglot countries in the world; race is certainly important in South Africa, but so too are language, ethnicity, class, and ideology. South Africa has no hope of ever becoming homogeneous; the South African "pot" will never "melt." The only viable strategy for survival in South Africa is therefore tolerance toward the political views of others. Although we are not oblivious to the other components of a democratic political culture, our overwhelming emphasis throughout this book is on finding ways to enhance the willingness of South Africans to put up with their political enemies, to allow open and widespread political competition, and to coexist in their diversity. If we contribute to that goal at all, we will consider this project to have been a success.

In light of the central importance of political tolerance for this research, it is useful to introduce this analysis from a somewhat more theoretical perspective.

POLITICAL TOLERANCE: AN INTRODUCTION

Perhaps the most pressing problem facing regimes attempting a trans-formation toward democracy is the problem of political intolerance. Tolerance is the endorphin of the democratic body politic; without tol-erance, it is impossible to sustain the sort of competition over political ideas that is essential to democratic politics.

Not surprisingly, then, political scientists have devoted considerable effort to understanding what makes people, and regimes, tolerant. The modern study of political tolerance began during a period of intense intolerance and repression in American politics – the era of the McCarthy/Truman Red Scare (Stouffer 1955; see also Carleton 1985). American McCarthyism was characterized by an extreme intolerance of all things left wing, from Communists to "too" liberal movie producers, but it was also characterized by an abiding suspicion of everything different or foreign, and by a pervasive demand for conformity. It is not surprising that Stouffer's path-breaking research on political intolerance has become one of the landmark studies in modern social science.

In the nearly fifty years since Stouffer's research, there have been myriad new studies and new approaches to studying political intoler-ance. Intolerance is not in short supply in contemporary polities, even in the established democracies, and political scientists, sociologists, and psychologists have consequently paid close attention to changes in levels of tolerance and to the factors that make people more tolerant. And what was once a largely U.S. enterprise has recently become crossnational and crosscultural, with important studies of political tolerance and intoler-ance conducted in Israel, New Zealand, Canada, Europe, Russia and the former Soviet Union, and several other countries, as well as multinational projects. At the most general level, these studies have documented con-siderable political intolerance even within largely democratic political systems. They have also taught us a great deal about what contributes to the development of a tolerant political outlook. It is fair to describe this body of research as one of the most developed areas of study within the field of public opinion and political psychology.

But despite the proliferation of large-scale studies of political intoler-ance, many important questions remain unanswered. These include:

Political Tolerance in the New South Africa

- How does political tolerance gain a foothold in polities with a history of governance by intolerant, authoritarian, or totalitarian regimes? Almost all research on political tolerance has been conducted within countries with considerable experience with democratic governance. Citizens who are tolerant are those who have learned about and accepted liberal democracy – majority rule, with institutionalized respect for minority rights. They are the citizens who most fully embrace the dominant ideology of society. But how do citizens who have never been exposed to the ideology of liberal democracy come to value tolerance? What of citizens in regimes that extol *intolerance*, either of the "infidels" or of the "enemies of the state" or "of the race" or of "liberation"? And most important, how do citizens of countries *beginning* the transition to democracy come to embrace tolerance? Tolerance, the most difficult and demanding of all democratic values, is nearly impossible to practice when it requires putting up with those holding the most repugnant political viewpoints, even those who would speak against democracy itself, and in favor of the *status quo ante*. There is a profound and unfortunate paradox of tolerance and democratization: Tolerance is most necessary during periods of democratic transition, when the institutions of democracy are themselves weak, unstable, and limited in their legitimacy. Yet during this transitional period, tolerance is likely to be in the shortest supply. Increasing the stock of tolerance is one of the most pressing needs of democratizing regimes.

- Most research on political tolerance is static; it fails to take into account that, while intolerance may be the initial reaction of citizens to a hated political enemy – their "opening bid" – tolerance sometimes emerges out of the rough and tumble of politics. Citizens can under some circumstances be convinced to change their views and accept a tolerant position in political disputes, even when their initial inclinations are intolerant. Research on political tolerance, like nearly all research on public opinion, places far too much (nearly exclusive) weight on the initial reactions of citizens, and far too little weight on the contextual factors that typically become mobilized in actual civil liberties disputes. Some of these factors may be capable of converting intolerance into tolerance, or otherwise altering people's viewpoints. After all, in many countries in the world, the standard U.S. approach to studying tolerance is neither interesting nor productive since the dependent "variable" is a constant – intolerance is widespread, there is little variance to explain, and the questions of the causes and consequences of intolerance become intractable. If we conceptualize intolerance as an "opening bid," one that can perhaps be counteracted and changed, then the problem

7

of fostering tolerance in intolerant polities becomes an interesting research question.

- One of the corollaries to our complaint about inattention to the dynamics of intolerance is that *change*, short-term or long-term, in tolerance attitudes is rarely examined. Some research treats tolerance as if it were a permanent attribute of people, perhaps grounded in obdurate personality attributes. Yet tolerance does change and it most likely changes primarily in response to environmental cues about the nature of the threat posed by various different groups. We do not gainsay that some portion of tolerance is rooted in relatively stable personality attributes. But without investigating change, no one can judge just how stable or unstable tolerance really is, and whether political systems are forever imprisoned by their cultural legacies.

- Those who study political tolerance pay little attention to the behaviors that flow from intolerant attitudes. It is by now well established that attitudes are often strongly associated with behavior,[1] so our grumble is not that intolerance is irrelevant because attitudes are so loosely connected to action (as in Weissberg 1998). But the fact remains that citizens seem to have little opportunity to act out their intolerance in the political arena. They may express demands for repressive public policy, but this is rare and occurs only among the most politically active segments of the society. Moreover, intolerance is often a matter of nothing more than acquiescing to repressive policy decisions adopted by elites – that is, *doing nothing*. Some researchers have attempted to bring behavior into the study of political tolerance, either by studying live political disputes (Gibson and Bingham 1985) or by asking citizens to respond to hypothetical controversies (e.g., Gibson 1989c, Marcus et al. 1995), but precious little research can be found that investigates the behavioral consequences of intolerant attitudes, even in terms of the reactions of citizens to civil liberties policy making by courts and other political institutions.

- Though very important exceptions can be found, tolerance research generally has been too insensitive to the role of context. By "context" we mean two things. First, national or cultural context is typically ignored, as is evident in research on single countries at single points in time. Second, we mean context in terms of the

---

1 A meta-analysis of 88 attitude-behavior correlations reported in social scientific papers concluded that the median correlation is .33, a sizable relationship since it is based on survey data. See Kraus (1995, 63).

specific attributes of civil liberties disputes. The question of whether "Communists should be allowed to march in your community" strikes us as much too sterile, as devoid of the contextual elements that turn simple civil liberties disputes into major political controversies (as when Nazis attempt to demonstrate in a community populated by Holocaust survivors). In the absence of inquiries into the role of context, we simply do not know what contextual factors are important, how important they are, and under what circumstances they are important.

Thus, much has been learned about political tolerance in fifty years of research. Pioneering studies by Stouffer, Sniderman, McClosky, Sullivan, Marcus, and others have taught us a great deal about the nature of political intolerance, where it comes from, and why it is important for democratic politics. Some questions within the tolerance literature are well understood (e.g., the attitudinal etiology of intolerance). The structure of tolerance and intolerance in some countries (e.g., the United States) has been well documented. And some bold and creative crossnational work has contributed much to our understanding of how national contexts affect and are affected by cultural attitudes such as tolerance.

Still, a host of important questions remain unanswered, and most of these questions have to do with the dynamics of change. Thus, our overriding goal in this book is to examine tolerance *as it might become* in South Africa, rather than tolerance as it exists today.

OBJECTIVES OF OUR RESEARCH

Consequently, we pursue several specific objectives in this research:

- First, we closely examine tolerance and intolerance in South Africa, a country struggling to emerge from decades of undemocratic rule. South Africa's courageous attempt at democratization provides an extremely fertile context for the study of political tolerance. By most accounts, South Africa has no possibility whatsoever of establishing and sustaining democracy. It lacks the level of wealth necessary (even if not sufficient) for democracy (Lipset 1994; Przeworski et al. 2000); it suffers from enormous economic inequality; in some respects, it hardly even qualifies as an industrialized country; and it is riven by the sort of cultural, ethnic, racial, and linguistic cleavages that make compromise and tolerance difficult if not impossible. South Africa presents enormous challenges to all theories of democratization and political tolerance. If we can understand how tolerance can be encouraged in South Africa, we will inevitably expand existing theories of tolerance considerably.

- Second, a portion of this project carefully replicates the research strategies and hypotheses of Western research. We are interested, for instance, in the degree to which threat perceptions contribute to tolerance; in the degree to which intolerance is "pluralistically" distributed; and whether the influential aspects of threat perceptions have to do with general threat to the country – to the South African "way of life" – rather than with the specific and immediate threat people feel from their political opponents ("sociotropic" versus "egocentric" threat perceptions). This portion of our research is not particularly novel, except that we analyze target groups such as the AWB (*Afrikaner Weerstandsbeweging*, the Afrikaner Resistance Movement), rather than conventional targets like Communists, Klansmen, and neo-Nazis. The value of this portion of our research is that it tests the generalizability of theories that have arisen in developed democracies and that have not been widely evaluated outside the West and developed democracies.

- Third, we ask whether intolerant attitudes are sensitive to a variety of contextual factors often thought to influence tolerance judgments. For instance, are promises of peaceful behavior influential in getting people to allow demonstrations to take place? As in some earlier research, we are constrained in investigating these hypotheses by the necessity of using hypothetical vignettes describing civil liberties disputes. But the immediacy of such conflicts in actual South African politics imbues our efforts with more realism than is typically found in such studies. In particular, we make use of a relatively new approach to studying public opinion, experimentally manipulated vignettes. These are experiments within the survey, experiments in which we directly manipulate such factors as the degree of threat posed by the political enemy. There are certainly limitations to this methodology, but its considerable advantage is that it yields a much more highly contextualized, concrete, and realistic approach to tolerance conflicts than has characterized previous tolerance studies.

- Fourth, it is unnecessary for us to spend a rand or a minute trying to figure out whether there is much intolerance in South Africa. Some rigorous research exists (e.g., Gouws 1993), but it is research that confirms the widely shared impression that intolerance is one of the most difficult problems facing South African society. If our objective were merely to document the levels of intolerance in South Africa, there would be no suspense to this book, and perhaps little reason for reading even a paragraph further.

But, as we have said, this book is not only about "what is," but about "what can be." It is about *persuasion and deliberation* – about ways in which citizens can be convinced to abandon their intolerance, to put up with their political enemies. Thus, we attempt to replicate the dynamics of civil liberties disputes within our survey, building debate into the interview. We do not promise spectacular success in this objective – and indeed an important and unfortunate finding of our study is that tolerance is more pliable than intolerance, that persuasion is asymmetrical – but we do report the results of a variety of efforts to persuade the intolerant to become tolerant. It is our hope that some of these strategies provide fruitful and practical means of constraining the widespread intolerance found in South African politics. Whatever the findings, research on the short-term dynamics of tolerance and intolerance provides a useful counterbalance to the largely static and crosssectional methodology that dominates the field:

- Many theories of political tolerance are deeply pessimistic about the possibility of creating tolerant citizens. This pessimism inevitably gives rise to an attempt to neutralize or ameliorate the "bad tendencies" of democratic citizens through institutional designs. Indeed, South Africa is the location of some of the most interesting efforts on this score in terms of the design of its basic electoral system (e.g., Lijphart 1985; Horowitz 1991). But what sort of institutions can block the intolerant propensities of South African citizens? Here, we devote considerable effort to investigating the impact of law and courts on controlling intolerance. If courts are predisposed to protect individual liberty, and if the judiciary has an unusual supply of institutional legitimacy, then perhaps courts can be successful in getting citizens to acquiesce to tolerant public policy. This is a time-honored hypothesis from Western research, but one that has been little investigated in existing tolerance research.

- Finally, anticipating the findings of widespread South African intolerance, what are the *prospects for change* in the political culture of South Africa? Culture is far less static than is typically thought, and especially during periods of intense institution building, the political beliefs, values, and attitudes of people can change fairly rapidly. Indeed, many theorists argue that institutional change is a major determinant of cultural change (e.g,. Muller and Seligson 1994). Consequently, one of our objectives is to assess the degree to which South African political culture has evolved over the period of the late 1990s, and to test hypotheses about the sources of individual-level change in commitment to democratic institutions and processes and in willingness to tolerate unpopular political minorities.

SUMMARY

Thus, we have two overriding concerns in this book. First, we care deeply at the macro level about the prospects for successful democratization in South Africa. But, although we will try to draw inferences about such possibilities, this study is not actually based on macro-level research. Instead, our specific attention here is on individual South Africans, at the micro level. Thus, our second and most important purpose is to assess levels of political tolerance and intolerance, and to determine the causes, consequences, pliability, and temporal stability of these important political attitudes.

THE DESIGN OF THIS BOOK

We have divided this book into three parts. The first part, comprised of this chapter and the next, sets the stage for the analysis. In Chapter 2, we provide an introduction to the South African context. Here we argue that South Africa differs from extant research in one overridingly important way: In South Africa, *tolerance matters greatly, it is a political problem of the greatest salience and urgency*. In South Africa, none of the aspects of tolerance and intolerance are hypothetical – the threats posed by political enemies, for instance, are not abstract threats, but are instead real and entirely concrete. In the absence of reliable institutional protections of the rights of political minorities, tolerance and intolerance become central to the lives of millions of ordinary South Africans. In Chapter 2, we lay out some of this context.

Appendix A is concerned with a variety of methodological details and issues surrounding the surveys on which this study is based. In addition to documenting our methodology, this chapter is important because it offers evidence that survey research in Africa can be conducted with as rigorous methods as are used in other parts of the world. In this chapter, we also discuss the difficulties of doing surveys in a multicultural country characterized by fairly widespread illiteracy.

With the details of our research design set, Part II of the book addresses the nature of tolerance and intolerance in contemporary South Africa. In Chapter 3, we present a detailed description of South African intolerance, relying on the "least liked" measurement technology found so useful in the West. This chapter also addresses important theoretical issues, such as whether intolerance in South Africa is pernicious because it is not distributed "pluralistically." Readers familiar with the Western literature on tolerance will find in this chapter data that can be readily compared to extant research on political tolerance.

Chapter 4 is one of the most important chapters in this book, since it addresses one of the most profound and longstanding puzzles in the tolerance literature: Why are some people threatened by their political enemies while others are not? Threat perceptions, as we document in Chapter 3, are strong predictors of intolerance – but from where do threat perceptions arise? In this chapter, we mobilize a body of theory – Social Identity Theory – that is rarely consulted in the tolerance literature. Social Identity Theory, which addresses the ways in which people come to understand their relationship to the groups making up South Africa's polyglot society, yields some useful insights into the origins of threat perceptions, and hence of intolerance.

Tolerance is typically studied using fairly abstract and context-free measures like "should a Communist be allowed to speak in your community?" Responses to these questions yield useful data for a variety of purposes. Yet most civil liberties disputes, including those in South Africa, are far more contextually dependent. It matters *who* is speaking, *what* will be said, and, perhaps most importantly, *where* the speech will take place. In Chapter 5, we assess how these various contextual elements influence judgments about whether to tolerate disliked political minorities.

Chapter 5 is important from a different perspective as well: It introduces the experimental methodology so central to much of the analysis we report in this book. In this chapter, we employ an experimental vignette – a short story about a civil liberties dispute. This vignette is useful precisely because it is experimental – it manipulates the attributes of the context of the dispute in order to determine how South Africans react (and is based on random assignment of respondents to treatment conditions). We contend that this new methodology can contribute mightily toward understanding many aspects of public opinion and political psychology.

The final third of the book – Part III – takes a much different tack, considering in more detail what the political culture of South Africa *may become*. We investigate three ways in which the current distribution of tolerance and intolerance might be altered.

First, we consider deliberation and persuasion. In Chapter 6, we report on a second experiment, actually a "quasi-experiment," aimed at getting South Africans to change their minds. After asking for an initial judgment on a civil liberties dispute, we present counterarguments to the respondents in an effort to replicate the deliberation that so often accompanies real controversies over civil liberties. We are indeed successful at changing attitudes – although more successful at changing the views of the tolerant than of the intolerant – and we report analysis of several hypotheses accounting for this change. It appears that persuasion is indeed a systematic phenomenon, rather than simple acquiescence to a demanding interviewer. We conclude that persuasion and deliberation are important parts of South African politics, and that understanding the dynamics of persuasion requires additional thought and empirical investigation.

In Chapter 7, we consider a different form of persuasion: the intervention of political institutions. Civil liberties disputes do not unfold in a vacuum; contestants often turn to courts and other political institutions in an effort to secure or to prohibit the exercise of rights, and institutions such as these often provide new – and perhaps persuasive – frameworks for understanding civil liberties disputes. Consequently, we examine the likely effect of a Constitutional Court intervention in a civil liberties dispute, simulating the distribution of opinion that would result from tolerant and intolerant rulings by the Court. We discover that judicial intervention can indeed have a substantial impact on the positions of South Africans, although as with interpersonal persuasion, the Court would be more successful at generating intolerance than tolerance.

In the final empirical chapter of this book, we examine change in political tolerance over the course of about one and one-half years, based on our 1996–7 panel survey. This chapter continues our interest in the dynamics of tolerance, assessing the degree to which South Africans adjust their attitudes in response to a changing political environment. Though some cultural theorists argue that attitudes change very slowly, our findings are quite to the contrary: change is fairly common, and is systematic. We report some success at understanding the sources of this change, tying change to perceptions of the South African environment, including perceptions of crime and satisfaction with the efforts at democratic reform.

Finally, in Chapter 9, we draw both micro-level and macro-level conclusions from our research. At the level of the individual, we consider the implications of our findings for enhancing political tolerance, and contributing to the further democratization of South Africa's political culture. At the level of the country, we speculate about the future of democracy in South Africa, based on our survey findings. In particular, we offer our judgments about what our various experiments on political tolerance portend for the South African democratic experiment.

2

The South African Context

One of the central themes of this book is that context matters for political tolerance. By "context" we mean several things, including the circumstances surrounding the efforts of unpopular political minorities to exercise their civil liberties. But we also mean context in the sense of national context. We contend, for instance, that tolerance has a different meaning and differing consequences in stable democratic societies as compared to transitional regimes. A study of tolerance in a regime such as South Africa can teach us much about what it means to tolerate and not to tolerate in a society attempting a transition to the democratic style of governance.

Our purpose in this chapter is therefore to describe the South African context at the time of our survey. We do this in part to provide a setting for our study, under the assumption that the particulars of recent South African political history are not well known to all. But we have several more theoretical purposes in providing these details. In particular, we assert that:

- One of the distinguishing features of South African politics is the intensity and multidimensionality of political conflict. Many transitional regimes are rent by strong divisions, but South Africa is typically considered to be a "deeply divided" society. Nor is conflict confined to a simple racial cleavage – although race is certainly important – but instead it implicates ethnicity and ideology as well. Consequently, groups perceive each other as highly threatening, with the threat being immediate and real rather than abstract and hypothetical.
- Consequently, tolerance is an uncommonly important and salient issue in South Africa, with controversy over whether to tolerate all competitors for political power being one of the most crucial issues for the consolidation of the country's attempt at democratization. Political tolerance is not an abstract issue; nor is it one of relevance

15

only to those on the periphery of the political system. Instead, tolerance concerns the main political actors in South Africa. Evidence of the consequences of intolerance is brought home daily to South Africans by the political violence that was so common at the time of our survey.

• South African intolerance must be understood within the context of weak democratic institutions. Not only are the institutions relatively new (especially at the time of the survey, 1996), but many still have the complexion of their old apartheid counterparts. Cultural tolerance is especially important in South Africa because the country's political institutions may be unable to defend the rights of unpopular political minorities successfully.

• Finally, the South African mass public played an uncommonly important role in the transition to democracy in that country. Popular mobilization not only contributed to forcing the state to the negotiating table, but it also constrained the options of the opposition leaders. The problem of managing the intolerance of the mass public – in part through "demobilization" – is one of considerable importance for the future of the South African democracy.

We turn now to further consideration of these claims. We begin with a review of the politics of the transition to democracy in South Africa.

SOUTH AFRICA'S DEMOCRATIC TRANSITION

The election of 1994 marked South Africa's transition from a state governed by apartheid and minority rule to one based on the democratic principle of majoritarianism and one person, one vote. That power would be transferred peaceably was unthinkable even as late as the 1980s. The context of the struggle and the transition is important for understanding the nature of intolerance in South Africa.

After more than forty years of coerced racial segregation, the leaders of the apartheid regime began to realize that the price they had to pay to maintain apartheid was becoming unacceptably high. The continued repression of the African National Congress (ANC), the South African Communist Party (SACP), the Pan Africanist Congress (PAC), and other political organizations, as well as the detention or exile of their leaders by the South African apartheid government, caused increasing international criticism and disinvestment, and an escalating economic crisis. Political liberalization could not take place in the context of a continued ban on these organizations.

The end of the Cold War had serious implications for the ANC and the apartheid government since the ANC lost the moral support it had been receiving from the Communist Bloc, and the apartheid government could no longer appeal to a wider crusade against Communism (Frost 1996, 20). The National Party (NP) merely became a minority government that attempted to maintain the status quo in the face of mounting national and international opposition. Changes in Moscow beget changes in Pretoria.

When the apartheid government unbanned political organizations on 2 February 1990 and freed Nelson Mandela on 11 February 1990, it started the process of political liberalization. The government believed it could still control the political agenda because it maintained sufficient cohesion and state capacity to apply repression where and when necessary. Yet, the ANC and its allies had popular and international support, and the initiative quickly started slipping from the government to the ANC.

Throughout 1991, the ANC and the NP attempted to find common ground for the South African transition. The NP wanted a grand consensus on democratic rule through power sharing (with amnesty for people who committed atrocities in the name of the apartheid regime), while the ANC wanted majority rule through a popular mandate from the population, settled through a constituent assembly and not the government's multiparty conference. Compromise was found in a multiparty forum, called CODESA,[1] that hammered out a negotiated settlement in the form of elite pacts (Lawrence 1994, 9). The agreement led to the first free elections in South Africa, in April 1994.

One of the most distinctive features of the South African democratic transition was the influence of popular mobilization (Marx 1997). When foreign pressure in the form of disinvestment and isolation could not dismantle the apartheid regime, and the armed struggle met with the limited success, large-scale mobilization of people occurred in many different sectors of the society: in the labor arena through the unions, in the education sector, in the urban areas through the civic organizations that imposed rent and services boycotts, and in the rural areas (see Cobbett and Cohen 1988). Not only was popular mobilization important in pressuring the white minority government to engage in negotiations, but the mass public also constrained the decisions of the ANC negotiators in many important ways. "Even though the final transition in South Africa was negotiated by elites, pressure from below helped to bring those elites

---

1 CODESA is an acronym for the Convention for a Democratic South Africa. CODESA started the negotiation process in 1991. At the beginning of the process, all political parties participated except for the separatist Afrikaner parties and the PAC. The South African government had two delegations – one representing the government of the day and the other representing the NP.

to the negotiating table in the first place" (Marx 1997, 491). Thus, the South African transition cannot be understood solely in terms of "pact-making" among elites. Ordinary South Africans played an important role in the transition and in politics before and after the transition.

The Context of Political Violence

The negotiation process, which was aimed at drafting a constitution safeguarding individual rights while providing for institutions to regulate an integrated society, took place against the backdrop of serious and ever-escalating violence. *The South African Institute of Race Relations (SAIRR) Yearbook* indicates that 3,706 people were killed between 1993 and 1994; 2,434 between 1994 and 1995; and 1,004 between 1995 and 1996 (see *SAIRR Yearbook* 1993–4, 24; 1994–5, 437; South African Survey 1995–6, 92).[2] Certain areas of the country were worse hit by violence than others. In Natal, the estimated deaths were 800 in 1989 and more than 1,500 in 1990, peaking with 2,000 in 1993. The Reef experienced 1,000 fatalities in 1990 and more than 2,000 in 1993 (Shaw 1994, 182). These figures should give pause to those who speak of the "peaceful" transition to majority rule in South Africa.

As Shaw observes, though violence rose in the year that the transition began and peaked in the year it ended, establishing the death toll is far easier than determining the causes of the violence. It is unclear whether the conflict in South Africa is between contending racial groups, between contending nationalisms (African and Afrikaner), between different ethnic groups focusing on certain primordial ethnic sentiments, or between warring political ideologies (Habib 1997). Very often, ethnic membership and ideology overlap in South Africa, and this volatile combination was behind much of the violence, as in the conflict between the ANC and Inkatha (renamed the Inkatha Freedom Party in 1990). A large percentage of the violence can be attributed to political rivalry between the ANC (and before its unbanning, the United Democratic Front [UDF]) and the Inkatha Freedom Party (IFP).

The rivalry of the ANC (and other predominantly more radical black political parties) with the IFP stemmed from perceptions that the IFP was coopted by the South African government (Meer 1994, 371). Inkatha developed alliances with moderate black leaders, supported capitalist initiatives, and committed itself to working within a white-dominated

---

2 Establishing the exact death toll due to political violence has been difficult. Police sources differ greatly, for example, from statistics kept by nongovernmental organizations. The statistics of the South African Institute of Race Relations are generally regarded as more reliable than most other sources.

system to find a nonviolent negotiated settlement (McCaul 1988, 165). These initiatives – combined with IFP's leader Dr. Mangosuthu Buthelezi's desire for political control over the territory of KwaZulu-Natal[3] – were seen by the ANC as undermining the liberation struggle.

As Lodge (1991, 161) argues, winning territorial hegemony was vital for Inkatha, and interparty rivalry became couched in ethnic terms.[4] For Inkatha, national influence would depend on the strength of its regional base and, according to the perceptions of the IFP leaders, there was no space for political competitors within the party's home territory. While Inkatha rejected violence against the state as a strategy for political liberation, the party's adherents were free to direct violence at their political competitors (Lodge 1991, 162). The potential for violence at the local level found its expression in attacks on the UDF and later the ANC. In the views of many, Inkatha violence was offensive, well organized, and involved fairly senior levels of its leadership (Lodge 1991, 163).

Violence also occurred in the 1980s between the UDF and the Azanian People's Organization (AZAPO). The explanation for this violence is also complex, but some of the major causes were the mobilization of the youth drawing their support from preexisting territorial networks, as well as the dogmatism of the UDF and AZAPO ideologues who would not accept any deviation from their organizations' ideologies (Lodge 1991, 150).[5]

Conflict and violence may have arisen for various reasons, but they inevitably became political as antagonists started to identify themselves with political parties. Shaw (1994, 184) argues that even though the violence had an ethnic "flavor" between 1990 and 1993, ethnicity never became the major cause of the violence. In Natal, the conflict remained between Zulu speakers who belonged to different parties (the ANC and the IFP), but on the Reef, all ethnic groups were the targets of violence. Thus, ethnicity *per se* cannot be considered the main cause of political violence and intolerance.

A plausible explanation (for which the Truth and Reconciliation Commission [TRC] found evidence) was that the KwaZulu government and the IFP acted as collaborators with the South African Police Security Branch and the South African Defence Force Military Intelligence. The TRC, for example, found that Inkatha/IFP colluded with the South

---

3 Dr. Buthelezi was the only leader of an independent bantustan homeland to appoint a commission looking into a regional political dispensation called the KwaNatal Indaba aimed at joint rule of KwaZulu and Natal (a South African province). This indicates the seriousness of the IFP's territorial aspirations.

4 For an incisive analysis of Zulu ethnicity and "nationhood," see Mare 1993.

5 For a superb account of youth politics in Diepkloof, see Marks 2001.

African government by the latter half of 1980 and formed a united front against a common enemy in the form of the UDF/ANC and its supporters (Truth and Reconciliation Commission 1998, Volume 5, 233). The TRC's database also shows that the IFP was responsible for the majority of deaths in KwaZulu-Natal – about 3,800 killings – while the ANC was responsible for 1,100 deaths and the South African Police for 700. The IFP was also blamed for 4,500 killings nationally (Truth and Reconciliation Commission 1998, Volume 5, 232).

Violence can also be explained by the involvement of state-sponsored clandestine forces such as units of the Security Force agitating in communities on a local level. Allegations have been made that different parties, individuals, and paramilitary structures were coopted by a "third force" designed to derail the negotiation process and to destabilize the country.[6] After 1994, the TRC found evidence of the involvement of Civil Cooperation Bureaus (CCBs)[7] in the violence (see Truth and Reconciliation Commission 1998, Volume 5, 237). The objective of the CCBs was to inflict the utmost damage on the enemies of the apartheid state, including the killing of political opponents, without regard for lawfulness (Truth and Reconciliation Commission 1998, Volume 5, 219). On the issue of the "third force," the TRC concluded:

. . . the success of "third force" attempts to generate violence was at least in part a consequence of extremely high levels of political intolerance, for which both the liberation movements and other structures such as the IFP are held to be morally and politically accountable.[8]

6 During the presidency of P. W. Botha, a "counterrevolutionary strategy" was developed to deal with the so-called onslaught against the apartheid state. This strategy led to the creation of a set of structures called the National Security Management System (NSMS), a cabinet committee on security, chaired by the state president, under the purview of the State Security Council. The NSMS initiated counter-insurgency measures through the National Joint Management Centre, Joint Management Centre, Sub-Joint Management Centres on regional and district levels, and (on the most local level of the community) the Mini-Joint Management Centres. At the community level, the mini-JMCs, together with the Civil Cooperation Bureaus (CCBs) – a clandestine security force unit, also called the "third force" – were involved in attacking and killing the local population suspected of being involved in insurgency. See Kotze 1989; Swilling and Phillips 1989; and the Truth and Reconciliation Commission 1998, Volume 5. For an account of the activity of one state employee, see de Kock 1998.

7 The Goldstone Commission of Inquiry into violence and intimidation found evidence of a "third force" as a clandestine security force fomenting violence between opposing black political organizations. See Strauss 1995.

8 We accept Kane-Berman's (1993) caution on blaming all violence on the third force. If too much emphasis is placed on the role of the third force, the complexity of the political violence in South Africa is ignored.

Others have suggested that violence was mainly the result of poverty. Conditions in hostels and townships as well as in rural areas, especially in Natal, meant that violence often stemmed from conflict over the control of resources, even if it was cloaked under the guise of politics (Shaw 1994, 183). Yet, not all poverty-stricken areas were enveloped by violence. Poverty therefore can account for only part of the problem. Nonetheless, most agree that poverty is one of the important contributors to political conflict and violence in South Africa.

It is plausible that the political violence in South Africa was a product of the transition process (and all the previously mentioned causes). Even if the democratization of South Africa did not cause the violence, the political turmoil and conflict associated with the transition made it difficult to extinguish (Shaw 1994, 184; see also Morris and Hindson 1992 for a detailed analysis of violence associated with the disintegration of apartheid). As a consequence, political violence continued in the run-up to the first democratic elections in South Africa. It was hoped that the first free election would curb the violence. But as Shaw (1994, 198) notes, there was no notable difference between patterns of violence in the four years preceding the election and that in the two months before the poll.

Parties blaming one another for South Africa's political violence became a central feature of the negotiation process. The NP blamed the ANC and IFP, and the ANC blamed the security forces and the KwaZulu police, and especially collusion between them. Parties were quite reluctant to blame those under their own control (Shaw 1994, 183).[9] There are different explanations for the violence, but regardless of what they are, the violence and its causes contributed to escalating intolerance among supporters of various parties.

Thus, one of the distinguishing characteristics of South African politics has been the intensity of political conflict. That conflict has often spilled over into violence. It has also begot a considerable amount of political intolerance.

Political Intolerance and the 1994 Election

From the perspective of political tolerance, the most alarming feature of the 1994 election was the declaration of "no-go zones" by members of the ANC and the IFP. No-go zones were areas in which the opponents of these parties were not allowed to enter for the purposes of campaigning, recruiting members, or holding political rallies. If opposing

9 Marks (2001) argues that the ANC lost control over many of its youth organizations, providing an opportunity for some "comrades" to transform themselves into "gangsters."

parties penetrated no-go zones, violence usually ensued and deaths often occurred. This significantly impeded the ability of parties to campaign freely. No-go zones are created when parties gain physical control of areas and all residents are then assumed to be supporters of the dominant party and rivals prevented from operating there (Friedman and Stack 1994, 310).

During the 1994 election, the Independent Electoral Commission (IEC) identified 165 no-go areas in which dominant parties excluded rivals. Opposing parties were completely denied access in 62 "hard" no-go areas. Of these, 39 percent were controlled by the ANC, 27 percent by the IFP, 15 percent by tribal authorities, and 12 percent by the white right wing. The PAC and NP controlled one area each (Friedman and Stack 1994, 310). Early in the campaign, 25 percent of all disruptions occurred in these no-go areas, but the disruptions later decreased as rival parties stopped trying to campaign in these areas.

The no-go zones continued to operate at least until the local government elections in November 1995. The information officer for the IFP, Ed Tillet, provided a list of eighty-seven areas which he claimed the ANC had designated as no-go zones. He also argued that these no-go zones evolved all the time in response to the pressure of the election and that there was constant struggle around them (*The Natal Witness*, 22 January 1996):

An editorial in *The Natal Witness* of 23 May 1995 commented on the prevalence of no-go zones:

... it must be remembered that no-go areas do not only exist in KwaZulu-Natal, nor only in areas which are disputed between the ANC and IFP. They are sadly a fact of life in many parts of the country, and they also restrict the free political activity of the DP, NP, PAC and the Freedom Front. Perpetuating political slanging (sic) matches serves nothing more than to reinforce the maintenance of political "kraals" full of hostile and suspicious groups locked in permanent enmity. Such a situation does nothing to advance the growth of democracy or the evolution of a national spirit in our country.

The no-go zones became a part of the South African political culture and their legacies live on in areas where ideological positions coincide with ethnic membership. No-go zones undermine the marketplace of ideas by making it impossible for ideas to be exchanged freely. Such political tactics obviously deny the rights of free movement and assembly to all South Africans.

The IEC also had to deal with numerous complaints of intimidation and violence; by the end of April, it had processed 3,594 allegations, of which 26 percent were in KwaZulu-Natal, 18 percent in the Pretoria-Witwatersrand-Vereniging (PWV) area, and 15 percent in the Western Cape. Complaints were made by all parties, but most of the charges were laid by individuals rather than parties (only 36 percent by parties and only 18 percent of the individual cases were proved against parties). As Friedman and Stack (1994, 311) argue, the volume of complaints and the fact that they were launched by individuals indicate that many voters felt themselves under threat.

The intolerance and intimidation that accompanied no-go zones found attitudinal manifestations among the citizens of South Africa. For example, attitudinal data from an omnibus survey conducted in KwaZulu-Natal during the period of the run-up to the election showed the following results for the question "whom would you fear most if it became known how you intended to vote?" – Seventeen percent said the IFP, 11 percent the ANC, 7 percent said the opposition party, and 8 percent mentioned their neighbors. Only 1 percent mentioned the South African Police or the KwaZulu Police (KZP). Moreover, 43 percent of the respondents said it would be impossible to live next to neighbors with political views different from their own. It was also clear that rural voters were more fearful than their urban counterparts of the level of intimidation to which they were subjected. Johnson and Zulu (1996, 193) concluded from these findings that violence and intimidation emanating from their communities were the most serious pressures on Africans during the election, rather than exterior forces represented by the police and employers.

More than half of the African respondents (52 percent) agreed that voters would be influenced at least to some extent by political groups controlling the local area. In rural parts of the province, 54 percent of Africans asserted that certain political parties should not be allowed to seek support in certain areas. This contrasts with a figure of 26 percent among urban Africans. Younger and less educated respondents also supported these sentiments (Johnson and Zulu 1996, 194).

In KwaZulu-Natal, a survey showed that 23.1 percent of respondents held the ANC responsible for starting violence and 27 percent the IFP, a very small difference between the two parties (see also Gouws 1996). Few voters blamed the "third force" (Johnson and Zulu 1996, 204). The results also showed that Africans found it very hard to disagree with family members on political issues, and 53.3 percent indicated that they found it very hard or nearly impossible to disagree with politicians. Chiefs were also very hard to disagree with, as were civics and street and area committees. Twenty-eight percent of Africans believed that their community would be hard on someone whose political views differed from their neighbors.

On a question directly testing tolerance – whether respondents thought it was right that political parties might be prevented from seeking support in their area – only 2.4 percent of Indians thought it was right,

30 percent of supporters of the white right thought it was right, and 21.4 percent of Africans supporting the ANC were of a similar view. A large majority of Africans wanted to hear messages of other parties and debates between parties; only 16.6 percent of the African respondents wanted to hear messages from only their party.

On questions of whether members of the party that the respondents most opposed should associate with their friends, operate businesses in their neighborhood, teach at their local school, or hold public protests or give a speech or canvassing political support, tolerance was low. Among Africans, tolerance never reached 40 percent on any of these questions. Tolerance was the lowest among rural IFP supporters. Intolerance increases the closer it gets to being relevant to the communiy. As Johnson and Zulu (1996, 208) argue, during the election, when communities were mobilized for political ends, any nonconforming behavior would not have been easy or safe.

Whereas the consequence of intolerance in other countries is often cultural conformity (see Gibson 1992b) or repressive policies, in South Africa it is more likely to involve political violence, as this discussion has shown. Within some communities, violence has become legitimized and substituted for the procedural norms and mechanisms of democracy. We therefore need to consider the possibility that political tolerance can act as an antidote to conflict in South Africa.

THE IMPORTANCE OF TOLERANCE AS AN ANTIDOTE TO CONFLICT IN A DIVIDED SOCIETY

Tolerance is more indispensable in heterogeneous societies than in homogeneous societies because in societies with deep divisions, the potential for conflict is so much greater. Diversity – represented in differences in culture, language, race, and religion – is a fundamental aspect of politics in divided societies, and these divisions have far more serious consequences for politics than mere differences in public policy preferences. In South Africa, the potential for conflict is embedded in the political culture, in that racial and ethnic groups were artificially separated from one another, leading to misunderstandings based on a lack of interaction with and knowledge of political differences connected to ethnicity.[10] Under such conditions, tolerance is necessary to foster peaceful coexistence.

---

10 The South African government adopted legislation that separated neighborhoods by race in urban areas and legislation that created ten bantustans – consisting of only 13 percent of the land area of the country – for the ten different ethnic groups (excluding whites, Coloured people, and those of Asian origin).

More mature democracies do not, however, necessarily have high levels of political tolerance (see Sullivan et al. 1985, and Duch and Gibson 1992). But the lack of tolerance in these societies has less serious consequences since the procedural aspects of democracy are not directly challenged. People may disagree with certain disliked minorities, but they do not want to change the nature of the regime itself in order to carry out desired political repression. Moreover, the "carriers of the democratic creed" (or political elites) tend to agree on most fundamental democratic values. Political leaders are in general more concerned with adhering to the most important democratic values and to set an example for their followers (but see Shamir 1991, and Gibson and Duch 1991).[11] Thus, whether the mass public supports the civil liberties of unpopular political minorities is of less consequence in established democracies compared to transitional regimes.

Where institutional guarantees are weak or ineffective, the primary inhibiting factor for violent conflict must be political tolerance. While institutional barriers to intolerance in the form of the judicial system (especially the newly formed South African Constitutional Court), as well as statutory bodies such as the Human Rights Commission, the Public Protector, and the Commission on Gender Equality, may be in place, management of conflict at the grassroots level still very much depends on the willingness of ordinary citizens to put up with their political opponents. Without political tolerance, majoritarian democracies can easily degenerate into majoritarian tyrannies (or so-called illiberal democracies – see Zakaria 1997).

The most prominent "carrier of the political creed" in South Africa, President Nelson Mandela, has pleaded for political tolerance numerous times during his tenure in office. For instance, in 1995 President Mandela ordered an investigation into the wounding of three people during an attempt by the IFP to launch a party branch in the ANC stronghold of Clermont. Mandela was deeply concerned about the clashes between the ANC and the IFP. He argued that no-go areas were totally unacceptable, whatever party may benefit from them. As he stated, "The ANC expects of all parties, and especially its own supporters, that they should set an example by according others the same political tolerance which they wish to enjoy themselves" (*Cape Times*, 11 July 1995). The pleas of Mandela and other political leaders were a recognition of the importance of political tolerance in the process of nation-building in South Africa.

---

11 The elitist theory of political tolerance has become contested since more recent findings have shown that political leaders are not necessarily more tolerant than ordinary people (e.g., Rohrschneider 1999; see also Gibson and Duch 1991; Shamir 1991).

In its campaign for political tolerance, the new government has been assisted by nongovernmental organizations (NGOs) that form part of South Africa's civil society. The Institute for Multi-Party Democracy (IMPD) was one of the NGOs whose main aim was to encourage political tolerance. This organization held workshops during the mid-1990s on political tolerance for local political leaders in the different provinces of South Africa (see IMPD Political Leadership Programme – Democracy Manual and Political Leadership Programme – Study Guide, no date). These workshops and popular campaigns were aimed at addressing the impediments to political tolerance, placing emphasis on techniques of political persuasion that might be effective with the South African mass public.

South Africa's social, political, economic, racial, and ethnic diversity is highly unlikely to dissipate in the foreseeable future. Consequently, political conflict is unlikely to moderate, even if overt political violence becomes less common. In light of this diversity, the leaders of South Africa have agreed that political tolerance is essential to the future of the country. Important impediments, however, exist.

IMPEDIMENTS TO TOLERANCE IN SOUTH AFRICA

One of the paradoxes of political tolerance is that tolerance is most difficult when it is most necessary; as Gibson (1996d, 10) has noted, political tolerance is a difficult value to adhere to in periods of transition. During a period of political transition, it may be especially difficult to tolerate one's enemies since so many fundamental conflicts over the nature of the regime dominate politics. Without guarantees that would allow peaceful contestation between political opponents, the price to pay for political tolerance may be too high, since the struggle is about the nature of the political regime and not about ordinary issues of public policy. It is not surprising that it is generally easier to learn majoritarian values than minoritarian values such as tolerance (Gibson 1996d, 11).

Especially in transitional countries like South Africa, intolerance may be of special significance. Dahl and other theorists have long argued that the early stages of democratic transitions are unlikely to be characterized by political tolerance (and certainly the U.S. case supports this hypothesis). The stakes of politics are simply too high, since political struggle focuses on the fundamental structure of the regime, not on ordinary issues of public policy. The prospect of losing is too fearsome to tolerate. And there is also the troublesome problem of retribution for political repression and other misdeeds under the old regime. The tolerance literature teaches us that one of the best and most consistent predictors of intolerance is the perception that one's political enemies are threatening (e.g., Sullivan, Piereson, and Marcus 1982; Marcus et al. 1995). Studies conducted in the United States (Sullivan, Piereson, and Marcus 1982, 191), in twelve Western European countries (Duch and Gibson 1992), and the USSR (Gibson and Duch 1993a) have all found that high levels of threat lead to intolerance. It seems as though intolerance is a natural response to perceptions of threat from one's enemies. To the extent that the perceived threat increases, the likelihood of tolerance decreases. During the transitional stages of democratization, perceptions of threat are likely to be heightened. Under these conditions, it is not surprising that few are willing to "put up with" their political foes.

In the case in which the opposition is not considered the "loyal opposition" but is instead viewed as enemies, it is important to develop what Dahl (1971, 217–18) has called mutual guarantees:

Opponents in a conflict cannot be expected to tolerate one another if one of them believes that toleration of another will lead to his own destruction or severe suffering. Toleration is more likely to be extended and to endure only among groups which are not expected to damage one another severely. Thus the costs of toleration can be lowered by effective mutual guarantees against destruction, extreme coercion, or severe damage. Hence a strategy of liberalization requires a search for such guarantees.

These mutual guarantees do not refer exclusively to institutional guarantees but include as well the mutual trust that is necessary to enable communication and the mutual promotion of goals. As Dahl (1971, 152) argues, because conflicts are more threatening among people who distrust one another, public contestation requires a good deal of trust in one's opponents. Only through the development of at least some level of trust can enemies be turned into opposition.

Perceptions of Group Threat in South African Politics

At the beginning of the negotiation process, the different parties clearly did not trust each other. In the words of Johnson and Schlemmer (1996, 9), a "stand off" existed in which no social or political group was sufficiently dominant to impose its "ideal project" on all the parties. They all had to contend with the second-best solution, with which few could identify. The common ground turned out to be liberal constitutionalism (see especially Klug 2000). Mutual guarantees of security did not arise out of this process.

South Africa is probably one of the few case studies of tolerance in which threat is unquestionably real and immediate. In the case of the United States, respondents in studies often have little if any personal experience with groups that they are asked to tolerate (like the Ku Klux Klan, for example). In the case of Europe, "fascists," with all of their historical connotations, have been used as a target group (Duch and Gibson 1992), which may be somewhat less hypothetical to people. Still, in the South African case, the target groups that threaten people are mainstream political parties with which people have regular contact, such as the ANC, IFP, and AWB[12] (see Gouws 1993).

In the case of South Africa, the political struggle against apartheid determined the context within which perceptions of threat have been shaped. Dissident groups have been viewed as undermining important values – such as the values of a political order that wanted to keep racial segregation in place, or the values opposing racial segregation, which covered a whole ideological spectrum depending on which liberation group people supported.[13] The choices of target groups were determined by this very same struggle, and that is why empirical evidence shows that the objects of intolerance are mainstream political groups. Gouws' (1992) research has shown that whites, for example, oppose the ANC and SACP (for fear of socialism), and that many Africans oppose the NP (because of its opposition to apartheid). These parties are the main political parties in South Africa that were embroiled in ideological struggles.

Threat in South Africa therefore stems from an environment that was tumultuous, violent, and undermining of the political order. And because the apartheid regime banned most of its opposition, there was no space for legitimate political contest through the exercise of civil liberties such as freedom of speech and assembly. In the absence of a legitimate space to compete for power, violence became a legitimate way of dealing with opposition on a grassroots level. In this way, threat became embedded in the very fabric of society.

When threatening conditions present themselves, people usually appeal to institutions to deal with the threat, such as asking for disputes to be settled or demanding that the civil liberties of groups be suspended or in extreme cases that groups be banned. In the case of South Africa, where the majority of the population was excluded from the political system, illegitimate institutions meant that people had to settle their own disputes, often in violent ways.

In the South African case, people have learned through the protracted struggle who their enemies are and why they should be feared. Research by Marcus et al. (1995) has shown that longstanding ideas about target groups play an important role in how political opponents are evaluated.

---

12 The AWB is the Afrikaner Resistance Movement, a right-wing paramilitaristic group.
13 This ideological spectrum covered socialism, Communism, liberal democracy, racial separatism, and others.

"Sociotropic" threat stems from evaluations of how groups may undermine the normative order of a polity. In this case, the ideas of the group present an affront to the community, such as being racist, inciting violence, or threatening democracy. But threat in the South African case may also be "egocentric" since individuals may feel their freedom threatened through their experience with specific groups. People may fear that groups may become powerful or threatening to their way of life. In South Africa, this type of fear is also a reality. Much of the violence in South Africa has occurred between neighbors, friends, and family members belonging to opposing groups, living in the same areas. In some instances, entire villages were wiped out (see Morris and Hindson 1992, 156). The enemy is literally in people's own midst.

This close contact that people have with dissident groups and the threat they pose contribute to the development of strong identities, because such groups provide their members psychic benefits such as security and self-esteem. Strong identities in the face of threat, however, often also produce strong negative feelings toward groups with whom people do not identify. People with strong identities therefore are more likely to be hostile toward outgroups, more likely to be threatened by political enemies (and more often see the world composed of enemies), and more likely to be intolerant of them. This division of the world into friends and foes can have serious negative effects for democracy, especially where threat is real and derived from the political environment. Though this relationship among identity, threat, and tolerance has rarely been investigated, it is of obvious importance.

Threat in South Africa is therefore heavily contextual and multidimensional since it involves a history of violence, longstanding ideas about groups, and social and personal as well as institutional aspects. The context of threat thus frames any study of political tolerance in South Africa.

The Ideological Underpinnings of South African Intolerance

Nor do many of the dominant ideologies in South Africa contribute much to political tolerance. The apartheid state itself was among the strongest advocates of intolerance, but so too were some aspects of the liberation forces. Ordinary South Africans of every color have long been exposed to strident arguments not to put up with their political enemies.

A synonym for *apartheid* is *intolerance*. The apartheid state engaged in countless instances of political intolerance, ranging from banning political organizations, imprisoning dissenters, and murdering its political opponents, to establishing a vast scheme of covert political disruption, trickery, and subversion of peaceful means of political protest.[14] It is thus not surprising that many South Africans learned from the actions of the government that the appropriate response to political difference was repression, not debate.

Moreover, the South African educational system had never been an effective agent of democratic social learning, at least for most South Africans. Social learning is crucial to inculcate democratic values (McClosky and Brill 1983, 232). This refers to the collective socialization experiences of people (Sullivan, Piereson, and Marcus 1982, 156). People learn the assumptions of political tolerance from the political culture of the polity. Where the norms of a political culture are not democratic, people will learn undemocratic values (Duch and Gibson 1992).

The majority of the population (who are not white) received a vastly inferior education.[15] As Nkomo (1990, 2) has argued, the consequences of apartheid education were high attrition rates, high failure, high illiteracy, and a general alienation from the schooling system (see also James and Lever 2000). Emphasis was not put on education to develop higher levels of political tolerance or democratic efficacy. On the contrary, differential education in South Africa led to quite illiberal outcomes since it bolstered apartheid principles (Alexander 1985, 79–91).

Apartheid inculcated a divided political culture based on the separation of racial groups. Findings based on attitudinal socialization research in South Africa comparing students of different racial groups have shown how deeply divided they are on political norms. For instance, Kotze et al. (1994) report that race was consistently the most powerful predictor of alienation, locus of control, and protest potential. African students were more alienated, lacked an external locus of control, and had a much higher protest potential than white students. Booysen's research has also shown how much Afrikaans- and English-speaking students differ from each other in their attitudes toward important political values. Afrikaner students were far more insulated from political change than their English counterparts and were more conservative (see Booysen and Kotze 1985; Booysen 1993; and Booysen and Fleetwood 1994). These findings suggest that no single set of political values predominates within South African political culture, undermining any notion of consensual democratic norms and making the acquisition of democratic values difficult.

---

14 For example, after the Sharpeville incident in 1960, the government banned both the ANC and the PAC, turning them into exile organizations. In 1977, the government banned seventeen Black Consciousness groups. The 1985–6 state of emergency was aimed at destroying the United Democratic Front.

15 Resistance to "Bantu education" was the impetus for the Soweto uprisings in 1976, in which school children started rejecting this type of education.

Social learning is also directly related to the development of self-esteem. Sniderman (1975) has found a strong relationship between self-esteem and political tolerance. According to him, democratic restraint (tolerance) is abstract, and not everyone is capable of abstract thought. People with low self-esteem may not be able to internalize or learn abstract values, since low self-esteem interferes with social learning. Apartheid was particularly destructive of citizens' self-esteem, through its system of differential education, through its ideology, and through other means.[16]

The state was not the only agent encouraging political intolerance among ordinary South Africans. Indeed, to understand political intolerance in South Africa, one must understand how the political struggle against apartheid shaped mass perceptions of rights, and more specifically the right to protest and freedom of speech. These perceptions developed in the midst of a political struggle to overthrow a repressive regime but did not necessarily coincide with the liberal democratic interpretation of rights.

Protest in the earlier decades of apartheid, specifically the ANC-led dissent of 1950s and 1960s, took the form of peaceful protest and defiance, such as direct mass action, boycotts, and demonstrations. This has been described as the "politics of mass mobilization" (Bundy 2000, 63–4). The aim of these protests was the inclusion of the majority of the population within a South African democracy based on the principles of majority rule and one person, one vote.

The Freedom Charter drawn up at Kliptown in 1956 became the guiding principles of the ANC for the duration of the liberation struggle. It combined the language of basic civil rights with social democratic tenets (Bundy 2000, 63). The supporters of the Freedom Charter, known as the Charterists, kept the vision of a multiracial nation united by common civil rights alive.

The banning of the ANC and the PAC after the Sharpeville incident in 1960 led to an armed struggle that changed the nature of mass mobilization against the apartheid regime. Protest was replaced by insurrection and military language through which the opposition (the apartheid regime) became defined as "the enemy," and the aim became defined as defeating and destroying the enemy. This elimination of apartheid

---

16 The levels of psychological abuse under apartheid led to the development of the Black Consciousness Movement in South Africa (e.g., organizations such as the South African Students' Organization, Black People's Convention, and Azanian People's Organization), which had as its main aim the psychological liberation of black people from feelings of inferiority and the restoration of their human dignity (see Leatt, Kneifel, and Nurnberger 1986, Chapter 7; and Sibisi 1991).

was to come about through the delegitimation of the government, the undermining of its military capability through guerilla warfare, the weakening of the economy through international sanctions, and general disruption of the body politic through boycotts, mass action, and stay-aways (Frost 1996, 19). As Frost (1996, 29) aptly describes it:

What South Africa did not have during this phase was a nuanced and normal democratic political practice. The practice of political power was still premised on threats of mass action, violence and counterviolence. In many ways it was still a militarized and polarized political culture.

Political divisions manifested themselves, according to Frost (1996, 30), in the following ways: If whites supported the ANC, they were supporting the enemy; if blacks supported the NP, they were viewed as "stooges of the regime." To aggravate circumstances, the territorial divisions of apartheid claimed its victims in that people believed that allowing an agent of an opposing party into one's area would be tantamount to allowing "enemy agents into the ranks of one's army" (Frost 1996, 30). In this period, there was no sense of "normal politics," including toleration of opposition.

The gap left by the banning of the ANC and the PAC was filled in the 1970s by the Black Consciousness Movement that organized around the idea of psychological liberation from apartheid's institutionalized racism. This form of organization took on an exclusivity that incorporated blacks (African, Coloured, and those of Asian origin) but excluded whites. The exclusion of whites from this type of liberation meant that the inclusivity of liberal democratic rights was, not surprisingly, not a priority.

In the 1980s, the UDF[17] mobilized the population against the tricameral government that, according to a new constitutional dispensation in 1983, included Coloureds and Indians in the government in separate chambers, but completely excluded Africans. The UDF became a front organization for the ANC in South Africa and its strategies of mobilization differed greatly from the strategies of the 1950s and 1960s.

The aim of the UDF was to make the country ungovernable through "people's power." People's power was the power of resistance and included an all-embracing range of actions such as consumer, rent, and transport boycotts; rallies, marches, and stay-aways; and the overthrow of illegitimate town councils and their replacement with civic organizations that provided the organizational impetus at the local level. It also

17 Its membership consisted of hundreds of affiliated organizations. For a detailed history of the UDF, see Seekings 2000.

included the establishment of the organs of people's power, such as people's courts and street committees.

The UDF was indeed successful in making the country ungovernable through waves of rolling mass action and township revolt, but also by mobilizing people in the rural areas. Yet, the same revolt that allowed for the advancement of democratization often led to the dilemma of protest that could not be controlled (Seekings 2000, 158). In response, the state became even more repressive, making it more difficult for UDF leaders to criticize and constrain popular violence (Seekings 2000, 159). UDF leaders later argued that their policy was one of nonviolence, but that violence became the unintended consequence of protest. Whatever the cause, protest and violence were often connected.

Inherent in the acceptance of "people's power" was also a shift from a focus on rights to a focus on power, even though the Freedom Charter was still the guiding policy document. For instance, Kane-Berman (1993, 43) quotes Alfred Nzo, an important ANC leader, as saying that "collaborators with the enemy must be eliminated" even if it includes "necklacing."[18]

Moreover, some openly advocated an ideology of intolerance. As Pallo Jordan, an ANC stalwart, has noted (1988), apartheid is a doctrine that is radically evil and therefore cannot be tolerated. Consequently, Jordan called for "liberatory intolerance." This theory rejects the liberal notion of tolerance – apartheid could not be viewed as just another idea in the marketplace of ideas. Liberatory intolerance divided supporters of apartheid and those struggling against it into categories of enemies and friends, evil and good, and lent a certain justification (if not imperative) to intolerance.

While liberatory intolerance against apartheid may have been a valid strategy in the liberation struggle, it has helped to create and sustain the belief that certain ideas are just not to be tolerated. To silence opposition because of disagreement with their beliefs is antithetical to tolerance as a central value of democracy. The silencing of opposition goes against procedural fairness in a democracy, especially the acceptance of the rules of democracy, such as claiming the right to free speech but also having to allow your opponents to claim the same right.

Two consequences of the "people's war" are important for this study: (1) that it got out of control, encouraging intolerance, and (2) that it provoked violent backlashes, setting off cycles of attack and counter-attack by people opposing each other (Kane-Berman 1993, 45). It is

---

18 Necklacing was a method of killing somebody by putting a gasoline-filled tire around the person's neck and then setting it alight. See Marks (2001, 98–9) for a discussion of some comrades' attitudes toward necklacing.

specifically through the organs of "people's justice" – the "people's courts," for instance – that it got out of control in a way that directly undermined political tolerance. Coercion in participation and boycotts became the *modus operandi* of the people's courts, as the examples given by Kane-Berman (1993, 34) show:

- Four men received five hundred lashes each for ignoring a stay-away call.
- A man was forced to swallow a bottle of tablets he bought during a consumer boycott and died of the overdose.
- A woman who bought fabric for a wedding dress during a consumer boycott was forced to cut it into little pieces.

The "people's war" was also successful in instilling fear into people through the use of *threat*. This could be done through the display of recognized symbols such as matches (reminding someone of being neck-laced). As Kane-Berman (1993, 36) argues, the initial investment in terror pays off by teaching people to behave in ways expected of them.[19]

Thus, the struggle over apartheid during the 1970s and 1980s contributed to legitimizing political intolerance. The ultimate expression of intolerance was of course the ideology of the apartheid state. But the people's power of the UDF often excluded political rivals or dealt with them with violence. Because there was no coherent discourse of rights and the acceptance of civil liberties, many South Africans thus came to accept that the most appropriate way to deal with political disagreements was through political repression. It would not be surprising, therefore, to find that intolerance is widely accepted within all segments of the South African population.

CONCLUSIONS AND IMPLICATIONS FOR THIS RESEARCH

The purpose of this chapter has been to outline the context for our study of political tolerance in South Africa and to highlight the conditions that make South Africa different from other countries. We have shown that political conflict in the country has been multidimensional, with the state and various political organizations using different strategies to oppose the apartheid regime. None of these strategies was particularly conducive to the extension of rights needed for a liberal democracy. The extension of rights of political opposition forms the bases of political tolerance. We

---

19 Seekings (2000, 322) is less critical of the liberation movement than others and argues that there were parallel discourses – emphasizing rights, diversity, and dis-agreement – within the coalition. According to him, the UDF accepted to a certain degree disagreement, self-criticism, and a discourse of rights.

contend that, especially as a transitional society, South Africa needs high levels of political tolerance to ease the transition to democracy; at the same time, however, it seems that tolerance is in short supply.

Certain contextual factors paint a bleak picture for political tolerance in South Africa, including:

- High levels of political violence in the past on the part of the state and among opposing groups through which enemies were clearly and rigidly defined
- High levels of threat from the political environment
- The undemocratic and intolerant practice of creating no-go zones to limit political competition
- The lack of mutual security guarantees among opposition groups
- Impediments to tolerance, as in social learning that legitimizes undemocratic political norms (such as liberatory intolerance), coupled with a breakdown of conventional agents of social learning about democracy, such as schools
- New political institutions, of untested legitimacy and effectiveness
- A mass public that played a major role in the transition and that resists demobilization

These various factors thus provide a context for the analysis of political intolerance that is quite unlike that employed in most earlier research.[20] It would not be far off the mark to say that in South Africa, "context is everything," and therefore this study has to display enormous sensitivity toward the context of threat and how that shapes perceptions.

A NOTE ON RACE IN SOUTH AFRICA

Whatever one's preferences, one cannot write about South African politics without writing about race. Since race is such a salient part of the South African context – and since race is such a contentious concept – we offer here our understanding of the meaning of the concept.

It is common in South Africa to divided the total population into four racial categories for the purposes of research or the explanation of demographic realities and/or socioeconomic conditions in the country, and we follow this practice throughout the analysis reported in this book. As James and Lever (2000, 44) note, "The use of these categories is unavoidable given the fixity that they have come to acquire both in popular

---

20 We of course recognize that the path-breaking study of Sullivan et al. (1985) included an analysis of intolerance within Israel, a country that shares many of the characteristics of South Africa. Perhaps the single most important distinction is that Israel is not engaged in a difficult transition to democratic governance.

consciousness and official business." The use of these racial terminologies, however, differs from the way racial categorization may by understood in other societies. It is therefore important to understand the historical development of these categories, especially the legal boundaries imposed on racial groups by the apartheid government.[21]

The four racial groups are African, white, Coloured, and South Africans of Asian origin (Indian). These groups are also often referred to as population groups, ethnic groups (although this term usually refers to African subcategories such as Xhosa or Zulu), or national groups. The African majority has been known by European settlers by different names over time, such as "native," "Bantu," or "Black," and some of these terminologies were later formalized by apartheid legislation. The Africans were the original inhabitants of the area now called South Africa and were descendants of Iron Age farmers speaking different variants of Bantu languages spoken in sub-Saharan Africa, east of Cameroon (James and Lever 2000, 44). Generally, we refer to these people as Africans or blacks.

The white inhabitants of South Africa (also formerly called Europeans) are descendants of Dutch, German, French (Huguenots who fled France due to religious persecution), English, and other European and Jewish settlers. Though South Africa was colonized by the Dutch and the British in different historical periods, the British colonization entrenched English as the most commonly spoken language.

"Coloured" is considered a mixed race category, although as James and Lever (2000, 44) argue, it is actually a residual category of people with quite divergent descents. Coloured refers to the children of intermarriages among whites, Khoi-Khoi (commonly referred to as "Hottentots"), the San (commonly referred to as "Bushmen"), slaves from Malagasy and Southeast Asia (Malaysia), and Africans (Thompson and Prior 1982, 34).

The Indian population came to South Africa as indentured laborers to work in the sugar plantations in Natal in the late nineteenth and early twentieth century. Yet, they came from different regions in the Indian subcontinent, adhered to different religions, and spoke different lan-

21 The editor of a special issue of *Daedalus* focused on South Africa had this to say about the use of racial terms in the articles in the journal: "Many of the authors in this issue observe the South African convention of dividing the country's population into four racial categories: white (of European descent), colored (of mixed ancestry), Indian (forebears from the Indian subcontinent), and African. The official nomenclature for 'Africans' has itself varied over the years, changing from 'native' to 'Bantu' in the middle of the apartheid era, and then changing again to 'black' or, today, 'African/black.' All of these terms appear in the essays that follow." See Graubard 2001, viii.

guages, so that they, like Coloured people, are not a homogeneous group. We refer to these people as South Africans of Asian origin, despite the fact that some Coloured people are technically of Asian origin.

When the NP came to power in 1948, it embarked on a legislative process aimed at securing white political power and keeping the white population group "pure." The Population Registration Act, 30, of 1950 (and its various amendments), legislated that all citizens of South Africa be classified according to racial or ethnic origins. Racial origin was determined by the natural father's classification (yet the policy was not consistently implemented, because when the father in a mixed-race marriage was African, the offspring was classified African, but if the father was white, the offspring was classified Coloured; see Brookes 1968, 24). Additional criteria were acceptance in the community and appearance. A 1967 amendment introduced descent (Thompson and Prior 1982, 36). Very often, mixed race families were split up due to the hues of their skin, causing immense suffering (Horrell 1982, 2).

The original act referred to the main groups as "white," "coloured," and "Native." In 1951, the South African government replaced "Native" with "Bantu," and in 1978 it officially changed the term to "Black." The most commonly employed term now used for the original inhabitants of South Africa is "African," while "Black" is often used inclusively to refer to everyone who is not white (and the term originated as a negative reaction to referring to groups other than whites as "non-whites"). In this sense, "black" is sometimes misleading, since it refers to Africans, Coloured people, and those of Asian origin. ("Black" is rarely if ever used in this way in this book.) The enforcement of the Population Registration Act was very important since it was the foundation for the Group Areas Act, 41, of 1950 (legalizing separate neighborhoods for each racial group), and the Separate Amenities Act, 49, of 1953 (legalizing separate public facilities for the different racial groups).[22]

A direct response to the fixed racial categorization of the apartheid regime was the ideological endorsement of nonracialism by the ANC. This policy rejected race as a social construct, supporting instead the underlying principle of equality for all, in which appearance and descent would play no role. Yet, the political and sociological realities that were created under apartheid – such as homogeneous neighborhoods and segregated schools, now coupled with political strategies such as Affirmative Action to undo past discrimination – still reinforce and politicize a racial consciousness, involving these specific categorizations

---

22 While many racial communities remained separate during the first part of the twentieth century, others developed into vibrant multicultural communities (such as District Six in Cape Town, for example).

(James and Lever 2000, 45). From the perspective of research on South Africa's political culture(s), it could therefore be justifiably argued that the subjective experience of these racial categorizations, the class positions, and sociological and historical realities of their members justify the general practice of reporting our results separately by these racial groupings.

Part II   South African Intolerance as It Is

3

The Nature of Political Intolerance in South Africa

One of the most vexing problems facing regimes attempting democratic transformations is political intolerance. With majoritarian sentiment at its peak, with political conflict intensified by struggles over the fundamental contours of the new regime, and with dark fears of the *status quo ante* returning, that intolerance would be rife is not altogether unexpected. But without tolerance, it is all too easy for transitional regimes to devolve, first, into majority tyrannies, and second, into simple, old-fashioned tyrannies.

Consequently, social scientists have devoted considerable effort to understanding the causes and consequences of political intolerance.[1] Defining tolerance as the willingness to allow all groups, irrespective of their political viewpoints, to compete for political power through legal and peaceful means, and relying upon a research tradition well established within relatively democratic polities, social scientists have investigated political intolerance as a crucial attribute of the political cultures of polities (see Almond and Verba 1963, 1980). The tool of this research is the opinion survey, and surveys have been conducted of mass and elite

---

1 Highlights in a fairly voluminous literature on political intolerance include Stouffer 1955; Prothro and Grigg 1960; McClosky 1964; Sniderman 1975; Lawrence 1976; Nunn, Crockett, and Williams 1978; Sullivan, Piereson, and Marcus, 1979, 1982; Gibson and Bingham 1982; McClosky and Brill, 1983; Shamir and Sullivan 1983; Caspi and Seligson 1983; Gibson and Bingham 1985; Sullivan et al. 1985; Gibson 1988, 1996c, 1997a; Barnum and Sullivan 1989; Gibson 1989a, 1989b; Fletcher 1989; Bobo and Licari 1989; Peffley and Sigelman 1989; Sniderman et al. 1989; Carnaghan and Bahry 1990; Fletcher 1990; Gibson and Duch 1991; Sniderman et al. 1991; Shamir 1991; Kuklinski et al. 1991; Guth and Green 1991; Gibson 1992a, 1992b; Duch and Gibson 1992; Gibson, Duch, and Tedin 1992; Gibson and Duch 1993a; Gouws 1993; Kuklinski et al. 1993; Kaplan 1995; Marcus et al. 1995; Bahry, Boaz, and Gordon 1997; and Gibson 1996c, 1997b, 1997c, 1998a, 1998b, and 2002.

publics in many countries throughout the world in an effort to assess the ways in which intolerance affects democratic governance.

Nowhere is the problem of political intolerance more pressing than in South Africa. South Africa began its attempt at democratization in the early 1990s, with the capstone of the initiation stage being the free elections of April 1994 that brought Nelson Mandela and the African National Congress (ANC) to power. By the end of the century, virtually all of the institutional components of democratic government had been installed in South Africa, including a strong constitution, an effective and representative parliament, and an independent and powerful judiciary. What has been slower to develop are the cultural components of democracy, and especially political tolerance. The lack of tolerance among South Africans may well be the most serious threat to consolidating democracy in the country.

Consequently, our purpose in this chapter is to investigate political intolerance within the South African mass public. We begin our analysis with a discussion of the significance of intolerance in the political culture of South Africa. Then we start the empirical portion of our research by assessing contemporary levels of intolerance. We also consider the degree to which intolerance is "pluralistically" distributed, since pluralistic intolerance is far less pernicious than focused intolerance. Our findings on both the level and distribution of intolerance in South Africa will not be welcomed by those favoring democratic governance.

We next consider the role of threat perceptions in fostering intolerance. Following a vast literature, we contend that a major key to dispelling intolerance is to reduce the threat that people perceive from their political enemies. We therefore investigate the connection between threat perceptions and intolerance with some vigor.

TOLERATING SOUTH AFRICANS?

By the accounting of macro-level statistical models, South Africa has little chance at a successful transition to democratic government (see Giliomee and Schlemmer 1994). It has little wealth, and what wealth exists is distributed quite unequally. It is one of the most culturally heterogeneous countries in the world, with the "simple" divisions over race being vastly complicated by linguistic, ethnic, and ideological differences. If wealth, economic equality, and subcultural homogeneity are the key predictors of a successful democratic transition,[2] then South Africa may well go the route of many failed African transitions.

2 See, for example, Lipset, Seong, and Torres 1993; Huntington 1991; Lipset 1994; and Diamond and Linz 1989.

Unless one is willing to endorse the policy of "ethnic cleansing," the only viable solution to subcultural pluralism is political tolerance. Ordinary people must come to accept that the marketplace of ideas must be a free market, with equal access to all ideas, even despicable and "wrong" ideas. This is certainly a difficult lesson to learn; putting up with one's enemies is something that people in even the most established democracies are often unwilling to do (e.g., Gibson 1997a). But without tolerance, efforts to democratize are unlikely to succeed.[3]

The system of apartheid contributed mightily to the uneven development of a democratic political culture in South Africa. Indeed, a principal heritage of apartheid is the unequal evolution of South Africa's political culture. As Esterhuyse (2000, 148) notes, "Apartheid left its mark on three fundamental dimensions of the South African political system: its value systems, its structure and its political culture." de Lange (2000, 29) agrees: "a lingering 'apartheid memory' continues to restrict the development of trust and allegiance in the new political dispensation and its institutions." Political consciousness developed disproportionately among South Africa's four main racial communities – Africans, whites, Coloured South Africans, and South Africans of Asian origin – with some acquiring the attitudes and skills necessary to playing the role of a citizen in a democratic state, but with others picking up few of the attributes of democratic citizens. Most South Africans (the non-white or "black" majority) were never taught the values necessary to participate in democratic politics – political efficacy, for instance, is as unequally distributed in contemporary South Africa as is housing – so it would not be surprising to find that vast inequalities in democratic values characterize the country, especially in the early days of the transition.[4] Thus, differences in attitudes toward democracy in a deeply divided society may not "naturally" occur but may instead be a product of state public policy.

---

3 We acknowledge that institutions may be designed to mitigate the impact of cultural intolerance (see Horowitz 1991; Gibson 1990). Nonetheless, if intolerance results in citizens repressing *one another*, rather than formal political institutions imposing limits on political freedom, then irrespective of institutional constraints, intolerance can significantly undermine the free and open exchange of ideas that is essential to democratic politics (see Gibson 1992b).

4 This is not to deny that many black South Africans learned well the skills of political protest, nor that institutions of self-governance and civil society were somewhat effective at the local level. Nor is it to assert that the internal governance of the ANC (a banned political party for most of the last forty years) necessarily precluded real political participation. But for the vast majority of blacks, the most important political decisions affecting their lives were made without their participation or consent, and without any political accountability. Such a system of governance is unlikely to lead to self-governance skills.

Not surprisingly, then, political intolerance continues to shape much of South African politics. For instance, in KwaZulu-Natal, one of the most violence-ridden provinces in South Africa, the death toll from political conflict in 1995 was as high as 110 people per week. In May 1995, the Inkatha Freedom Party (IFP) declared eighty-four no-go areas, claiming retaliation for the ANC's no-go areas (Gouws 1996, 28).

In July 1997, a explosive incident of political intolerance once more shook the country and evoked public outcries. In the town of Richmond, in KwaZulu-Natal, an ANC member was expelled from the party. Just before the by-election, he joined a newly formed opposition party called the National Consultative Forum (NCF). He did so in the belief that NCF candidates could win the majority of the wards in this town. The ANC, however, won the election. The day after the election, five elected ANC council members were shot and killed by assailants thought to be supporters of the NCF. ANC members now had to move around under armed protection, and supporters of the different parties are said to be living in two separate "refugee camps." Some are leaving town in fear of their lives (*Weekly Mail and Guardian*, 25–31 July 1997).

Not all of South African politics is characterized by this sort of intolerance and political violence. Yet the unwillingness of many to allow free and open access to the political marketplace is a problem of considerable importance for the struggling South African democracy.[5] Consequently, our objective in this chapter is to examine the nature of political intolerance within the South African mass public. Despite some earlier scientific work (and much anecdotal evidence), little is known about the extent to which South Africans are willing to put up with their political enemies. Our survey data reveal an interesting, but complicated, picture of intolerance in the country.

THE MEANING OF INTOLERANCE: CONCEPTUAL DISCUSSION

Previous scholars have devoted a great deal of attention to conceptualizing political intolerance (see especially Sullivan, Piereson, and Marcus

---

5 In a survey conducted by the Institute for a Democratic South Africa (Idasa) in October 1994, a few months after the election, attitudinal levels of political intolerance were still high. In Gauteng (a South African province), 65 percent of the respondents would not allow their target groups free speech and 61 percent would not allow public protest. In the North West Province, 75 percent would not allow free speech and 71 percent would not allow public protest. And in the Northern Province, the percentage who would not allow free speech was 66 percent, with 77 percent not supporting the right to public protest, and 74 percent opposing canvassing for votes (see Gouws 1996, 29).

Table 3.1. *The Relationship between Tolerance and Antipathy*

	Attitude toward the Political Group or Idea		
Tolerance	Friend	Neutral – Indifferent	Foe
Allow activity	(a)	(b)	(c) tolerance
Not allow activity	(d)	(e)	(f) intolerance

1982), and by now the basic contours of the concept are well understood. *To tolerate is to allow.* But as simple as this seems, a host of difficult issues surrounds the conceptualization of political tolerance. To tolerate is to allow, but thorny questions arise when we try to specify *what* should be allowed, *by whom*, and *under what conditions*.

A widely accepted definition of political tolerance claims that tolerance is putting up with that with which one disagrees (Sullivan, Pierson, and Marcus 1982). Crucial to this definition is the so-called *objection precondition*: One cannot tolerate (i.e., the word does not apply) that of which one approves. Tolerance is forbearance; it is the restraint of the urge to repress one's political enemies. Democrats do not tolerate democrats, but they may or may not tolerate Communists. Tolerance, then, refers to allowing political activity (considered in the following paragraphs) by one's political enemies.

Table 3.1 outlines the relationship between tolerance and antipathy. One can view a political movement or its supporting ideology as a friend or a foe, or one can be indifferent toward it. Those who would allow political activity by a foe (cell *c*) we would readily deem to be tolerant. Similarly, those who would not allow a foe to engage in political activity (cell *f*) are easily categorized as intolerant. But what of the other cells in the table? Cell *a* would clearly not qualify as an instance of tolerance (just as one is rarely said to "tolerate" a fine South African shiraz).[6] This is the point most forcefully made by Sullivan, Pierson, and Marcus (1982): We should regard only those who would allow political activity as tolerant when allowing is mixed with at least some antipathy toward the group or idea.

Presumably, cell *d* would not occur very often – why would one refuse to allow one's political friends to engage in political activity?[7] However, those who would not allow friendly groups to engage in such activity would most likely not allow their enemies such behavior either, and

6 Sniderman et al. (1989, 26) refer to these people as "pseudo-tolerant."
7 For analyses relevant to this cell, see Barnum and Sullivan 1989 and Hurwitz and Mondak forthcoming.

therefore it would not be too far off the mark to argue that cell *d* is an instance of intolerance, albeit a special and uncommon one.

How does neutrality toward a group or idea affect our understanding of tolerance? To deny political activity to a group about which one is neutral is intolerant because those who would not allow neutral groups to act surely would not allow hated groups to act. Thus, we have little difficulty in describing cell *e* as composed of intolerant people. But should those in cell *b* be considered tolerant? Sullivan, Piereson, and Marcus (1982) would probably say no, because there is no objection to the group, and we probably agree.

Those who oppose the group – cells *c* and *f* – are easily characterized as tolerant or intolerant, respectively, because the antipathy precondition is satisfied. These are the most readily understood cells of the table. Thus, political intolerance is fairly easy to measure so long as we ensure that there is at least some negative affect toward the group about which the respondent is questioned.

But what exactly must the tolerant allow? Obviously, every society places some limits on the kinds of political activities in which groups can engage. Few would claim that tolerance requires putting up with terrorism or other acts of political violence. But there is a wide range of other actions, short of terrorism, about which people disagree. The difficult part is to identify a principled position from which tolerated behaviors can be derived.

Perhaps democratic theory can be of some assistance here. When we speak of tolerance, we mean in every instance "political" tolerance. More specifically, we mean "democratic political tolerance," or to be even more specific, "liberal democratic political tolerance." That is, our understanding of tolerance derives primarily from theories of liberal democracy. The key defining characteristic of a liberal democracy is that all political movements have institutionalized opportunities to compete for political power – that is, to try to become a political majority. With Dahl, we believe that democracy is a system that must grant unimpaired opportunities for all full citizens

- To formulate their preferences
- To signify their preferences to their fellow citizens and the government by individual and collective action
- To have their preferences weighed equally in the conduct of the government – that is, weighted with no discrimination because of the content or source of the preference (Dahl 1971, 1, 2)

Unless all political interests have the opportunity to persuade the majority, the marketplace of ideas is unnecessarily constrained and competition among ideas cannot flourish. Without such competition, citizens may be denied the opportunity to support the political movements of their choice, political freedom may be lost, and democratic accountability may be undermined. Thus, the activities that must be tolerated in a liberal democracy are those that involve political competition – organizing, taking one's message to the people, competing in elections, and so forth.[8]

Generally, the tolerance literature is indeed primarily interested in such activities. For instance, the U.S. General Social Survey (GSS) routinely asks about whether speeches ought to be allowed, and whether a book advocating unpopular ideas should be removed from a public library.[9] Speeches and books are obviously means by which groups try to convince others of the rightness of their ideas.

But the GSS also asks whether members of disliked political groups ought to be allowed to teach in a college or university. Democracies probably profit from having professors with widely diverse political viewpoints (and certainly academic freedom profits), but whether democracy *requires* that people of all viewpoints be allowed to be university

8 Jung and Shapiro (1995) have argued that a serious flaw in the interim institutions negotiated as part of the transition to democracy in South Africa was the absence of an institutionalized political opposition. They argue that "democratic systems rely on institutionalized oppositions, and it is doubtful that any regime could long survive as minimally democratic without them," and, "Such opposition requires both the permissive freedoms of speech and association, and the presence of institutions and practices that make it possible for counterelites to organize and inform themselves so as to be able to contest for power" (1995, 272). The government of national unity instituted by the 1993 Constitution was antithetical to the development of such an opposition. See also Koelble and Reynolds (1996), who object to this argument, and the reply of Shapiro and Jung (1996). In any event, the government of national unity was short-lived.

9 Note that the item does not ask whether books should be purchased, decisions that are legitimately shaped by many factors (all books do not have an absolute right to be purchased), but instead focuses on removing a book that has already been placed into circulation. There is in fact a difference between the two stimuli, based on Gibson's two-wave panel on tolerance conducted in the United States in 1987. Among those giving a tolerant response at t_1 to a question about whether a book written by an advocate of military dictatorship should remain in the library, 78.0 percent were tolerant at t_2 when asked the identical question, but only 66.0 percent of the t_2 sample were tolerant when asked whether they would support the purchase of such a book. Among those intolerant at the first interview, 29.4 percent did not favor removing the book (at the second interview), while only 20.2 percent favored purchasing the book. Thus, tolerance decreases by roughly 10 percentage points when the stimulus referred to the decision about whether to purchase a disliked book.

professors is not so clear to us.[10] So long as the activities about which we ask are clearly directed as competition in the marketplace of political ideas, then we are on safe ground in treating those who do not allow such activity as intolerant.

Finally, there is the matter of context. Few democratic theorists would deny to the state some rights to regulate the context within which political views are expressed. Considerations of public safety and convenience are relevant; it seems quite legitimate not to close motorways so that groups can demonstrate. Yet invariably states attempt to quash freedom under the guise of regulation, and the threat of a disorderly reaction from onlookers at demonstrations is often used to justify the prohibition of marches (the so-called heckler's veto – see Gibson and Bingham 1985). Democracies require that any restrictions upon political expressions be applied equally to all political points of view, and that such restrictions be reasonable.

One other theoretical issue is of importance. Though our concern for tolerance is heavily molded by democratic theory, we do not *equate* democracy and tolerance. A reasonable hypothesis is that as political tolerance increases, the likelihood of successful democracy increases. But the relationship may not be entirely linear (see Gibson and Bingham 1985). At very high levels of tolerance, for instance, an increment in tolerance may not produce an increment in democracy, and indeed some even believe that at extreme levels, tolerance undermines democracy (see Rohrschneider 1996). We do not care to enter that debate, and in fact it is unnecessary to do so since South Africa is in no danger whatsoever of approaching extreme levels of tolerance. We simply stipulate that tolerance and democracy are not the same thing, and hypothesize that under most but perhaps not all circumstances, tolerance contributes to democratic government.

Thus, tolerance means putting up with that with which one disagrees. It means allowing one's political enemies to compete openly for political power. A tolerant citizen is one who would not support unreasonable or discriminatory governmental restrictions on the rights of groups to participate in politics. This conceptualization offers some pretty clear guidelines for operationalizing political tolerance.

---

10 The problem is compounded with this item because respondents are often left wondering whether the member of the group will teach the group's ideology. For many, there is a big difference between a fascist teaching chemistry and a fascist teaching fascism in a political science or philosophy department, and respondents are often confused about this aspect of the question.

The Nature of Intolerance in South Africa

MEASURING POLITICAL INTOLERANCE

Precursors to Intolerance – The Objection Precondition

Nearly all who have studied political tolerance in the past impose some sort of antipathy precondition: One cannot tolerate something one likes. A valid measure therefore requires that respondents be presented with a stimulus that is objectionable, a group that is disliked. Assessing attitudes toward various political groups is therefore one of the first empirical tasks in investigating political intolerance.

We asked our survey respondents to express their views toward a variety of competitors for political power in contemporary South Africa. (For details on the survey, see Appendix A.) The groups were selected in part on the basis of earlier research in South Africa (see Gouws 1993) and in part by our assessment of which groups were likely to be common targets of intolerance. The distribution of affect toward the groups – measured on an eleven-point scale – is reported in Table 3.2.

Table 3.2 reports both the percentage of respondents rating the group at the most extreme disliked point on the continuum, as well as the means and standard deviations for the affect scale.[11] Clearly, the most disliked group active in South African politics is the AWB – the Afrikaner Weerstandsbeweging (Afrikaner Resistance Movement, AWB), a far-right movement led by the notorious Eugène Terre Blanche. Two-thirds of the South Africans rate the AWB at the most extreme point on the antipathy scale. This radical group generates a great deal of hatred among South Africans.

The AWB is clearly on the fringe of the South African political spectrum (and may even qualify as a terrorist group). On the other hand, the second most hated group in South Africa – the Inkatha Freedom Party (IFP) – is far from extreme; it is one of the primary competitors for political power in South Africa and was represented in the government at the time of our survey. Over one-half of the respondents rated the IFP as extremely disliked.

Large percentages of South Africans also hate Afrikaners and (perhaps surprisingly, in light of their irrelevance to the intense political struggles in South Africa) homosexuals. Antipathy toward Afrikaners – the architects of apartheid – is perhaps understandable, but the reason for the

---

11 Note that we explicitly encouraged the respondents to tell us when they had no opinion toward the group. For purposes of this analysis, those without opinions were scored at the neutral point (6) on the eleven-point scale.

Table 3.2. *The Distribution of Affect toward Political Groups in South Africa, 1996*

Group	% Dislike Very Much	Mean[a]	Std. Dev.	N	% Most Disliked[b]
African National Congress & Supporters	8.3	8.5	3.4	2,514	6.4
Trade Unionists	8.6	7.0	3.1	2,524	.7
Muslims	13.9	5.5	2.8	2,525	.9
South African Communists	18.8	5.7	3.2	2,523	4.4
Advocates of a One-Party State	20.2	5.5	3.4	2,524	1.9
Pan-Africanist Congress & Supporters	20.4	5.3	3.1	2,524	3.5
Democratic Party & Supporters	22.7	4.4	2.7	2,525	1.3
National Party & Supporters	25.9	4.7	3.2	2,525	4.1
Afrikaners	40.6	3.9	3.2	2,525	10.2
Homosexuals	40.9	3.5	2.7	2,518	3.6
Inkatha Freedom Party & Supporters	57.3	2.9	2.8	2,515	25.2
Afrikaner Resistance Movement (AWB) & Supporters	66.2	2.1	2.0	2,526	34.8
Other	–	–	–	–	.7
None	–	–	–	–	2.2

Notes:

[a] High scores indicate greater positive affect.

[b] This is the percentage of respondents naming the group as most disliked.

intense antipathy toward homosexuals is less clear.[12] With so many South Africans expressing negative attitudes toward homosexuals, it is perhaps fortuitous that the South African constitution, unlike any other constitution in the world, gives political protection to gays.

After these four most disliked targets, a variety of groups draws the antipathy of smaller segments of the South African population. About

12 Expressions of homophobia are relatively common among South Africans. More traditional African South Africans insist that homosexuality does not exist among Africans, a view endorsed by the president of neighboring Zimbabwe, Robert Mugabe. Neither are whites in general supportive of the gay movement in South Africa.

one-quarter of the sample dislikes the National Party (NP) a great deal; slightly less hate the Democratic Party, the Pan Africanist Congress, and advocates of a one-party state. Unlike in many Western countries, Communists are not widely hated (due surely to their role in the struggle against apartheid). The least hated group in South Africa (of those about which we asked) is the ANC, with only 8.3 percent of the respondents giving the ANC the most extreme score on the antipathy scale.

Most South Africans express extreme hatred for one of these groups. Only 8.5 percent of the respondents failed to rate any group at the most extreme disliked score (1); nearly one-half of the respondents rated four or more groups at 1 on the eleven-point scale. Conversely, only 32.1 percent of the respondents did not assign the most positive score to one of the groups, with a plurality (35.5 percent) naming only a single group as extremely liked. The extent of antipathy toward groups is *not* strongly dependent upon one's racial/linguistic group, although white Afrikaners hate significantly more groups on this list than do others, and South Africans of Asian origin hate significantly fewer groups.

As we expected, racial and ethnic differences in affect toward specific groups are substantial. How one feels about Afrikaners is extremely dependent on one's race ($\eta^2 = .44$) and/or ethnic group ($\eta^2 = .47$), as are attitudes toward the ANC, the South African Communist Party (SACP), the Pan Africanist Congress (PAC), and even unions.[13] On the other hand, attitudes toward homosexuals, Muslims, and the AWB are not a function of race or ethnicity. The two most racially charged groups are Afrikaners and supporters of the ANC. Moreover, there are considerable differences in the structure of group hatred across the various racial groups in South Africa. For instance, among Africans, there is a very strong negative relationship ($r = -.61$) between affect toward the ANC and the IFP; those who like the ANC tend to dislike the IFP (and vice versa). For Coloureds and South Africans of Asian origin, affect polarizes around the NP and the ANC ($r = -.55$ and $-.37$, respectively). For whites, the strongest negative correlation is between attitudes toward Afrikaners and attitudes toward homosexuals, although this relationship is relatively weak ($r = -.20$).[14] In light of the tortured history of race in South Africa, it is not surprising that whom one hates depends at least to some degree on skin color.

---

13 For all of these groups, knowing the respondent's racial and/or ethnic group can account for at least one-fourth of the variance in affect toward the group.

14 This correlation means that whites who are positively predisposed toward Afrikaners tend weakly to be negatively predisposed toward gays. This likely reflects greater tolerance of homosexuality among the English-speaking white community in South Africa.

South African Intolerance as It Is

The Most Disliked Groups

The primary purpose of the group affect questions is to set up the selection of target groups for the consideration of political intolerance. Consequently, after the respondents rated each group, they were asked to indicate which group they disliked the most, second most, third most, and fourth most.[15] Table 3.3 reports the distribution of these disliked groups.[16]

A large majority (78.6 percent) of South Africans rated the AWB as among their four most disliked groups. Nearly two-thirds of the respondents named the IFP and its supporters as one of their most disliked groups. After these two groups, consensus declines markedly, with only a third of the respondents naming Afrikaners and the NP and its supporters as among their most disliked groups in South African politics.

The selection of target groups is, not surprisingly, racially polarized (see Table 3.4). For instance, 77.5 percent of the African respondents named the IFP and its supporters as among their most disliked groups, but only 16.5 percent of the whites and about one-half of the Coloureds and Asians named the IFP as a hated group.[17] Very large majorities of non-whites named the AWB as among the most hated groups, but only one-half of the whites did so. Africans were most likely to name the AWB and IFP as groups they disliked a great deal; whites were most likely to name the PAC and the Communists; and Coloured people and Asians were united in hating the AWB.

Within racial groups, there are also some important differences in the structure of group hatred. For instance, Zulu people are more likely than other Africans to name Afrikaners as among their most disliked groups, and are less likely to name the IFP and its supporters. Still, a majority (58.1 percent) of the Zulu respondents put the IFP among their most disliked groups (compared to about 85 percent of those of other African ethnicity). And Zulu-speaking South Africans were little different from

15 Note that the respondents were also allowed to nominate a group not on the list. As in earlier research based on this measurement strategy, only a very small percentage elected to do so.

16 For the tiny proportion of the sample unable to name a highly disliked group, we used as the group stimulus either "those who would re-impose apartheid in the country" or "those who would force all whites to leave South Africa," depending upon which of these two groups was disliked the most by the respondent.

17 We refer to these groups as "hated" even though they are really only among the groups most disliked by the respondents. Note, however, that 84.0 percent of the respondents rated this most disliked group at 1 on the 1 through 11 affect scale, and fully 91.7 percent rated the group at 1 or 2. The other highly disliked group is less hated, but still 59.7 percent scored it at 1, and 74.2 percent gave it either a 1 or a 2. Thus, we think it fair to argue that these groups are at least quite disliked, and are most likely hated.

Table 3.3. *The Distribution of Disliked Groups*

Group	Percentages[a]				
	Among Most Disliked	Most Disliked	2nd Most Disliked	3rd Most Disliked	4th Most Disliked
Afrikaners	33.9	10.2	9.4	8.9	5.4
African National Congress & Supporters	12.1	6.4	2.4	1.7	1.6
Afrikaner Resistance Movement (AWB) & Supporters	78.6	34.8	27.8	9.7	6.4
South African Communists	17.3	4.4	5.2	4.5	3.2
Pan-Africanist Congress & Supporters	23.1	3.5	7.2	7.7	4.6
National Party & Supporters	33.6	4.1	8.9	12.6	8.1
Democratic Party & Supporters	21.9	1.3	4.2	9.1	7.2
Inkatha Freedom Party & Supporters	65.9	25.2	21.3	11.8	7.6
Advocates of a One-Party State	10.5	1.9	2.5	3.8	2.4
Homosexuals	22.7	3.6	5.0	7.0	7.0
Trade Unionists	5.0	.7	.9	1.5	2.0
Muslims	6.3	.9	1.1	1.9	2.4
Other	3.1	.7	1.9	2.4	1.2
None	–	2.2	2.2	17.6	40.9
N		2,559	2,559	2,559	2,559

Note:

[a] The percentages for the most disliked, second most disliked, third most disliked, and fourth most disliked groups total to 100 percent down the columns (except for rounding errors). The percentages for the "Among the Most Disliked" column total to 100 percent across the four rows (except for rounding errors).

other Africans in their tendency to like the ANC. Whites divide the most over the AWB (named by 61.7 percent of the English-speaking whites but only 37.0 percent of the Afrikaans-speaking whites, data not shown), and, to a lesser degree over the ANC (with greater antipathy among Afrikaans-speaking whites). Whites are not divided, however, on their attitudes toward the SACP. Xhosa-speaking South Africans were somewhat more likely than other Africans to put the NP and its supporters on their list of hated groups. Thus, as in so much of this research, race is only a part of the explanation of group antipathy; strong intraracial differences exist.

Table 3.4. *The Distribution of Disliked Groups by Race*

Whether Named as Among Most Disliked	Race of Respondent			
	African	White	Coloured	Asian Origin
Afrikaners	42.5	1.6	11.7	21.1
African National Congress & Supporters	4.9	39.6	27.0	21.1
Afrikaner Resistance Movement (AWB) & Supporters	84.6	49.0	79.3	77.0
South African Communists	4.6	72.1	33.2	35.9
Pan-Africanist Congress & Supporters	10.8	72.7	48.0	37.0
National Party & Supporters	41.8	3.0	18.0	9.3
Democratic Party & Supporters	25.9	4.8	19.1	10.4
Inkatha Freedom Party & Supporters	77.5	16.5	50.8	52.2
Advocates of a One-Party State	5.2	39.2	6.6	20.4
Homosexuals	22.1	20.9	26.2	31.9
Trade Unionists	1.4	23.9	3.5	10.7
Muslims	4.6	14.3	5.1	10.0
Other	3.4	1.0	4.7	2.6

Note: Entries are the percentages of each racial group naming the political group as among its most disliked groups.

An important limitation of most applications of the least-liked measurement approach is that it places too much emphasis on a single extreme stimulus – the least liked group. It is important to know whether such an extreme stimulus generates intolerance; but it is also important to know whether less extreme groups are tolerated, and, in general, to know the *breadth* of intolerance (see Gibson 1985, Gouws 1992). It is quite plausible that some people would not tolerate their most hated political enemy while tolerating virtually all other political competitors. This person is less intolerant than one who would not tolerate many political groups. For many, there may well be a "special" political enemy who "deserves" no tolerance – Nazis in Europe, the AWB in South Africa – but this indeed is a special case. It it therefore essential that tolerance of groups that are not *most* disliked by the respondent be considered.[18]

18 To anticipate the findings that follow, confining the discussion of tolerance to the least liked group also has the undesirable effect of constraining the variance in the tolerance measures since those who would not tolerate many groups are scored the same as those who would not tolerate only their most disliked group.

Consequently, we queried the respondents about their tolerance of their most disliked group and another highly disliked group. The respondents were asked to tell us the four groups they disliked the most. Most were able to do so, but a significant proportion could not. Respondents unable to name four groups were asked about their third most disliked group; those unable to name three groups were asked about their second most disliked group; and those unable to name two disliked groups were asked about either "those who would re-impose apartheid in the country" or "those who would force all whites to leave South Africa," depending on which of these two groups was disliked the most. For most of the sample (59.0 percent), the stimulus was in fact the fourth most disliked group, but for 23.3 percent we used the third most disliked group, and for 15.4 percent it was the second most disliked group (no group was named by 2.3 percent of the respondents).[19] We will refer to this second group throughout as "another highly disliked group." It is these groups that provide the "objection precondition" for the respondents, a necessary condition for valid measurement of political intolerance.

Levels of Political Intolerance

To hate a group is not necessarily to be intolerant of it. Consequently, it is necessary to determine the degree to which the antipathy we have observed begets intolerance.

Political tolerance is "putting up with" one's political enemies. But putting up with what? As we noted previously, the key activities that we believe must be tolerated in a democracy concern competition for political power. Democratic theory does not necessarily contend that homosexual sex must be tolerated, for instance, but it does require that activity designed to persuade others on political matters be protected. Consequently, we asked the respondents whether their disliked groups should be allowed to

19 Note that there is very little difference in the degree of negative affect toward the group that is related to the specific rank assigned to it. η between the rank and affect is .03, and indeed the mean affect score for the fourth most disliked group is slightly (but insignificantly) more negative than the mean score for those only able to name a second or a third most disliked group. Similarly, on the perceptions of threat factor score (discussed in the following section), the fourth most disliked group is more threatening (slightly and insignificantly) than the second or third most disliked groups. For practical purposes, the rank of the group is entirely unimportant and will be ignored in the remainder of this analysis.

Table 3.5. *Levels of South African Political Intolerance*

Group/Activities Tolerated	Percentage			Mean	Std. Dev.	N
	Intolerant	Uncertain	Tolerant			
Most Disliked Group						
Allow candidates	61.8	10.7	27.4	2.4	1.4	2,512
Allow demonstrations	74.3	10.5	15.2	1.9	1.2	2,512
Do not ban	65.3	12.1	22.6	2.2	1.3	2,510
Tolerance Index	–	–	–	2.2	1.0	2,515
Another Highly Disliked Group						
Allow candidates	53.7	11.7	34.6	2.6	1.4	2,509
Allow demonstrations	66.8	11.2	22.0	2.3	1.2	2,508
Do not ban	54.0	13.7	32.3	2.6	1.4	2,507
Tolerance Index	–	–	–	2.5	1.1	2,508

- Stand as a candidate for an elected position
- Hold street demonstrations in the respondents' community
- Exist as a political group (not be officially banned)

Obviously, democratic tolerance requires that all groups be permitted to organize, to proselytize others, and to attempt to control the government.

All of these activities are elements of peaceful competition for political power; none concerns illegal behavior, terrorist activity, or other forms of violence. Thus, even when our questions are framed about so-called extremist groups (like the AWB), they refer to the group engaging in behavior that is entirely legal and a legitimate means of competing for political power and influence. We do not contend that tolerance requires that violence be countenanced. Rather, democracy profits from a free and open marketplace of ideas. It is important to keep this in mind as we discuss our findings. Table 3.5 reports the responses to these tolerance items for the most disliked group and another highly disliked group.

The data in the table are unambiguous: South Africans tend to be quite intolerant. About two-thirds of the respondents would ban their most disliked group and nearly three-fourths would prohibit the group from demonstrating. Nor is the other highly disliked group tolerated much more; two-thirds would prohibit demonstrations, and over one-half would ban the group and forbid the group to run candidates for public office. South Africans who are tolerant are in a distinct minority.

Significant racial and ethnic differences exist in levels of intolerance (data not shown). In general, the English-speaking whites are the most tolerant South Africans, and either the Xhosa- or Zulu-speaking Africans

Table 3.6. *Political Tolerance in Great Britain, the United States,*
Russia, and South Africa

	Percentage Tolerant			
Activity	Great Britain	United States	Russia	South Africa
Be banned from running for office[a]	27	27	–	27
Be banned (outlawed)[a]	31	32	7	23
Be allowed to hold a public rally	34	33	6	15
Be allowed to make a public speech	51	50	10	25

Note:

[a] For these items, disagreement was the tolerant response.

Sources: The British data are taken from Table 1, Barnum and Sullivan, 1989, p. 139, and are from a survey of mass opinion conducted in 1986. The U.S. data are taken from Table 3, Gibson, 1989b, p. 567, and are from a 1987 survey of mass opinion. The Russian data are from a survey conducted by Gibson in 1996.

are the least tolerant. Both Coloured and Asian people tend to be slightly more tolerant than Africans. Afrikaans-speaking whites are decidedly less tolerant than English-speaking whites, but are slightly more tolerant than other South Africans. We will return to racial/ethnic differences when we consider the impact of threat perceptions, but for the moment it appears that one's tolerance is to some degree dependent upon one's race or ethnicity.

How tolerant are South Africans compared with the people of other countries? Tolerance surveys have not been conducted in most countries in the world, but some limited comparative data are available. Table 3.6 reports comparable tolerance scores for the United States, Great Britain, Russia, and South Africa. These figures are comparable since they are based on the least-liked methodology.

These data provide useful perspective on the South African findings. On most items, the South Africans are indeed less tolerant than the British or the Americans, although they are equally as likely to oppose banning members of the most disliked group from running for elected office. But the South Africans are considerably *more tolerant* than the Russians, which is perhaps a surprising finding since Russia profits from universal literacy. From the perspective of these comparative data, South Africans are indeed intolerant, but they are far from being the most intolerant people imaginable.

We have constructed an index of intolerance from the responses to these six items measuring tolerance toward the most disliked and another highly disliked group. Based on two groups and three activities, this index is a broader measure of intolerance than is normally produced in research using the least-liked methodology. The index meets the conceptual requirement of the objection precondition and is grounded in democratic theory. The reliability (internal consistency) of the six items is quite high; Cronbach's alpha is .77. The six items are strongly intercorrelated, and when factor-analyzed, they produce a single strong factor.[20] The factor loadings range from .50 for the question of whether the most disliked group should be allowed to demonstrate, to .70 for the item concerning whether the other highly disliked group should be banned. For purposes of analyzing tolerance of each group separately (e.g., when group-specific controls for perceptions of threat are necessary), we have calculated simple summated indices of the responses to the three tolerance items for each group. Tolerance of the most disliked and another very disliked group is strongly related; the correlation between these two indices is .48, indicating a strong tendency for those unwilling to tolerate their most disliked group not to be willing to tolerate the other highly disliked group. Otherwise, to indicate general intolerance, we use the factor score from the first unrotated factor produced from the six-item factor analysis.

Pluralistic Intolerance?

A crucial question about the nature of intolerance is whether it is pluralistic or focused (Sullivan, Piereson, and Marcus 1982). Focused intolerance refers to agreement among people on which groups are threatening and therefore worthy of intolerance. When most agree on the identity of the menace to society, then concerted action taken against the group is more likely. When there is disagreement – that is, when the groups named as highly disliked are distributed widely and pluralistically across the political spectrum – then the pernicious effects of intolerance are less likely to materialize. If people cannot agree on who presents a threat to society, then they are unlikely to join in concerted action to deny rights and freedoms to the group.

This theory of pluralistic intolerance has been used to explain the connection between intolerance and political repression in politics in the United States. According to Sullivan, Piereson, and Marcus (1979, 1982), intolerance was directed in the 1950s in the United States at Communists and so-called fellow travelers. As a result of widespread agreement that Communists were a menace, demands to do something about the Communist threat were voiced and heard, and political repres-

---

20 The eigenvalue of the first factor is 2.81, accounting for 46.8 percent of the interitem variance; the eigenvalue for the second factor is .99, explaining only 16.5 percent of the variance.

sion resulted.[21] On the other hand, contemporary U.S. politics is less repressive not because Americans are more tolerant, but rather because contemporary intolerance is not focused. Some hate and would repress groups on the left, but others hate and would repress groups on the right. In the absence of agreement on where the threat lies, intolerance is diffused and dispersed, and concerted demands for repression are not widely heard. Thus, whether intolerance has pernicious effects on politics is in part dependent upon whether it is pluralistically distributed.[22]

What conclusions can we draw about the distribution of antipathy and intolerance in South Africa? Unfortunately, to assess fully and directly the thesis of pluralistic intolerance requires that tolerance questions be asked of a wide variety of groups, a costly proposition indeed. Consequently, the thesis has typically been addressed indirectly, concentrating on whether there is consensus on the groups named as most disliked. The data in Table 3.3 allow us to assess this thesis.

There are two groups active in South African politics who are potential targets of political repression, according to the theory of pluralistic intolerance. The AWB and its supporters, and the Inkatha Freedom Party and its supporters, are both highly disliked by large majorities of South Africans. For the AWB, nearly four in five South Africans name it among their four most disliked groups, and for the IFP, nearly two-thirds give it such a rating. This is a considerable degree of agreement among South Africans, the sort of agreement that has often given rise to effective demands for political repression.

It should also be noted that were we to consider only the most disliked groups, as is often the strategy in research of this sort, we would draw badly mistaken conclusions about the structure of intolerance in South Africa. Only 34.8 percent of the respondents named the AWB as most disliked, even though 78.6 percent put the AWB as among the four most disliked groups. The second column in the table gives the impression of pluralistic intolerance since no group draws a majority naming it as most disliked. *But groups that are not most disliked are nonetheless disliked a great deal*, and considerable intolerance is present even when the target group is not the respondent's most disliked group (see Table 3.5). Even though only 25.2 percent named the IFP as the most disliked group, the IFP was rated at the most disliked end of the

---

21 Gibson (1988) challenges this interpretation of the simple linkage between mass intolerance and repression during McCarthyism, arguing instead that repression was largely a function of elite intolerance, not the intolerance of ordinary Americans.

22 For an assessment of the degree of pluralism in Russian intolerance, see Gibson 1998b.

antipathy scale by 57.3 percent of the respondents (see Table 3.2), and the mean antipathy score was 2.9 on the eleven-point scale. These data strongly suggest that examining only the structure of antipathy toward the most disliked group often leads to erroneous conclusions about whether intolerance is pluralistically distributed.

Analyzing the distribution of antipathy is an indirect approach to assessing the hypothesis of pluralistic intolerance. The important question is whether significant majorities of South Africans support the repression of any particular political groups. To the extent that there is widespread intolerance of a group, then the theory predicts that repression will materialize.

We did not ask tolerance questions about all of the groups shown in Table 3.2, so it is not possible to ascertain directly where intolerance begins and ends. However, some statistical manipulations of these data may allow estimates of the breadth of intolerance. The analysis begins by assessing how much negative affect is necessary to stimulate intolerance.

For both the most disliked group and another highly disliked group, we have data on the degree of affect toward the group and on the willingness to tolerate political activities by it. Considering both groups so as to maximize the variability in affect toward the groups (i.e., "stacking" the two data sets on top of each other), we regressed the tolerance index on affect. The resulting equation was:

Predicted Tolerance = 2.056 + (.165 * Group Affect)

This equation indicates that for every unit change in positive affect toward the group, tolerance increased by .165 units.[23] Since the tolerance index ranges from 1 to 5, and the affect measure ranges from 1 to 11,[24] a unit increase in tolerance is produced by a change of about 6 units of positive affect. This is not necessarily a strong relationship, but perhaps we can still use the equation to generate predicted tolerance scores for each group for which affect scores are available.

We applied this equation to the affect scores of each of the groups, with the result shown in Table 3.7. For each group, we have reported the percentage of respondents with a predicted tolerance score greater than 3.0 on the five-point tolerance index, a score indicating relative tolerance. Scores less than 3.0 indicate at least some intolerance directed toward the group. Thus, the figure for the AWB is 9.9 percent, which means that only 9.9 percent of South Africans support, on average, little

---

23 The standardized regression coefficient is .21.
24 Although practically speaking, the empirical range is from 1 to 6, with nearly all of the respondents scoring on the negative end of the affect scale.

Table 3.7. *Predicted Levels of Tolerance, Based on Group Affect*

Target Group	Percentage Relatively Tolerant	Political Tolerance		
		Mean	Std. Dev.	N
Afrikaner Resistance Movement (AWB) & Supporters	9.9	2.40	.33	2,527
Inkatha Freedom Party & Supporters	21.4	2.54	.47	2,515
Homosexuals	30.7	2.63	.44	2,519
Afrikaners	30.8	2.69	.53	2,526
Democratic Party & Supporters	40.1	2.78	.44	2,525
National Party & Supporters	40.2	2.82	.53	2,525
Pan-Africanist Congress & Supporters	52.7	2.93	.52	2,525
Advocates of a One-Party State	54.1	2.97	.56	2,525
Muslims	57.2	2.96	.46	2,525
South African Communists	60.2	3.00	.53	2,523
Trade Unionists	72.5	3.21	.52	2,525
African National Congress & Supporters	80.8	3.45	.55	2,514

repression against the AWB. We also report the means and standard deviations for these predicted tolerance scores. We should reiterate that these scores are based solely on levels of affect toward the groups.

Several groups would not be tolerated by two-thirds or more of the South African mass public, including the AWB, Inkatha, homosexuals, and Afrikaners. And at least two other political groups (the Democratic Party [DP] and the NP) would not be tolerated by a majority of South Africans. These data are not compatible with a conclusion that intolerance is pluralistically distributed. It is true that many groups are the objects of intolerance in South Africa, *but large majorities of South Africans do not want to put up with a variety of political enemies.*

Summary

Thus, we have seen that political intolerance is fairly widespread in South Africa, although it is perhaps not as common as in some other transitional regimes (e.g., Russia). In addition, South African intolerance has two other characteristics that make it particularly worrisome. First, not all targets of intolerance are located on the fringes of South African politics. Certainly the AWB is not in the political mainstream, but just as certainly the IFP is. The danger of South African intolerance is that it is not confined to the extremes of South African politics, as it seems to be in many other countries.

Nor is South African political intolerance pluralistic. Nearly everyone would support repression against groups like the AWB, and, by our projections, only 21.4 percent of South Africans are relatively tolerant of the IFP, a major competitor for power in South Africa. Homosexual organizations and Afrikaners fare little better. Intolerance is dispersed across the political landscape, but this dispersal *does not* dissipate it, as supposed by the theory of pluralistic intolerance. "Multifocused" is perhaps a better description of intolerance in South Africa than "pluralistic."

PERCEIVED THREATS FROM TARGET GROUPS

The research literature has demonstrated that one of the best predictors of political intolerance is the perception that a target group is threatening. Even within the confines of the "least-liked" measurement approach – in which all target groups are greatly disliked – perceived threat is typically a powerful predictor of intolerance. Consequently, we have devoted some effort to assessing the role that threat perceptions play in causing intolerance.

The most significant and sustained investigation of the role of threat in producing intolerance is the work of Marcus and his colleagues. Marcus et al. (1995, 36) distinguish among threat perceptions as predispositions (generalized attitudes), standing decisions (established, concrete opinions), and contemporaneous information (perceptions):

Conceptually, we . . . distinguish among three different types of threat. The first, threat as a predisposition, is a general assessment that is independent of any specific group or context but generates a tendency to perceive the world as dangerous. The second, threat as a standing decision, is meant to summarize respondents' attitudes about the belligerence and untrustworthiness of their least-liked group and other similarly situated groups. In this respect, threat as standing decision is a far more specific measure of threat than the predispositional measure. Finally, threat as contemporary information refers specifically to a sense of threat with reference to the interaction between a specific group and a context that is available from the immediate environment (1995, 106–7).

For them, contemporary judgments can be further distinguished as referring to either the perceived strength of the group or direct normative judgments of the group.

Their findings indicate that perceptions of the strength of the group are unrelated to tolerance, while normative judgments have significant effects on willingness to put up with threatening enemies (1995, 102). The strength findings are puzzling since they indicate that groups that are perceived to be stronger are not necessarily perceived to be more threatening, and hence less tolerated. Their argument is that, "we ... question whether people are driven primarily by pragmatic considerations when it comes to tolerance. If people were merely pragmatically tolerant – being tolerant only when the group in question was weak and ineffectual – they would rely heavily on probability to determine their tolerance judgments" (Marcus et al. 1995, 79). Their data clearly indicate that people do *not* rely on such judgments.

However, their empirical analysis reveals only a very weak direct effect of threat on intolerance. The impact of threat as a standing decision (the conventional measure of threat) is statistically and substantively insignificant, while the impact of predispositional threat is only marginally significant (1995, 110). Because both of these variables had substantial bivariate correlations with intolerance, they conclude that "the influence of threat antecedent considerations is encapsulated, to some extent, in a standing decision to be intolerant" (1995, 109), one of the other independent variables in the model. Thus, their empirical results are somewhat disappointing.[25]

Gibson and Bingham (1985) also investigated the role of threat perceptions in their research on reactions to efforts of the American Nazi Party to hold a demonstration in Skokie, Illinois, a community populated by a large number of Holocaust survivors. They discovered that those perceiving a greater threat from the Nazis were more likely to take action to prevent them from demonstrating, thus increasing the correlations between their attitudes and their behavior. Similarly, Gibson and Duch (1993a, 307) also found that where the target group is perceived to be extremist and engaged in illegal activity, it is less likely to be tolerated.

In South Africa, Gouws (1992, 84) measured threat perceptions with the following indicators: fear that the group would change the economic system, that it lacks a democratic belief system, that it is violent, or racist, or that the group would not allow its opponents civil liberties. She found a significant relationship between intolerance and the perceptions that the group is violent, racist, lacks democratic beliefs, or would not allow civil liberties.

In a more recent study on intolerance and violence in KwaZulu-Natal, Gouws (1996, 31) found that respondents believed that it was their

---

25 They also test for a conditional effect – and conclude that "those who are most threatened are most attentive to contemporary information and thus are able to be either reassured or threatened by new information" (1995, 113) – but the statistical evidence supporting their conclusions is extremely weak.

target group that was causing the violence in the province. In the highly politicized context of South Africa, perceptions of imminent danger still play an important role. We consequently hypothesize that people who perceive their target groups as threatening will be more intolerant.

As we argued in Chapter 2, the threats posed by political enemies in South Africa are more realistic and less abstract than in most other political systems. After all, domestic Communists have killed very few people in the United States, while the violent struggle between the ANC and the IFP has killed thousands of people. And even those whom apartheid did not affect physically were far more touched by the vicious hand of the government and its agents than is true in established democracies.[26] Thus, we must be mindful that threat perceptions take on a more true-to-life meaning in South Africa than might ordinarily be the case.

What does it mean to say that a target group is threatening? The first distinction to be made is between the object of the threat – is the threat to institutions, to the larger political system, or is it directed specifically toward the individual? These various types of perceived threat may be quite different. Following a well-established tradition in research on perceptions of the performance of the economy, we will refer to perceived threats to the political system as "sociotropic threats" and perceived threats to the individual as "egocentric threats."[27]

The political economy literature also distinguishes between retrospective and prospective perceptions, between views of the past and views of the future. In our assessments of threat perceptions, we similarly distinguish between contemporary threat and potential threat. People may support the repression of groups not currently powerful as a preemptive strike, designed to keep the groups from becoming powerful. Or they may believe that the contemporary impotence of the group makes it unnecessary to implement repression.

Table 3.8 reports the perceptions of the threats posed by the respondent's most disliked and the other highly disliked group. The perceptions were measured using semantic differential scales and nine antipodal descriptors of the group. For instance, endpoints of the continuum used to collect the data for the first row in the table were "not dangerous to society" and "dangerous to society." Though the data were collected through balanced scales, all responses have been recoded so that a high score indicates a more threatening response.

26 See, for example, de Kock 1998.
27 Kinder and Sears make a similar distinction when they conclude that, "Our findings imply that the white public's political response to racial issues is based on moral and symbolic challenges to the racial status quo in society generally rather than on any direct, tangible challenge to their own personal lives" (1981, 427, 429).

Table 3.8. *The Perceived Threat of Highly Disliked Groups*

Perception	% At Most Extreme Score	Mean[a]	Std. Dev.	N
Most Disliked Group				
Dangerous to society	68.2	6.2	1.5	2,503
Unpredictable	57.1	5.8	1.8	2,502
Not committed to having democracy in South Africa	63.4	6.0	1.6	2,503
Dangerous to the normal lives of people	54.2	5.7	1.9	2,503
Likely to gain a lot of power in South Africa	6.1	2.5	1.9	2,504
Likely to affect how well my family and I live	32.1	4.6	2.2	2,502
Angry toward the group	53.3	5.4	2.1	2,498
Unwilling to follow the rules of democracy	62.6	6.1	1.5	2,499
Powerful	13.0	3.2	2.2	2,499
Another Highly Disliked Group				
Dangerous to society	43.4	5.1	2.1	2,492
Unpredictable	43.4	5.3	1.9	2,491
Not committed to having democracy in South Africa	43.1	5.2	1.9	2,491
Dangerous to the normal lives of people	34.2	4.8	2.1	2,493
Likely to gain a lot of power in South Africa	4.7	2.6	1.8	2,491
Likely to affect how well my family and I live	21.7	4.0	2.2	2,498
Angry toward the group	36.1	4.8	2.2	2,498
Unwilling to follow the rules of democracy	44.1	5.3	1.9	2,493
Powerful	10.5	3.0	2.1	2,492

Note:
[a] High scores in every instance indicate greater degrees of perceived threat.

The least-liked group is clearly perceived as very threatening. Large majorities of the respondents rated the group at the most extreme point on the scale regarding its dangerousness to society, its lack of commitment to having a democracy in South Africa, and its unwillingness to follow the rules of democracy. A majority of the respondents used the extreme end of the scale to describe the group's unpredictability, its dangerousness to ordinary people, and the respondent's degree of anger toward the group. Only about one-third of the respondents were certain that the group would affect their personal well-being, however. Most interestingly, there was great variability in the perceived power – contemporary or potential – of the group, with only a tiny percentage of the respondents putting the group at the extreme ends of these continua. In general, it is clear that the least-liked measurement approach succeeded in generating target groups that are extremely threatening to the respondents.

The picture is much the same regarding the other highly disliked group, although at a somewhat less extreme level of threat. The other highly disliked group was perceived as considerably less dangerous than the least-liked group, although there is little difference in the predictability of the two groups, and perhaps even in the degree of anger toward the groups. Perhaps unexpectedly, the two disliked groups were not rated much differently on their powerfulness, current or future. We shall return to this finding later in the analysis.

As we noted previously, Marcus et al. distinguish between threat perceptions based on the perceived strength of the group and simple normative objections to the group. The data in Table 3.8 certainly suggest such a distinction as well. For instance, 68.2 percent of the respondents believe that their least-liked group is as dangerous as could be rated on the scale, although only 13.0 percent view the same group as extremely powerful, and 6.1 percent view it as quite likely to gain a lot of power in South Africa. Power is obviously not a prerequisite to danger. Similar discrepancies exist with regard to the other highly disliked group. Clearly, there is a difference between perceiving a group as dangerous and perceiving it as powerful, and we must be mindful of this difference in the following analysis.

A factor analysis of the two sets of threat perceptions further supports this view. In both instances, a two-dimensional factor structure emerged, and in both instances the second factor was overwhelmingly defined by the items referring to the power and potential power of the group. Indeed, the two power items typically correlate *negatively* with the other threat perceptions.[28] The other seven items all derive from a single factor, and the pattern loadings differed little depending on whether the most disliked or the other highly disliked group was rated. The best indicator of threat perceptions was sociotropic danger – the dangerousness of the

28 It is possible that the weak correlations between the power items and the rest of the set are a function of the skewed distributions of all items except those measuring power. We have, however, no means by which to test that hypothesis since the least-liked technology, as a matter of principle and theory, necessarily generates groups that are highly threatening to the respondent.

group to society.[29] For both groups, the strongest correlate of the degree to which the group makes the respondent angry is the dangerousness to ordinary people.

These specific groups, while all highly disliked, vary considerably in the degree of threat presented to the respondents. The identity of the group accounts for 19 percent of the variance in perceived threat from the most disliked group and 24 percent of the variance in threat from the other highly disliked group. At one extreme, those naming Muslims (N = 23) or homosexuals (N = 92) as their most disliked group are not very threatened by them, while at the other extreme, those naming the IFP (N = 644) or the AWB (N = 884) are very threatened.

Perceptions of threat are also to some degree dependent upon the respondent's racial/ethnic group. For the most disliked group, η is .33; for the second most disliked group, η is .21. The greatest distinction is between Africans and all other South Africans; blacks are considerably more threatened by their most disliked group and somewhat more threatened by the other highly disliked group. Zulu-speaking Africans are the most threatened group in the sample when it comes to the least liked group[30]; English-speaking whites and South Africans of Asian origin are the least threatened. For the other highly disliked group, Xhosa-speaking Africans are the most threatened, while the Indian and Coloured respondents are the least threatened. Indeed, some of the difference across groups in levels of tolerance is surely due to differences in the perceived threat of groups named in the tolerance questions.

CONNECTING THREAT PERCEPTIONS AND INTOLERANCE

Table 3.9 reports the results of regressing each of the tolerance indices on the various measures of the perceived threat posed by the group. For both target groups, the equation is a reasonably strong predictor of intolerance, although because there is greater variability among the groups named as disliked but not most disliked, threat perceptions explain more variance than usual. Note also that many of the variables with strong bivariate effects have rather weak independent effects, a finding influenced by the strong intercorrelations among the various independent

29 The perceived dangerousness of the group to society is moderately to strongly correlated with the perceived dangerousness of the group to ordinary people (r = .38 and .56, respectively), but it less strongly correlated with estimates of the group's likely effect on the respondent and her or his family (r = .25 and .34, respectively).

30 This is partly a function of Zulu being the dominant language of Africans living in KwaZulu-Natal.

Table 3.9. *The Relationship between Threat Perceptions and Political Tolerance*

Threat Perceptions	Most Disliked Group				Another Highly Disliked Group			
	b	s.e.	Beta	r	b	s.e.	Beta	r
Individual Indicators								
Dangerous to society	−.06	.02	−.10*	−.24	−.06	.01	−.13*	−.37
Unpredictable	−.06	.01	−.11*	−.21	−.04	.01	−.08	−.29
Not committed to having democracy in South Africa	−.03	.02	−.04	−.21	−.03	.01	−.05	−.32
Dangerous to the normal lives of people	−.02	.01	−.04	−.21	−.05	.01	−.10*	−.36
Likely to gain a lot of power in South Africa	−.06	.01	−.10*	.13	.05	.01	.08	.19
Likely to affect how well my family and I live	−.02	.01	−.05	−.17	−.02	.01	−.04	−.22
Angry toward the group	−.07	.01	−.14*	−.25	−.07	.01	−.14*	−.35
Unwilling to follow the rules of democracy	−.03	.02	−.05	−.21	−.03	.01	−.05	−.33
Powerful	−.03	.01	−.06	.01	.02	.01	.04	.12
Negative affect	−.08	.02	−.07	−.13	−.07	.01	−.11*	−.23
Intercept	3.74	.13			3.63	.09		
R^2			.14*				.24*	
Standard error of estimate	.95				.93			
Standard deviation	1.02				1.06			
N	2,478				2,478			
Factor Score and Indicators								
Perceived threat	−.37	.02	−.31*	−.34	−.47	.02	−.41*	−.46
Powerful	−.03	.01	−.06	.01	.02	.01	.04	.12
Likely to gain a lot of power in South Africa	.05	.01	.09*	.13	.05	.01	.08	.19
Negative affect	−.08	.02	−.07	−.13	−.08	.01	−.11*	−.23
Intercept	2.04	.05			2.15	.04		
R^2			.13*				.23*	
Standard error of estimate	.95				.93			
Standard deviation	1.02				1.06			
N	2,479				2,478			

Note:

* Standardized regression coefficient is significant at $p < .0000$.

variables. For both the most disliked and another highly disliked group, two variables have consistently significant effects: groups that are rated more dangerous to society and groups that anger the respondents are groups that are less likely to be tolerated. For the most disliked group, tolerance is also related to the predictability of the group. For the other highly disliked group, the perceived dangerousness of the group enhances intolerance, and, even in the multivariate equation, greater negative affect increases intolerance. Generally, perceptions of threat are strong but not overwhelming predictors of intolerance.

Two of the threat variables are related to tolerance in an unexpected direction: As the least-liked group is perceived as more likely to achieve power in South Africa, tolerance *increases* ($r = .13$, $\beta = .10$). A similar relationship exists for the other highly disliked group ($r = .19$, $\beta = .08$). Further, for the other highly disliked target, groups that are perceived as more powerful now are tolerated *more* ($r = .12$, $\beta = .04$), although the relationship is not the same for the most disliked group. These are indeed most curious and unexpected relationships. It appears that some respondents are reluctant not to tolerate their enemies because their enemies' power (or potential for power) makes it dangerous to do so. Thus, these items may capture the perceived repercussions of intolerance more than the degree of threat posed by the group.

We have also investigated the hypothesis that perceptions of group power have a conditional effect on the relationship between perceived threat and intolerance. That is, we expected that as the perceived power (contemporary or future) of the group increases, perceived threats more readily translate into intolerance. When groups are not powerful, the perceived threat takes on a different, less virulent quality, leading to a weaker relationship with intolerance, we hypothesized. No such conditional effect was found for either of the two groups or for either of the two power variables. Thus, like Marcus and his colleagues, we are left with the puzzling finding that the power of a group has little to do with the level of tolerance expressed toward it.[31] So, especially in light of the finding that only one of the multivariate coefficients is statistically

---

31 We should also reiterate the finding that perceptions of the power of the group are generally negatively correlated with the other threat variables. For instance, the correlations between the perceived power potential of the most disliked group and the other threat perceptions are $-.25$ for the perceived willingness to follow democratic rules, $-.20$ for the perceived commitment to democracy, and $-.11$ for the degree of anger (groups perceived to have the potential for power make the respondent slightly *less* angry). The two power variables are strongly and positively interrelated, but groups perceived as more powerful are generally somewhat less threatening.

significant, perhaps it is prudent to treat these relationships as substantially insignificant and indistinguishable from zero.

As a consequence of the unexpected performance of the power perceptions, we have excluded them from the perceived threat measures. When the remaining seven threat perceptions are factor-analyzed without the two power perceptions, a unidimensional factor emerges for the other highly disliked group and an almost unidimensional factor is extracted for the most disliked group.[32] The variables with the strongest loadings for both the most disliked group and another highly disliked group factor analyses are the perceptions of the group's commitment to democracy and its dangerousness to society, both sociotropic aspects of threat perceptions. Factor scores from these two analyses will be used as summary measures of the threat posed by the group. This summary index of threat perceptions is strongly related to tolerance of the most disliked group ($r = -.34$, $b = -.40$) and the other highly disliked group ($r = -.46$, $b = -.53$).

The groups identified as least-liked vary significantly in terms of the degree to which they engage the emotions of the respondents. When we regressed tolerance on the threat perceptions *within the group*, we discovered a substantial range of effects of the variable "angry versus indifferent," ranging from a high of $-.26$ for the ANC (standardized regression coefficient; unstandardized coefficient $= -.13$) to a low of $-.04$ for supporters of a one-party state (unstandardized coefficient $= -.01$). In addition to the significant coefficient for the ANC, anger toward the following groups had some impact on tolerance: Afrikaners ($-.11$, $-.05$), AWB ($-.15$, $-.07$), the Democratic Party ($-.10$, $-.05$), the IFP ($-.14$, $-.07$), and Muslims ($-.15$, $-.07$). Anger toward the South African Communist Party, the PAC, the National Party, supporters of a one-party state, and homosexuals has no impact on willingness to tolerate the group. Why anger is relevant to some groups and not to others is unclear to us at the moment, but variation in the degree of emotional engagement is surely an important component of the process connecting threat and intolerance.

DISCUSSION

Observers of South African politics will not be surprised by the widespread intolerance we have reported in this chapter. For most South

---

32 For the most disliked group, the eigenvalues of the first two factors are 2.73 and 1.03, accounting for 39.0 and 14.7 percent of the variance respectively. For the other highly disliked group, the eigenvalues are 3.47 and .94, and the variance explained by the first two factors is 49.5 and 13.4 percent respectively.

Africans, the idea of putting up with their political enemies is distasteful and/or foreign. And indeed, most South Africans have political enemies, enemies they dislike a great deal, and these enemies are perceived as quite threatening. The combination of disliking a group and feeling threatened by it is a powerful source of political intolerance.

The structure of hate, fear, and intolerance in South Africa is not simple. It is certainly not simplistically racial, with whites fearing and refusing to tolerate Africans, and Africans fearing and refusing to tolerate whites. Deep divisions exist among Africans themselves, and Coloured people and South Africans of Asian origin do not hold the same views as Africans. There is certainly agreement among *all* South Africans that certain political movements are threatening and undeserving of political rights (e.g., the AWB), but there is also much specialization in choosing one's enemies.

We also note that South African intolerance is not limited to "fringe" political groups. While we agree that the AWB is on the extreme of South African politics, the Inkatha Freedom Party is not. One of the great dangers of South African intolerance is that many of the central competitors for political power are unwilling to tolerate one another. It is as if Democrats in the United States would support efforts to deny Republicans the opportunity to compete for political power, or as if Tories would seek to repress Labour in Britain. Intolerance is not a sideshow in South African politics, as perhaps it is in more established and stable democracies; instead, the main stage of politics is littered with intolerance. This is indeed one of our most important and disconcerting findings.

Finally, South Africans, like most people, rarely resist the impulse to translate perceptions of threat into intolerance. The type of threat motivating South African intolerance is sociotropic – it is the threat to the respondent's idea of what constitutes a desirable South African political system. Understanding better the origins of this threat is the objective of the next chapter.

4

Social Identities, Threat Perceptions, and Political Intolerance

As we have argued, South Africa faces a host of impediments to the successful consolidation of its efforts at democratizing its political system. Grinding poverty, extreme inequality, and the "lost generation" of young warriors against apartheid are just some of the most pressing difficulties facing the new regime. Optimism about the future of democracy in South Africa is in short supply (e.g., Giliomee 1995).

Among the impediments to democratic consolidation is the high degree of subcultural pluralism within South Africa. The country is divided, and deeply so, along a variety of racial, ethnic, and linguistic lines. Race is certainly central to South African politics, but intraracial (or ethnic) divisions are terribly significant as well. "Subcultural pluralism" has often been found to be a major impediment to successful democratization (e.g., Dahl 1989; Bollen and Jackman 1985; Horowitz 1985; Weingast 1997), and South Africa has an extreme case of such pluralism (e.g., Smooha and Hanf 1992; Horowitz 1991).

One important consequence of subcultural pluralism is political intolerance. In deeply divided polities, people typically develop strong ingroup positive identities, often leading to strong outgroup animosities. This psychological division of the world into friends and foes can undermine tolerance. Thus, Social Identity Theory (SIT, see Tajfel 1978; Tajfel and Turner 1979) is a micro-level complement to macro-level theories about the role of cultural pluralism in the development of democratic institutions and processes. Cultural pluralism contributes to strong group identities, leading to an unwillingness to put up with one's political foes, which impedes the free and open political competition so essential to democratic governance.

Or so it seems. Despite wide agreement among scholars that strong group identities are inimical to democracy, little systematic empirical research supports that viewpoint. Researchers have tended to *assume* that intolerance is a natural consequence of group identities, but that

72

relationship has rarely been investigated empirically and has never been conclusively established. Indeed, the literature on political intolerance seldom even considers Social Identity Theory (perhaps in part because it has been so heavily dominated by research on the United States). The micro-level process undergirding the hypothesis that subcultural pluralism impedes democratization is badly in need of empirical assessment.

The purpose of this chapter is therefore to examine the connection between social identity and political intolerance in South Africa. We begin by exploring the structure of group identities among ordinary South Africans. This is an important descriptive task, with several counterintuitive findings. Because our sample includes representative subsamples of the major ethnic/racial/linguistic groups in South Africa, we are able to assess how social identities vary across groups. The primary contribution of the chapter is a test of the hypothesis that those with stronger group identities are more likely to hold antipathy toward other groups, are more likely to be threatened by their political enemies, and are more likely to be intolerant of those enemies. Our results indicate that South African social identities do indeed have important consequences for democratic values among ordinary people, and perhaps as well for the consolidation of democracy in South Africa.

SOCIAL IDENTITY THEORY

Social Identity Theory[1] argues:

... our sense of who we are stems in large part from our membership of affiliation to various social groups, which are said to form our social identity. This identity is thought to be maintained through evaluative comparisons between in-groups and relevant out-groups. When these comparisons are favorable, that is, when some positive distinctiveness has been achieved, our social identity is said to be positive and, by implication, our more general self-concept. Since it is assumed that there is a general preference for a positive rather than negative self-concept, this introduces a motivational element into our comparative activity; we will be more disposed to look for and recognize intergroup differences which favour our in-groups over out-groups (Hinkle and Brown 1990, 48).

According to the most influential theorist in the field, social identity is "that *part* of an individual's self-concept which derives from his

---

1 The literature on social identities is vast. For useful reviews, see Messick and Mackie 1989; Brewer and Kramer 1985; and Hinkle and Schopler 1986. Though it is not directly relevant to the work reported here, the "classic" applications of SIT to political behavior are Miller et al. 1981; Gurin, Miller, and Gurin 1980 (see also Kelly 1988). Studies of racial politics in the United States often rely on SIT, at least as a heuristic (e.g., Bobo and Gilliam 1990; Tate 1993; Allen, Dawson, and Brown 1989; Sidanius and Pratto 1999).

knowledge of his membership of a social group (or groups) together with the value and emotional significance attached to that membership" (Tajfel 1978, 63, emphasis in original). Thus, social or group identities are psychological attributes of individuals; they may be grounded in objective characteristics, but they take on political significance only to the extent that individuals are cognizant of their membership in a group and attach value to it.

Four major processes developed out of Tajfel's experiments are important for understanding the political relevance of Social Identity Theory (Taylor and Moghaddam 1994, 78):

- Social categorization – the segmentation of the world so as to impose order on the environment and provide a locus of identification for the self
- Social identity – the self-concept developed out of a person's membership in a social group and the emotional value attached to that membership
- Social comparison – the comparison of the ingroup characteristics with outgroup characteristics
- Psychological distinctiveness – the distinctive and positive identity that group members experience in comparison with other relevant groups

Membership in a group, and especially the subjective evaluation of that membership, forms the basis for an individual's social identity. Because group membership is value-laden, it is psychologically important for individuals to belong to positively evaluated groups (Taylor and Moghaddam 1994, 79). What is crucial for this particular research is social comparison – the process through which individuals arrive at an assessment of their group's relative social position, and the value and status they acquire through their membership in the specific group.

From social comparison, a strong desire may develop to achieve distinctiveness, or to be different from other groups, rather than to become more similar, so that an identity is achieved that is unique and positive in comparison with other groups. The stronger people identify with their group, the more they will attempt to achieve intergroup differentiation. Differentiation in turn contributes to psychological security and self-esteem (Taylor and Moghaddam 1994, 86).

IDENTITIES, SUBCULTURAL PLURALISM, AND DEMOCRACY

Social identities have serious consequences for political systems. According to Dahl, "the prospects for polyarchy are greatly reduced if the fundamental beliefs and identities among the people of a country produce political conflicts and are correspondingly increased if beliefs and identities are compatible and therefore not a source of conflict. Thus, as the strength and distinctiveness of a country's subcultures increases, the chances for polyarchy should decline" (Dahl 1989, 254). Subcultural pluralism can be an especially serious threat to democracy because

... subcultural conflicts threaten personal and group identities and ways of life, because such threats evoke deep and powerful emotions, and because the sacrifice of identities and ways of life cannot readily be settled by negotiation, disputes involving different subcultures often turn into violent, nonnegotiable conflicts. In a country where conflicts are persistently violent and nonnegotiable, polyarchy is unlikely to exist (Dahl 1989, 255).[2]

It is not surprising, therefore, that scholars have long argued that strong group loyalties and identities undermine democracy, especially if those identities are based on ascriptive (and therefore exclusionary) rather than achieved characteristics (e.g., Lijphart 1977). The basic process is fairly simple – strong ingroup identities are said to give rise to strong outgroup "anti-identities." To the extent that a political majority is formed from ascriptive characteristics such as race, politics generates permanent majorities and minorities, a most unwelcomed state of affairs for democracies. Consociationalism is one possible solution (e.g., Lijphart 1977), and others advocate institutions that are capable of ingroup policing (e.g., Fearon and Laitin 1996), but some scheme must be implemented to impede the institutionalized dominance of any particular group. Even the theorist John Stuart Mill recognized this problem long ago when he asserted "free institutions are next to impossible in a country made up of different nationalities" (quoted in Lijphart 1977, 18).

Some social scientists view strong group identifications as anathema to democratic governance in part because ingroup identifications can be closely connected to authoritarianism. For instance, Duckitt argues that the greater the identification, "the greater will be the emphasis on behavioral and attitudinal conformity with ingroup norms and rules of conduct – that is, conventionalism" (a dimension of authoritarianism), "the greater the emphasis will be on respect and unconditional obedience to ingroup leaders and authorities – that is, authoritarian submission" (another dimension of authoritarianism), and "the greater will be the intolerance of and punitiveness toward persons not conforming to

---

2 In his earlier book on "polyarchies," Dahl claimed that only 15 percent of countries with extreme pluralism had even semidemocratic political systems (Dahl 1971, 110–11).

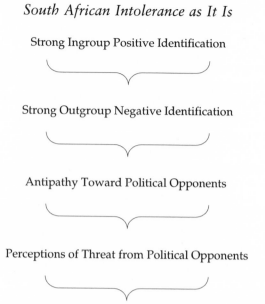

Strong Ingroup Positive Identification

Strong Outgroup Negative Identification

Antipathy Toward Political Opponents

Perceptions of Threat from Political Opponents

Political Intolerance

Figure 4.1. Hypothesized Pathways from Social Identity to Political Intolerance

ingroup norms and rules – that is, authoritarian aggression" (Duckitt 1989, 70). Authoritarianism is obviously anathema to a democratic political culture.

Earlier thinking clearly implies a linkage between strong social identities and political intolerance. The process is straightforward: Strong identities, tinged with authoritarianism, lead to anti-identities. These in turn lead to the perception that outgroups are threatening. Since authoritarianism and closedmindedness involve making harsh distinctions between friends and foes, those who are dogmatic are more likely to see the world as comprised of ingroups and outgroups, with a rigid divide between the two. Since the perception of threats from a group is one of the strongest predictors of intolerance, strong identities therefore lead to intolerance. Figure 4.1 depicts this process. Especially in deeply divided societies, group identities and intolerance most likely go hand in hand.

Surprisingly, little earlier research on political tolerance has tested this hypothesis. Perhaps because the tolerance literature is so strongly dominated by research on the United States, social identities have not been investigated as a source of intolerance. The tolerance literature teaches us that perceptions of threat from one's political enemies quite readily translate into intolerance (Stouffer 1955; Sullivan, Piereson, and Marcus

1982; Sullivan et al. 1985; Duch and Gibson 1992; Gibson and Duch 1993a; Shamir 1991; Gibson 1992a, 1998a), but has generally been unsuccessful at identifying the etiology of threat perceptions (but see Marcus et al. 1995). Thus, Social Identity Theory also offers the promise of addressing one of the central paradoxes emerging from the contemporary tolerance literature (see Gibson 1996d): the psychological origins of threat perceptions.

EMPIRICAL DIMENSIONS OF SOCIAL IDENTITY

Table 4.1 reports the primary social identities of the four major racial groupings in South Africa.[3] Virtually everyone accepted one of the offered terms as her or his social identity. Among black South Africans, the most attractive label by far was "African," claimed by nearly one-third of the respondents. White South Africans were most likely to think of themselves as just "South Africans," as was true of Coloured South Africans, and South Africans of Asian origin. Few whites were attracted to the term "white," although 28.5 percent of the Coloured respondents claimed the label "Coloured," and 15.9 percent of the Asians selected the term "Indian" (with another 12.2 percent identifying with "Asians"). As we have noted in the last row in the table (which combines primary and secondary responses to our question), roughly one-third of the Africans think of themselves as "South African"; over one-half of whites, Coloureds, and Asians embrace that term.[4]

We also asked the respondents to identify the groups with which they most strongly do *not* identify. Nearly 20 percent claimed not to have any "anti-identities" (and virtually no respondents claimed multiple

---

3 The respondents were asked, "People see themselves in many different ways. Using this list, which of these best describes you? Please take a moment to look at all of the terms on the list." The respondents were then asked, "Still looking at the card, do you think of yourself in any of the other terms as well?" The next question asked, "Still looking at the card, which would you say most strongly does NOT describe you?" "Primary" social identities are the initial responses given. Our measure is similar to the question used recently by Miller, Hesli, and Reisinger (1993, 3) to measure group identifications in the former Soviet Union.

4 These findings are somewhat at odds with other survey research discussed by Mattes (1999). He reported survey data indicating that between one-tenth and one-quarter of South Africans claim a national identity. However, he also notes that this percentage increased significantly from 1994 to 1995 (and it is unclear whether multiple responses to the identity question were recorded). Perhaps our 1996 data reflect the continuation of a trend toward greater acceptance of a national identity among South Africans.

Table 4.1. *The Distribution of Primary Positive Social Identities*

Primary Identity	% All South Africans	% – Within Racial Group[a]			
		African	White	Coloured	Asian-Origin
African	24.2	31.6	.8	3.9	1.5
South African	21.3	19.0	27.9	29.7	31.1
Black	10.5	13.7	0.0	2.7	.4
Zulu	7.4	9.5	0.0	0.0	0.0
Christian	6.7	2.6	22.1	15.2	13.0
Xhosa	5.8	7.3	0.0	.4	0.0
Afrikaner	3.9	0.0	23.9	4.3	0.0
Tswana	3.7	5.2	0.0	0.0	0.0
North Sotho-Sepedi	2.9	4.0	0.0	0.0	0.0
Coloured	2.4	.2	0.0	28.5	0.4
South Setho-Sesotho	2.0	2.8	0.0	0.0	0.0
English	1.4	0.0	10.6	.8	0.0
Moslem	1.1	0.0	0.0	11.3	8.1
Seswati-Swazi	1.0	1.2	0.0	0.0	0.0
Venda	.9	1.1	0.0	0.0	0.0
Tsonga-Shangaan	.8	1.0	0.0	0.0	0.0
White	.7	0.0	4.6	0.0	0.0
European	.6	0.0	4.8	0.0	0.0
Boer	.5	0.0	2.8	0.0	0.0
Hindu	.5	0.0	0.0	0.0	16.7
Indian	.5	0.0	0.0	0.0	15.9
Asian	.4	0.0	0.0	0.0	12.2
Brown	.3	0.0	0.0	3.1	0.0
Other	.3	.1	1.2	0.0	.7
% "South African"[b]	39.6	35.2	53.0	56.6	53.0
N	2,563	2,006	502	256	270

Notes:

[a] χ^2 for differences across race = 4,434.9; $p < .00000$.

[b] Percentage of respondents claiming "South African" identity as a primary *or* secondary identity.

anti-identities). Table 4.2 reports the distribution of the responses to this question.

Significant racial differences exist ($p < .00000$) in the willingness to declare an anti-identity, with 21.9 percent of the African respondents asserting no anti-identity, but with only 5.5 percent of the whites being unable to identify a group with which they negatively identify. Among African South Africans, the most common anti-identity was "Boer," followed by "Afrikaner," which is perhaps not surprising. Interestingly, "white" is not the primary anti-identity of Africans; instead, they focus

Table 4.2. *The Distribution of Primary Negative Social Identities*

Primary Negative Identity	% All South Africans	% – Within Racial Group[a]			
		African	White	Coloured	Asian-Origin
None	18.7	21.9	5.5	15.9	11.6
Boer	16.4	18.7	8.9	10.7	7.5
Black	14.4	9.5	36.7	17.5	19.4
Afrikaner	11.5	13.7	3.7	3.6	13.4
White	5.7	6.9	.6	6.0	1.5
European	3.7	3.9	1.6	4.8	4.5
Zulu	3.6	3.8	2.8	1.2	7.1
Moslem	3.4	1.6	12.2	4.4	2.2
African	2.1	1.0	5.3	4.0	9.7
Hindu	2.1	1.3	5.9	2.4	2.6
Coloured	2.0	1.5	1.6	7.5	1.9
Indian	2.0	2.2	1.6	0.0	1.9
Xhosa	1.9	1.7	2.0	2.8	2.2
Brown	1.8	2.1	.2	2.0	1.5
Other	1.5	.8	4.5	2.4	1.1
Kaffir	1.4	1.4	.4	3.2	0.0
Jewish	1.3	1.1	1.4	2.8	3.4
Asian	1.0	1.1	.6	0.0	1.9
English	1.0	1.0	1.0	.8	.4
Christian	.9	.9	.4	1.2	1.1
Malaysian	.8	.7	1.4	.4	.7
Tsonga-Shangaan	.6	.7	.2	.4	.7
South Sotho-Sesotho	.5	.5	.2	.8	0.0
Venda	.5	.5	.4	.4	.4
North Sotho-Sepedi	.4	.4	.4	.4	.4
Tswana	.3	.2	.4	0.0	.4
Boesman-Hotnot-Hottentot	.3	0.0	0.0	4.0	0.0
Seswati-Swazi	.2	.1	0.0	.4	.4
South African	.2	.2	0.0	.4	0.0
Coolie	.1	0.0	0.0	0.0	.2
N	2,550	2,002	493	252	268

Note:
[a] χ^2 for differences across race = 949.0; $p < .00000$.

on an ideologically defined subset of whites. Still, African anti-identities are strewn across the political landscape.

Whites are much more likely to select a single group with which they disidentify; for over one-third of the whites, "blacks" are their anti-identity. A plurality of Coloured and Asian South Africans also dissociate with "black," but at rates roughly half that of whites. These distributions of identities and anti-identities suggest significant racial polarization in contemporary South Africa, and also indicate that race in South Africa is not just a matter of "black" and "white."

Just because the respondents answered our questions about identity does not mean they vest these terms with psychological significance. We therefore asked them to rate the degree of importance of their social identities.

For South Africans of every race, these identities are indeed important. Roughly three-fourths of each group rated their identity as "very important," the highest point on the five-point scale. Racial differences in the importance of the identity are trivial. Whites, for instance, ascribe as much importance to their identities as do Africans. Group identification seems to be a powerful force throughout South Africa.

We measured the psychic benefits the respondents derive from their social identities by asking them whether they received any security, importance, or self esteem as a result of their group identifications. The results can be found in Table 4.3. Roughly two-thirds of the respondents claimed to derive each of these psychic benefits, with fully 51.5 percent of the respondents claiming strong benefits of all three types. The measure of benefits received is fairly strongly correlated with the rated importance of the respondent's identity ($r = .36$).

Significant racial differences exist in the perceived benefits of group identification, with whites substantially less likely to derive these benefits from their group identifications. For instance, while at least two-thirds of Africans, Coloured people, and South Africans of Asian origin assert that they think better of themselves because of their group identifications, less than one-half of the whites derive a similar benefit. On each of the three measures, non-white South Africans hold similar views; white South Africans stand out as being less likely to claim the psychic benefits of group membership.

Finally, we asked the respondents to evaluate a series of items about the political significance of their group identifications. Their responses are reported in Table 4.4.

Several of the items in Table 4.4 refer to what may be termed "group solidarity." For instance, the second proposition in the table is an assertion about subordinating individual interests to the interests of the group. A large majority of South Africans proclaim the importance of following the group's view, even when it differs from the individual's view. Variability across racial groups in the responses to this proposition is not great, with only a somewhat larger percentage of Coloured respondents asserting greater importance for the group than the individual. Overall, the data in Table 4.4 reveal considerable perceived political importance of these group identities.

Table 4.3. *Perceived Benefits of Group Membership*

Benefit/ Group	Percentage			Mean	Std. Dev.	N
	No Benefit	Uncertain	Benefit			
Feel Secure[a]						
All South Africans	14.6	17.7	67.7	2.53	.74	2,525
African	11.3	17.0	71.7	2.60	.68	1,980
White	36.7	19.8	43.5	2.07	.89	490
Coloured	9.1	18.7	72.2	2.63	.65	252
Asian Origin	12.7	24.3	62.9	2.50	.71	267
Feel Important[b]						2,540
All South Africans	14.7	17.2	68.0	2.53	.74	
African	9.5	17.1	73.4	2.64	.65	1,995
White	44.9	17.5	37.6	1.93	.91	492
Coloured	13.1	17.9	68.9	2.56	.72	251
Asian Origin	15.7	18.0	66.3	2.51	.75	267
Think Better of Myself[c]						
All South Africans	18.4	15.3	66.2	2.48	.79	2,558
African	14.4	15.6	70.1	2.56	.73	1,970
White	41.5	15.4	43.1	2.02	.92	494
Coloured	19.9	13.5	66.5	2.47	.81	251
Asian Origin	17.3	13.5	69.2	2.52	.77	266

Notes:
[a] $\eta^2 = .07; p < .0000.$ [b] $\eta^2 = .12; p < .0000.$ [c] $\eta^2 = .06; p < .0000.$
The questions read:
People have different sorts of feelings as a result of being a member of a group. Which of the following characteristics describes how you feel about being a [GROUP NAMED IN THE OPEN-ENDED QUESTION]
It makes me feel very secure to be a . . .
It makes feel very important to be a . . .
It makes me think much better of myself to think of myself as a . . .

When the items in Table 4.4 are factor analyzed, two significant factors emerge.[5] The first factor, based on the first four items in the table, clearly

5 The results of the initial factor extraction are:
Eigenvalue$_1$ = 1.97, variance explained = 32.8 percent
Eigenvalue$_2$ = 1.21, variance explained = 20.1 percent
Eigenvalue$_3$ = .88, variance explained = 14.6 percent
The items in Table 4.4 are ordered by the size of the factor loadings. The loadings on the first factor range from .47 to .55, and the loadings on the second factor are .59 and .60.

Table 4.4. *Attitudes toward Groups and Social Identity*

Attitude/ Group	Percentage			Mean	Std. Dev.	N
	Agree	Uncertain	Disagree			
My group is best[a]						
All South Africans	68.9	12.2	18.9	2.23	1.13	2,550
Black	70.8	11.2	18.0	2.18	1.14	1,999
White	61.1	15.5	23.4	2.38	1.17	496
Coloured	64.6	15.4	20.1	2.45	.96	254
Asian Origin	61.5	15.9	22.6	2.44	1.08	270
Support my group's view[b]						
All South Africans	69.6	12.7	17.6	2.28	1.07	2,555
Black	68.5	13.4	18.1	2.29	1.09	2,002
White	68.5	10.0	21.5	2.33	1.12	498
Coloured	80.8	11.0	8.2	2.14	.76	255
Asian Origin	72.2	12.2	15.6	2.25	.99	270
Group fate affects me[c]						
All South Africans	79.7	10.8	9.5	1.96	.96	2,555
Black	77.4	12.2	10.4	1.99	.99	2,001
White	83.6	7.8	8.6	1.88	.91	499
Coloured	89.8	5.1	5.1	1.89	.72	255
Asian Origin	88.1	5.9	5.9	1.90	.78	270
Group should stand together[d]						
All South Africans	79.5	10.1	10.4	1.93	1.00	2,557
Black	78.9	11.2	9.9	1.92	1.00	2,002
White	76.0	7.6	16.4	2.03	1.10	500
Coloured	87.8	5.5	6.7	1.84	.83	255
Asian Origin	84.4	7.4	8.1	1.92	.90	270
Can't get much without group[e]						
All South Africans	35.5	28.1	36.3	2.99	1.13	2,552
Black	33.4	29.6	36.9	3.03	1.14	2,000
White	36.9	22.4	40.7	3.02	1.20	496
Coloured	50.2	24.7	25.1	2.71	.97	255
Asian Origin	46.3	21.1	32.6	2.86	1.11	270
Fate has to do with politics[f]						
All South Africans	38.2	25.4	36.4	2.99	1.21	2,555
Black	37.0	28.8	34.2	2.98	1.19	2,000
White	36.6	12.4	51.0	3.19	1.33	500
Coloured	52.5	18.0	29.4	2.71	1.08	255
Asian Origin	44.1	13.0	43.0	3.02	1.21	270

Notes:
[a] $\eta^2 = .01$; $p < .0000$ [b] $\eta^2 = .00$; $p > .05$ [c] $\eta^2 = .00$; $p < .05$
[d] $\eta^2 = .00$; $p > .05$ [e] $\eta^2 = .01$; $p < .0001$ [f] $\eta^2 = .01$; $p < .0000$
The items read:
Of all the groups in South Africa, [MY GROUP] is best.
Even though I might sometimes disagree with the standpoint/viewpoint taken by [MY GROUP], it is extremely important to support [MY GROUP'S] point-of-view.
What happens to [MY GROUP] in South Africa will affect my life a great deal.
When it comes to politics, it is important for all of [MY GROUP] to stand together.
Unless you are a member of a group like [MY GROUP] it is very difficult to get much out of South African politics.
The well-being of [MY GROUP] has more to do with politics than it does with our own hard work.

emphasizes the "group solidarity" items, while the second factor (based on the last two items) refers more to the political relevance of the group. Not surprisingly, these two factors are strongly related ($r = .47$), indicating that those who believe in greater group solidarity are more likely to perceive greater political relevance for groups in South African politics. Racial differences on the group solidarity factor are trivial and insignificant, while racial differences on the perceived political relevance of groups are slight ($\eta^2 = .01$, $p < .0000$) and mainly attributable to Coloured South Africans.

HYPOTHESES CONCERNING THE INTERCONNECTIONS OF SOCIAL IDENTITY SUBDIMENSIONS

Before considering the relationship between social identifications and political intolerance, several hypotheses about the interconnections of these various dimensions of group identities should be tested. Table 4.5 reports the intercorrelations of these six aspects of social identities in South Africa.[6]

Several interesting conclusions emerge from these data. First, claiming a South African identity is *unrelated* to the other aspects of identity. Though a couple of the correlations achieve statistical significance, none of the relationships of South African identity with the other aspects of identity is at all strong. Africans who assert they are "South African" are somewhat more likely to name a group with which they disidentify and to favor strong group solidarity, although these correlations are very weak, and the direction is surprising since we expected that South African identity would be related to *unwillingness* to name an antigroup rather than willingness. White South Africans who identify with the nation tend to derive fewer psychic benefits from their identity, but again

---

6 Note that analysis based on survey data, collected in interviews in numerous languages, with a very large proportion of very poorly educated respondents, will never result in large correlations. Survey data, from any country or context, are rarely capable of producing large relationships because measurement error is so substantial. Indeed, the only way in which large coefficients can be generated is through corrections for attenuation due to measurement unreliability. We have not made such corrections since we are unconvinced that we gain anything by simply bloating the coefficients, especially when reliabilities are relatively low. We therefore rely on tests of statistical significance as an aid to interpreting the coefficients reported in the analysis.

Table 4.5. *Intercorrelations of Social Identity Measures*

Social Identity Dimensions	Dimensions					
	1.	2.	3.	4.	5.	6.
All South Africans						
1. South African Identity	1.00					
2. Strength of Primary Identity	.01	1.00				
3. Psychic Benefits of Identity	−.03	.36*	1.00			
4. Any Anti-Identity	.09*	.01	−.03	1.00		
5. Group Solidarity	.07	.25*	.25*	.12*	1.00	
6. Political Relevance of Groups	.01	.10*	.15*	.06	.48*	1.00
African South Africans						
1. South African Identity	1.00					
2. Strength of Primary Identity	.03	1.00				
3. Psychic Benefits of Identity	.03	.38*	1.00			
4. Any Anti-Identity	.10*	−.00	−.03	1.00		
5. Group Solidarity	.11*	.23*	.21*	.12*	1.00	
6. Political Relevance of Groups	.01	.09*	.14*	.05	.45*	1.00
White South Africans						
1. South African Identity	1.00					
2. Strength of Primary Identity	−.04	1.00				
3. Psychic Benefits of Identity	−.16*	.31*	1.00			
4. Any Anti-Identity	−.07	.09	.14	1.00		
5. Group Solidarity	−.13	.31*	.41*	.16*	1.00	
6. Political Relevance of Groups	−.12	.15*	.19*	.13	.55*	1.00
Coloured South Africans						
1. South African Identity	1.00					
2. Strength of Primary Identity	−.02	1.00				
3. Psychic Benefits of Identity	.06	.41*	1.00			
4. Any Anti-Identity	−.06	.03	.24*	1.00		
5. Group Solidarity	.05	.37*	.34*	.24*	1.00	
6. Political Relevance of Groups	.10	.07	.08	.16	.51*	1.00
South Africans of Asian Origin						
1. South African Identity	1.00					
2. Strength of Primary Identity	.03	1.00				
3. Psychic Benefits of Identity	−.14	.32*	1.00			
4. Any Anti-Identity	−.04	−.11	−.08	1.00		
5. Group Solidarity	.04	.24*	.29*	.10	1.00	
6. Political Relevance of Groups	.06	.15	.14	.08	.56*	1.00

Note:

* *p* < .000. Entries are bivariate correlation coefficients.

the relationship is weak. Generally, these data indicate few consistent consequences of claiming a national identity.[7]

We expected that strong group identifications are more likely to produce stronger anti-identities. In fact, this hypothesis can be strongly *rejected* ($r = .01$). For instance, of those rating their primary identities as "very important," only 18.4 percent were unable to name a group with which they disidentify, compared to 20.6 percent of those for whom their primary identity was "not very important." How strongly one identifies with one's group has little to do with the formation of disidentities, and this is so of each of the racial groups in South Africa.[8]

But are particular attributes of social identities more conducive to the formation of anti-identities? A central hypothesis found in the literature suggests that as the strength of social identities increases, greater emphasis will be placed on group solidarity (e.g., Duckitt 1989). Stronger identification with a group seems to produce a need for internal group conformity. This hypothesis is testable using the data at hand.

The hypothesis receives moderate support – those with stronger primary identities are more likely to hold attitudes favoring group solidarity ($r = .25$). We observe the same correlation when using the psychic benefits index as the predictor of solidarity attitudes ($r = .25$), and these relationships hold within each racial group. Thus, this analysis confirms an important portion of the conventional wisdom on social identities.

Further, support for group solidarity contributes somewhat to the formation of anti-identities, especially among Coloured South Africans ($r = .24$). People who are more concerned with internal group cohesion are more likely to be able to identify a group enemy. This same tendency can be found among all racial groups, although it is quite weak among South Africans of Asian origin and Africans.

---

7 A substantial literature on nationalism and patriotism exists, and the speculation in that literature is that these attitudes have consequences for tolerance (e.g., Feshbach and Sakano 1997; see generally the papers in Bar-Tal and Staub 1997). We resist, however, making very direct references to that body of work because our measure of national identity is neither an indicator of nationalism nor patriotism. We agree with Feshbach and Sakano when they assert, "Clearly, national feelings can be intertwined with intense hostility toward an out-group. Whether such linkage is inevitable, or whether it is only characteristic of a particular subgroup of nationalists who strive to impose their ideology and affect on other patriots, are questions that require systematic empirical study" (1997, 93).

8 Like many aspects of SIT, the hypothesis that strong ingroup attachments automatically generate strong outgroup detachments is controversial (e.g., Hinkle and Brown 1990). We will return to this issue in the following discussion, but it seems clear that it is the attitudes and values associated with claiming a strong ingroup identity that are associated with outgroup antipathy and intolerance, not identity *ipso facto*.

Finally, as we noted previously, those more concerned about group solidarity are more likely to assert the political relevance of groups in South African politics.

Generally, these data suggest that those who ascribe more importance to their group identification derive greater psychic benefits from it, and are in turn more likely to assert the need for group solidarity (and, to a lesser degree, to recognize the political relevance of groups in South Africa). The desire for solidarity is associated with the ability to identify an outgroup, and makes identities politically relevant. Thus, these data in fact confirm several of the basic micro-level processes assumed by Social Identity Theory.

HYPOTHESES CONNECTING IDENTITIES WITH ANTIPATHY, THREAT, AND INTOLERANCE

One hypothesized implication of strong group identifications is that people will tend to see the world as composed of political enemies. Those with stronger identities will therefore be more likely to judge a variety of political movements negatively, and perhaps to be threatened by them, and to be unwilling to tolerate their political activity. This hypothesis is directly testable with the data at hand.

The respondents were asked to rate a variety of groups "currently active in social and political life" in South Africa. The groups were selected in part on the basis of earlier research in South Africa (see Gouws 1993) and in part by our assessment of which groups were likely to be common targets of antipathy. A sampling of groups from the left and right was presented, and the respondents were asked to score each on an eleven-point scale ranging from 1, indicating disliking the group very much, to 11, which means that the respondent likes the group very much.[9] We constructed a general measure of group antipathy by determining the number of groups rated at the most extreme negative point on the scale. We hypothesize that stronger group identities are associated with more outgroup antipathy.

We also measured the level of intolerance of the political group that the respondent hates the most, relying on the "least-liked" measurement approach (see Sullivan, Piereson, and Marcus 1982, and Chapter 3). After rating each group, the respondents were asked to indicate the group they disliked the most, second most, third most, and fourth most. We then asked the respondents whether their disliked groups should be

---

9 See Table 3.2 for the frequencies on these ratings.

allowed to (a) stand as a candidate for an elected position, (b) hold street demonstrations in the community, and (c) exist as a political group (not be officially banned). Obviously, democratic tolerance requires that all groups be allowed to organize, to proselytize others, and to attempt to control the government.

As we have noted in Chapter 3, South Africans tend to be quite intolerant. About two-thirds of the respondents would ban their most disliked group and nearly three-fourths would prohibit the group from demonstrating. Tolerant South Africans are in a distinct minority.

To simplify the analysis that follows, we will use an index of the three items focused on the most disliked group as our principal measure of intolerance. Most generally, we hypothesize that intolerance will be most commonplace among those more firmly attached to their own group.

Since intolerance typically flows from perceptions that groups are threatening, we have also measured the degree of threat posed to the respondent by the most disliked group. The perceptions were measured using semantic differential scales and nine antipodal descriptors of the group (see Chapter 3). For instance, the endpoints of the continuum used to collect the data for sociotropic dangerousness perceptions were "not dangerous to society" and "dangerous to society." Though the data were collected through balanced scales, all responses have been recoded so that a high score indicates a more threatened response.

A factor analysis of the set of threat perceptions reveals a two-dimensional factor structure, but the second factor was overwhelmingly defined by the items referring to the power and potential power of the group. Indeed, the two power items typically correlate *negatively* with the other threat perceptions. The other seven items all derive from a single factor, and the pattern loadings differed little depending on whether the most disliked or the other highly disliked group was rated. The best indicator of threat perceptions was sociotropic danger – the dangerousness of the group to society. For this analysis, our measure of threat perceptions is the factor score derived from analyzing the seven principal measures of threat perceptions.

To reiterate, we hypothesize that those with stronger group identifications will hold higher levels of group antipathy, will perceive their political enemies as more threatening, and hence will be less tolerant of them. The correlations relevant to these three hypotheses are reported in Table 4.6.

Consider first the relationships between the dimensions of identity and the summary measure of group antipathy (the first data column in Table 4.6). There are indeed some important consequences of identity for antipathy – for instance, those who more strongly believe in the need for group solidarity are more likely to hate a wider variety of political groups

Table 4.6. *Intercorrelations of Social Identity and Political Intolerance*

Attitudes	Group Antipathy	Threat	Intolerance
All South Africans			
South African Identity	−.02	.02	−.05
Strength of Primary Identity	.09*	.07*	.05
Psychic Benefits of Identity	.15*	.13*	.11*
Any Anti-Identity	.09*	.08*	.08*
Group Solidarity	.16*	.15*	.12*
Political Relevance of Groups	.06*	.00	.03
African South Africans			
South African Identity	.02	.08*	.00
Strength of Primary Identity	.08*	.06	.01
Psychic Benefits of Identity	.15*	.08*	.04
Any Anti-Identity	.08*	.13*	.12*
Group Solidarity	.14*	.16*	.07*
Political Relevance of Groups	.02	.02	−.04
White South Africans			
South African Identity	−.20*	.05	−.15*
Strength of Primary Identity	.15*	.07	.19*
Psychic Benefits of Identity	.24*	−.01	.17*
Any Anti-Identity	.14*	.02	.13
Group Solidarity	.22*	.16*	.31*
Political Relevance of Groups	.20*	.07	.25*
Coloured South Africans			
South African Identity	−.09	−.07	−.04
Strength of Primary Identity	.13	.09	.17
Psychic Benefits of Identity	.23*	.18	.13
Any Anti-Identity	.20*	.25*	.13
Group Solidarity	.25*	.11	.13
Political Relevance of Groups	.15	.15	.12
South Africans of Asian Origin			
South African Identity	.09	.04	.02
Strength of Primary Identity	−.04	.04	.11
Psychic Benefits of Identity	−.14	−.02	.11
Any Anti-Identity	−.02	.02	−.02
Group Solidarity	.18*	.19*	.24*
Political Relevance of Groups	.10	.14	.11

Note:

* $p < .001$. Entries are bivariate correlation coefficients.

in South Africa. The overall relationship is .16, but the correlation exceeds .20 for both white and Coloured South Africans. This finding supports the proposition that group identities are associated with political hatreds that may be inimical to democratic politics.

There is also some correlation between group antipathy and the degree of psychic benefits derived from group attachments, with those receiving more benefits being more likely to hate more groups ($r = .15$). Again, the association is stronger among white and Coloured people. Surprisingly, the direction of the relationship is reversed among South Africans of Asian origin, with those deriving more psychic benefits from group membership holding *less* group antipathy. This may be a function of the relatively high prevalence of religious identifications among Asian South Africans.[10]

Several of the other aspects of group identity have selective connections to group antipathy. For instance, beliefs about the political relevance of groups are related to higher levels of antipathy among white and Coloured South Africans, but not among Africans, and only weakly so among South Africans of Asian origin. South African identity is associated with less antipathy among white and Coloured South Africans, but (slightly) more hatred among South Africans of Asian origin, and is unrelated to levels of antipathy among Africans. White and Coloured South Africans who hold an anti-identity tend to hate more political groups, although this is less true of Africans and not true of Asian South Africans. We will defer considering the implications of these findings until the multivariate analysis we present in the next section.

A more direct test of the main hypothesis can be found in the second data column, which reports the correlations with the summary index of perceived threat from the most disliked group. Here we also find similar, interesting relationships. Deriving greater psychic benefits and asserting more need for group solidarity are associated with a greater perceived threat from one's most hated political enemies ($r = .13$), as is the group solidarity variable ($r = .15$). A few additional idiosyncratic relationships are significant (e.g., among Coloured South Africans, higher perceptions of threat are found among those claiming an anti-identity).

Finally, stronger group attachments are associated with greater political intolerance, although the relationships are slightly weaker (perhaps because they are more distal). Those who derive greater psychic benefits

---

10 For instance, among those claiming a religious self-identity, the correlation between psychic benefits and group antipathy is .12; for those holding a nonreligious identity, the relationship is −.23. The relatively small numbers of respondents, and the skewed distributions on the psychic benefits variable, make it unwise to try to untangle these relationships further.

from their group identity and who believe more strongly in group solidarity are more likely to be intolerant. Among Africans, the only aspect of identity that relates to intolerance is being able to name an anti-identity group, but among the other three racial groupings, virtually all aspects of group identity are connected to intolerance. Some of these relationships are quite strong – for instance, among whites, a stronger belief in the necessity of group solidarity is significantly associated with intolerance ($r = .31$). Generally, except perhaps among the African majority, those who hold more meaningful group identities are more likely to be intolerant.

MULTIVARIATE ANALYSIS

Not all of the aspects of social identity performed equally well in predicting antipathy, threat, and intolerance. Generally, and across all South Africans, beliefs about the importance of group solidarity are the strongest predictors of these antidemocratic attitudes, followed by the psychic benefits derived from group membership. To consider the multivariate relationships more fully, we therefore confine our attention to these two variables. Table 4.7 reports a multivariate analysis of the interconnections between these two aspects of identity and the three dimensions of attitudes toward hated political groups.

Perhaps the most important finding from the coefficients reported in the various parts of this table is the contribution of attitudes toward group solidarity to antipathy, threat, and intolerance.[11] Among all four racial groups, solidarity attitudes are significantly related to group antipathy; among all but Coloured South Africans, heightened group solidarity is significantly associated with greater perceived threats; and

---

11 Our analytical strategy calls for testing the null hypotheses connecting aspects of social identities with political intolerance within each of these racial/ethnic/linguistic groups. Thus, for each coefficient in Table 4.7, we report a significance test indicating whether we can reject the hypothesis that the coefficient comes from a population in which the parameter is zero. The most important comparison across groups is simply whether the coefficients are significant within each group. It is that comparison that we consider in the text.

Some readers may be interested in other forms of crossgroup analysis – for instance, a test of whether the difference between the coefficients from two groups is statistically significant. Such tests are readily calculable using data reported in the table. For instance, a t test for the difference in regression coefficients can be conducted on the basis of the sample coefficients, the standard errors, and the numbers of cases within each group. Those conducting such tests should be cognizant of the different sample sizes for the various groups and especially the large sample of African South Africans.

Table 4.7. *Multivariate Analysis of the Interconnections of*
Social Identity and Political Intolerance

Attitudes	Group Antipathy			Threat Perceptions			Political Intolerance		
	b	s.e.	Beta	b	s.e.	Beta	b	s.e.	Beta
All South Africans									
(N = 2,477; * standardized regression coefficient is significant at $p < .0001$)									
Threat Perceptions	–	–	–	–	–	–	.36	.02	.31*
Group Antipathy	–	–	–	.06	.01	.14*	.04	.01	.08*
Group Solidarity	.35	.06	.13*	.12	.02	.11*	.06	.03	.05
Psychic Benefits	.21	.04	.11*	.06	.02	.08*	.04	.02	.05
R^2			.04*			.05*			.13*
Standard Deviation		2.18			.87			1.02	
Standard Error of Estimate		2.14			.85			.95	
African South Africans									
(N = 1,951; * standardized regression coefficient is significant at $p < .001$)									
Threat Perceptions	–	–	–	–	–	–	.36	.03	.30*
Group Antipathy	–	–	–	.07	.01	.16*	.04	.01	.08*
Group Solidarity	.25	.06	.09*	.14	.02	.13*	.01	.03	.01
Psychic Benefits	.24	.04	.13*	.03	.02	.04	.00	.02	.01
R^2			.03*			.05*			.11*
Standard Deviation		2.07			.83			.97	
Standard Error of Estimate		2.04			.81			.92	
White South Africans									
(N = 476; * standardized regression coefficient is significant at $p < .01$)									
Threat Perceptions	–	–	–	–	–	–	.30	.06	.21*
Group Antipathy	–	–	–	.05	.02	.15*	.08	.02	.16*
Group Solidarity	.46	.14	.16*	.15	.05	.16*	.31	.06	.23*
Psychic Benefits	.36	.09	.19*	-.07	.03	-.11	.03	.04	.03
R^2			.08*			.05			.17*
Standard Deviation		2.47			.82			1.18	
Standard Error of Estimate		2.37			.80			1.08	
Coloured South Africans									
(N = 242; * standardized regression coefficient is significant at $p < .05$)									
Threat Perceptions	–	–	–	–	–	–	.25	.06	.26*
Group Antipathy	–	–	–	.09	.03	.23*	.02	.03	.06
Group Solidarity	.77	.26	.20*	.01	.10	.01	.11	.10	.07
Psychic Benefits	.34	.12	.18*	.09	.05	.12	.02	.05	.04
R^2			.10*			.09*			.10*
Standard Deviation		2.40			.91			.90	
Standard Error of Estimate		2.29			.88			.86	
South African of Asian Origin									
(N = 264; * standardized regression coefficient is significant at $p < .05$)									
Threat Perceptions	–	–	–	–	–	–	.48	.07	.39*
Group Antipathy	–	–	–	.10	.02	.29*	.06	.03	.15*
Group Solidarity	.74	.20	.24*	.16	.07	.15*	.16	.08	.12*
Psychic Benefits	-.39	.12	-.20*	-.01	.04	-.02	.09	.05	.11
R^2			.07*			.12*			.26*
Standard Deviation		2.40			.84			1.03	
Standard Error of Estimate		2.32			.79			.90	

among whites and South Africans of Asian origin, there is even a significant direct connection to political intolerance. (And note that, as in all earlier research, threat perceptions directly contribute to political intolerance, among each of the groups.) The connection between solidarity and threat is especially important since earlier research has *not* been successful at identifying useful predictors of perceived threat. Group identity *per se* does not contribute to perceptions of threat, but *among identifiers who believe in the necessity of internal group conformity, the threat posed by their political enemies is perceived as more substantial.* Thus, attitudes toward group solidarity (which in all instances flow directly from the psychic benefits of identity) play a substantial role in contributing to political intolerance.

We also note that those deriving psychic benefits from their group identity are more likely to express higher levels of group antipathy (except among South Africans of Asian origin). These relationships hold even when controlling for attitudes toward group solidarity.

It is perhaps noteworthy that the effects of social identities on intolerance are most strongly felt among *white South Africans*. That is, variability in social identities among whites is more closely connected to antipathy, threat, and intolerance than among any other group in South Africa (e.g., compare the unstandardized regression coefficients across groups).

These findings might have something to do with the relative status of the different groups in South Africa. Sidanius and his colleagues (e.g., Sidanius 1993) have proposed Social Dominance Theory (SDT) as a means of accounting for differences across groups in the importance of social identities. According to this theory, social identities are more significant for socially dominant groups. Their concept "asymmetrical ingroup bias" – which asserts that the link between ingroup favoritism and outgroup hatred is stronger for the socially dominant group (Sidanius, Pratto, and Rabinowitz 1994) – may provide an explanation of why the relationships between the identity and tolerance variables are stronger among whites in South Africa. This is certainly a finding that warrants additional investigation, but it appears that the deleterious effects of group identities are not confined to any single segment of the South African population.

In sum, we have found that those who derive psychic benefits from their social identities are more likely to assert the need for group solidarity. These two attributes of identities – benefits and solidarity – in turn structure antipathy toward groups in general and perceptions of threat from political enemies in specific. Antipathy and especially threat lead to political intolerance. Thus, the combined effects, direct and indirect, of these two attributes of social identity are considerable.

DISCUSSION

In this research, we have supported several important deductions from the existing literature on social identities and democratization. Most important, stronger and more developed group identities are associated with greater intergroup antipathy, threat, and intolerance. Strong group identities and their associated attitudes are therefore inimical to democratic politics in South Africa. Thus, we have made at least some progress in understanding the process through which subcultural pluralism undermines democracy.

Critics of the social identity literature have suggested that identity is a multidimensional concept, and that not all aspects of group identification fit neatly within Tajfel's original formulation of the theory (e.g., Hinkle and Brown 1990). Our findings certainly support this view. Simple social identities do not directly and automatically turn into intolerance. More important, we have been successful in identifying the specific aspects of social identity that do lead to intolerance; it is not identity *per se* but the collateral attitudes that sometimes arise from identities that are consequential for democratic values. More research must be conducted on the dimensionality of identities, but our analysis clearly points to attitudes toward group solidarity and the perceived psychic benefits of group membership as crucial aspects of the group identities that people hold.

Our most important findings characterize each of the major racial/ ethnic/linguistic groups in South Africa. Nonetheless, some group-specific anomalies have emerged, and we have not been entirely successful at explaining them. It may be that group is a surrogate for other important moderating variables that influence the relationship between identities and intolerance. For instance, some research has suggested that differences along the individual–collectivism continuum may play an important conditional role, with the dominant effects of strong social identities being confined to those who hold collectivist orientations (e.g., Hinkle and Brown 1990). Empirical evidence on this score is spotty and inconsistent (e.g., Lee and Ward 1998), and we are not certain that the most important difference across these South African groups is in fact on this dimension. Nonetheless, this is an issue worthy of further consideration (see also Berry 1984).

These findings are drawn of course from a single point in time – 1996. There is some evidence that South Africans are developing a greater sense of national identity, and perhaps this process will continue. Unfortunately for those favoring a democratic South Africa, however, we have not found much support for the view that such identities contribute to lower levels of antipathy, threat, or intolerance. Though developing a sense of national identity is surely important, it is not clear that those who think of themselves as South African will necessarily be any more tolerant of their fellow South Africans.

This research supports what appears to be a fundamental aspect of social interactions: People who identify with a group tend to develop attitudes about the nature of individual allegiance to and solidarity with the group, and these attitudes often give rise to a form of xenophobia – political intolerance. Yet, given the limited analysis of these data to date, we cannot be certain whether group identities are a cause or an effect of xenophobia. It may well be that those who are more fearful of their political enemies seek solace and protection from groups, rather than groups contributing independently toward antipathy and xenophobia. The entire causal structure of identities is a question worthy of considerable additional research.

Finally, these data reinforce the view that intolerance is a social process, and is not entirely an attribute of individual psychology. People learn where they belong in society, and this knowledge of belonging often leads to beliefs about not belonging. This process of adjustment results in people learning who their enemies are, which then leads to perceptions of threat and ultimately to intolerance. It perhaps does not follow that social isolation contributes to tolerance and democratic values, but the way in which individuals come to understand their location in social and group space is crucial for the attitudes they form. Future research on South African identities should be especially mindful that individuals do not live in splendid isolation, but instead are part of a complex and intricate social fabric.

The analysis reported in this chapter relies upon a fairly abstract and context-free measure of political intolerance. Since real civil liberties often turn on contextual factors – such as who is speaking, what is being said, and where the speaking takes places – the next chapter moves away from this primary focus on the individual citizen to consider how circumstances – local and national – influence the judgments people make about whether to tolerate their political enemies.

5

Making Tolerance Judgments:
The Effect of Context, Local and National

In most studies of political tolerance, researchers investigate relatively abstract and context-free attitudes, using measures such as: "Suppose [an] admitted Communist wanted to make a speech in your community. Should he be allowed to speak, or not?" Tolerance is conceptualized as a generalized willingness to allow unpopular political views to be expressed. Such questions are asked annually in the General Social Survey (GSS), for instance, and are widely analyzed by social scientists (e.g., Gibson 1992a; Bobo and Licari 1989; Karpov 1999).

Attitudes of this kind are no doubt important, but they may not tell the full story of how people form opinions when it comes to actual civil liberties disputes. Actual civil liberties controversies may well be more contextualized than suggested by the relatively abstract measures that are typically employed by researchers. Disputes over civil liberties typically turn on context – *who is speaking* is important, *what is being said* is important, and *where the speaking will take place* is important. People certainly employ general predispositions in judging actual civil liberties controversies,[1] but their general predispositions are thought by many to interact substantially with a variety of contextual elements. Consequently, knowing one's predispositions on matters of political tolerance may not necessarily generate successful predictions about whether one will tolerate a specific group acting within a particular context (Marcus et al. 1995).

---

1 Marcus et al. (1995) refer to these general tolerance attitudes as "standing decisions." They argue (1995, 21) "that over time, people will tend to make similar tolerance judgments when faced with a highly disliked group within a particular context. In essence, this standing tolerance decision is something of a habit that people can fall back on when a new but similar situation demands a judgment concerning civil liberties." This approach is similar to that adopted by Gibson and Bingham (1982).

Some earlier research on controversies over civil liberties explicitly incorporates this concern with context. For instance, Gibson and Bingham (1985) analyzed the dispute in Skokie, Illinois, over the attempt of members of the National Socialist Party of America, a Nazi group, to hold a demonstration in the village. Gibson (1987) demonstrated that contextual factors had much to do with support for the right of the Ku Klux Klan to hold an antihomosexual demonstration in Houston. Similarly, Gibson and Tedin (1988), analyzing support for gay rights in Houston, incorporate several contextual variables into their analysis. Sniderman et al. (1989) address the question of contextual influences through an analysis of consistency in tolerance responses across groups and activities. Chanley (1994) examines a particular aspect of context – the personalization of threat. Marcus et al. (1995) have devoted the greatest amount of effort to understanding how context influences decisions, developing a model that involves both predispositions and perceptions of the context of civil liberties disputes. Nelson, Clawson, and Oxley (1997) also treat context quite seriously in their analysis of the role of the mass media in framing civil liberties disputes. Even longitudinal work on political tolerance (e.g., Davis 1975; Sullivan, Piereson, and Marcus 1982) may be thought of as contextual in the sense that changes over time in the perceived threat from political enemies are incorporated in the understandings of intolerance. And Stouffer's (1955) original research on intolerance in the United States was very heavily contextual since it was a case study of the Red Scare. Thus, scholars recognize that the context of a civil liberties dispute is important when it comes to understanding the dynamics of political intolerance.

Crossnational research also typically treats context as necessary to understanding tolerance judgments. Sullivan et al. (1985), for instance, demonstrate that national circumstances shape the identification of hated political enemies, even if substantial crossnational commonalities exist in the etiology of intolerance. Sullivan et al. (1993) address the way in which elite–mass differences are shaped by systemic attributes. Some quite useful non-U.S. case studies of tolerance exist, and these too rely heavily on incorporating context into their analysis (e.g., the Canadian Charter of Rights study by Sniderman et al. 1996). The small but growing crossnational literature on tolerance has contributed significantly to our understanding of different contextual influences on political tolerance (as in the analysis of the effect of education on tolerance in Russia; see Gibson and Duch 1993a).

Nonetheless, earlier research has left many important questions unanswered. We do not know very much about which specific contextual factors are important and why. For instance, Marcus et al. (1995) have left us with the unexpected puzzle that the perceived power of a group has nothing to do with willingness to tolerate it: Powerful and power-less groups are tolerated (or not tolerated) at equivalent levels. More-over, we are unclear about the role of deliberation in civil liberties disputes. In most real controversies, people talk with one another, try to convince opponents to change their views, and attempt to frame events in particular ways. In real disputes, the role of leaders is often crucial. Our understanding of the precise role of contextual factors in the making of a decision to tolerate or not is limited indeed.

Moreover, one major contextual variable has received little attention in extant research: the nature of the political system. Most research on political tolerance is based in the United States, an unusual political system in which questions of political tolerance are concentrated on the fringes of the country's ideological space. Tolerance in Bosnia, Kosovo, Rwanda, and is South Africa most likely has quite different characteristics than it does in the United States.

The purpose of this chapter is therefore to investigate the influence of contextual factors on tolerance judgments. Based on a highly realistic experimental vignette presented to our representative sample of the South African public, we test the hypotheses that willingness to tolerate a demonstration by one's political enemies is affected by: (a) the community's antipathy toward the proposed demonstration; (b) whether the demonstration is expected to result in law breaking and violence; (c) the role of community leaders; and (d) the effect of deliberation and debate. Our general findings are quite unexpected: The specific context of the civil liberties controversy matters little to South Africans. Instead, atti-tudinal predispositions – in particular, preexisting threat perceptions – seem to shape all aspects of tolerance judgments. We conclude that context probably matters for tolerance, but that it is the South African context – the immediacy and realism of the threat posed by political com-petitors – that is more influential, not the elements of the situation itself. In short, context matters, but not always in direct and simple ways.

THE ROLE OF CONTEXT IN CIVIL LIBERTIES DISPUTES

Actual civil liberties disputes differ a great deal from the simplistic sce-nario depicted by the question, "Should a Communist be allowed to make a speech in your community?" Consider the famous (or infamous) case of Nazis attempting to demonstrate in Skokie, Illinois, the home of a large number of Holocaust survivors (see Gibson and Bingham 1985; Barnum 1982; Downs 1985; Strum 1999). Many elements of that context were crucial to understanding how people felt about the dispute. Some anticipated violence at the march; others did not. Some thought the march would be an opportunity to demonstrate community strength and solidarity; others thought irreparable harm would be done to those seeing or thinking of the hated Nazis marching in their community. Some framed the issue around Nazis; other framed it around the ordinances passed by the village, and their impact on First Amendment rights (on framing in civil liberties controversies, see Nelson, Clawson, and Oxley 1997). The role of the courts was crucial in the dispute, as was the intervention of the American Civil Liberties Union (Gibson and Bingham 1985). Perhaps most important, opinion was dynamic; it evolved over the course of the squabble as different aspects of the context became more or less salient (Barnum 1982). Not many of the highly significant details of this civil liberties battle could be captured in the simple question, "Should Nazis be allowed to hold a demonstration in your community?"

How is it that contextual influences become so powerful in civil liberties controversies? Most likely, contextual aspects of disputes evoke value conflict. Most people, when confronted with a stimulus like, "Should a Communist be allowed to give a speech in your community?" react fairly simply according to how despicable and threatening they perceive Communists to be. They probably do not engage in a cost/benefit analysis of policies to repress Communists, since the question encourages people to think simplistically about "whether to do bad things to groups that are threatening." Earlier work has shown that if people are encouraged to process the stimulus in more complete, multidimensional terms, they often change their view based on the relative weight they assign to the multiple values implicated by disputes (Gibson 1996d, 1998a). Thus, those who are tolerant may not initially think about the possibility of violence were a demonstration to be held, just as those who are intolerant may fail to consider the implications of allowing the authorities to say who can and cannot protest. Context is inevitably multidimensional, requiring people to evaluate and judge aspects of the dispute they might not otherwise consider when reacting to hypothetical and abstract survey questions.

This way of thinking about contextual influences comports well with recently developed theories of the survey response that emphasize the process of making judgments in politics. Instead of understanding responses to survey questions as a simple act of recall – in which the respondents search their memories to retrieve a thought that can serve as the basis for a reply – this viewpoint posits that many respondents are actually *creating* opinions, deriving them from the particular values stimulated by the question. In actual political disputes, people must do far more than "look up" the appropriate attitude in their minds and draw a conclusion, and especially when asked to consider complex topics like whether one should put up with one's enemies, many people may not find looking up the answer in their memories an altogether easy task. The point is that civil liberties controversies require people to make judgments, often based on multiple values, not all of which are of equal importance. Thus, instead of conceptualizing people as holders of attitudes and values, it may be useful to view them as makers of judgments and choices.

Thus, real politics is contextual; it involves attitudes and values, but it also involves facts and circumstances. It involves figuring out how incidents in the political environment connect with attitudes and values, and, more important, how conflicts among competing values get managed. A contextual model of tolerance is therefore a deliberative model of tolerance. Consequently, to understand the nature of mass opinion, it is necessary to try to reproduce something of the structure of real politics within our surveys; respondents must be asked not simply to recall attitudes and values, but to apply them to concrete circumstances involving ambiguity, uncertainty, and conflict. That is, it may be useful to examine how citizens make political judgments. Simple, abstract questions like those used in the GSS surely do not accomplish this.

One purpose here is to move beyond studying citizens as little more than holders of attitudes and values, and look instead at the ways in which people make concrete judgments in contextualized circumstances. Perforce, we employ hypothetical (and highly simplified) conflicts, a strategy inferior in many important ways to case studies examining actual political conflicts.[2] But what we lose in depth we perhaps gain back in the strength of the causal inferences that can be drawn from our experimental research design. By combining survey and experimental methods, we are able to gain considerable purchase on the role of contextual factors in tolerance judgments. Our general hypothesis is that people are influenced by contextual factors when making decisions about whether to tolerate political activity by their hated political enemies.

USING VIGNETTES TO STUDY CONTEXT

Contextual processes are not easily investigated within the context of mass public surveys. Instead, the purpose of such surveys is usually to measure general predispositions (such as attitudes and values) or overall propensities (such as the likelihood of voting). For surveys to address contextual problems, it is necessary to turn to the methodology of experimental vignettes.[3]

---

2 Sniderman (1993) refers to these case studies as "firehouse" studies. See, for examples of this genre of research, Gibson and Bingham 1985; Gibson 1987.

3 On experimentation in general, see McGraw 1996; Kinder and Palfrey 1993.

South African Intolerance as It Is

Experimental vignettes embedded within representative national samples provide a promising means for understanding contextual influences on mass opinions.[4] A vignette is a short story about a political event.[5] The value of vignettes is first that they allow the contextualization of opinions. Instead of asking an abstract question about political tolerance, a concrete story provides the respondents with a context containing many important details about a civil liberties controversy. These details are often quite consequential for the opinions that people form.

The power of vignettes such as these derives from their experimental nature, and the consequent ability to test hypotheses about causal effects. If the investigator can identify specific attributes of the context as potential causes of civil liberties judgments, then those attributes can be varied in the vignettes. With the random assignment of respondents to the various treatment conditions (the different versions of the vignettes), strong causal conclusions are possible. If respondents make different choices, and if all other differences among the respondents have been randomized, then the most likely causal source of the choices is the attribute that is manipulated in the vignette. In this sense, internal validity (whether the dependent variable was in fact caused by the independent variable – see Campbell and Stanley 1963, 3) is unusually strong.[6]

MODELING CONTEXT

Civil liberties disputes involve myriad contextual elements. In the South African context, such disputes typically often include the circumstances such as those described in this section.

Experimental Manipulations and Hypotheses

This portion of the interview began with a short story about a dispute over the civil liberties of a group that the respondent disliked a great

---

4 Sniderman and Grob (1996, 378) argue that a revolution has taken place in survey research methodology: "... the principal breakthrough has been to combine the distinctive external validity advantages of the representative public opinion survey with the decisive internal validity strengths of the fully randomized, multifaceted experiment."

5 Rossi and his collaborators probably deserve the most credit for developing the use of experimental vignettes. See, for example, Rossi and Anderson 1982; Rossi and Nock 1982. In political science, Sniderman and his colleagues have been instrumental in developing the technique (e.g., Sniderman et al. 1996). For an excellent example of applying experimental vignettes to the study of political tolerance, see Marcus et al. 1995.

6 The distinction between internal and external validity was first made by Campbell. For an explication, see Cook and Campbell 1979.

deal.[7] In the stories, four contextual characteristics were manipulated, resulting in sixteen versions of the vignette. Each respondent heard only a single story, and respondents were randomly assigned to vignette versions. The manipulations were orthogonal to each other, and the four dummy variables representing the manipulations are therefore uncorrelated. Table 5.1 reports the attributes we varied in the stories. Thus, the most threatening version of the vignettes read:

As an election approaches, members of the [DISLIKED GROUP] want to hold a rally in a community where most people support their opponents. People in the community are worried that the [DISLIKED GROUP] will not follow all of the laws during the rally. The [DISLIKED GROUP] intends to give speeches that will make most people in the community very, very angry. Local community leaders aren't sure whether the rally should be allowed to take place since they say the speeches will be pretty dangerous and threatening. Some people are saying that the [DISLIKED GROUP] shouldn't be allowed to speak because their speeches will only recruit more people to the [DISLIKED GROUP].

The least threatening version read:

As an election approaches, members of the [DISLIKED GROUP] want to hold a rally in a community where most people support their opponents. The [DISLIKED GROUP] promises that it will follow all of the laws during the rally. The [DISLIKED GROUP] intends to give speeches, but not many people in the community care one way or the other about what they have to say. Local community leaders urge that the rally be allowed to take place since they say the speeches aren't really very dangerous or threatening. Some people are saying "let them speak because when they speak they show everyone just how foolish their ideals are."

After hearing the story, the respondents were asked to make a judgment about whether the rally should be allowed to take place. We expected that version 1 would generate the most intolerant responses and that version 16 would produce the highest level of tolerance.

The degree of antipathy toward the political enemy also varies. Some respondents were asked to judge a potential demonstration by the group they identified as their most disliked political enemy, while others were asked to respond to a scenario involving another highly disliked group.

---

7 The vignette relies upon the "least-liked" methodology developed by Sullivan, Piereson, and Marcus 1982 (and explicated in Chapter 3). This approach is sometimes referred to as "content controlled" because it allows the respondents to identify the groups that are most relevant to them. The degree of antipathy toward the group is a fifth experimental manipulation, with half of the respondents hearing a story about the group they dislike the most, and the other half hearing a story about another highly disliked group. Because the identity of the group was not randomly designated, some might consider this experiment to be a "quasi-experiment" (see McGraw 1996).

Table 5.1. *The Structure of the Vignette's Experimental Manipulations*

Manipulation	Versions	Hypotheses
Anticipated Lawlessness	0. People in the community are worried that the [GROUP] will not follow all of the laws during the rally. 1. The [GROUP] promises it will follow all of the laws during the rally.	No promise of lawfulness → Intolerance
Community Antipathy	0. The [GROUP] intends to give speeches, but not many people in the community care one way or the other about what they have to say. 1. The [GROUP] intends to give speeches that will make most people in the community very, very angry.	Community anger → Intolerance
Role of Leaders	0. Local community leaders aren't sure whether the rally should be allowed to take place since they say the speeches will be pretty dangerous and threatening. 1. Local community leaders urge that the rally be allowed to take place since they say the speeches aren't really very dangerous or threatening.	Intolerant leaders → Intolerance
Deliberation	0. Some people are saying that the [GROUP] shouldn't be allowed to speak because their speeches will only recruit more people to the [GROUP]. 1. Some people are saying "let them speak because when they speak they show everyone just how foolish their ideals are."	Antitolerance deliberation → Intolerance

Note: The opening sentence of all vignettes read, "As an election approaches, members of the [GROUP] want to hold a rally in a community where most people support their opponents."

Because this is a true experiment (with random assignment of individuals to vignettes), doubts about causality, which frequently concern social sciences, are minimized.[8]

The four experimental manipulations represent the various hypotheses under consideration.

Anticipated Lawlessness. A key contextual variable in many civil liberties disputes is expectations about whether the exercise of the liberty will be disruptive. Many of those who would not object to a private meeting held by their political enemies would nonetheless object to a demonstration being held on public streets. The threat of disorder, even violence, is often given as one of the key justifications for denying political groups access to public places for political purposes (Gibson and Bingham 1985; Gibson 1987). Though opponents of a group have no legal right to veto a demonstration by threatening violence (e.g., the so-called heckler's veto), anticipations of violence often color reactions to attempts to hold demonstrations. Thus, we told half of the respondents that the people in the community were worried about potential lawlessness, while we told the other half that the group promises to follow all of the laws. Of course, even in the latter case respondents may anticipate violence at the demonstration, either because the group breaks its promise or because the violence originates elsewhere. This possibility we consider more fully later in this Chapter.

Community Antipathy. Demonstrations are often planned for "enemy territory" in a bid for publicity for the demonstrators' cause. An obvious example is the Skokie/Nazi dispute. The Nazis were from Chicago, and were embroiled in a controversy over the desegregation of a local neighborhood. Skokie had absolutely nothing to do with the original conflict. The Chicago Nazis sought to demonstrate in Skokie in a bid, entirely successful, for publicity for their cause.

In South Africa, rival political parties often try to demonstrate in communities dominated by the opposition. Indeed, no-go zones are areas of the country (many in KwaZulu-Natal) where the appearance of members

---

8 The experiment gets its external validity, first, from being embedded in a representative sample of South Africans, and, second, by the highly realistic nature of the story. At the time of the survey, South Africa was experiencing numerous conflicts precisely over the issue of whether political parties could demonstrate in "enemy" territory (the issue of no-go zones; see Chapter 2). We are virtually certain that nearly all of the respondents found it easy to imagine and understand the circumstances portrayed in the vignette.

of an opposition party regularly incites violence. Parties attempt such demonstrations not only as a means of gaining publicity, but also as an effort to recruit local support. Campaigning in "enemy territory" is thought to be more beneficial to the party than campaigning in areas where support already exists. Thus, one of our contextual manipulations has to do with the reaction of the community to the proposed demonstration. In one version of the vignette, the community is indifferent; in the other, it is incensed.

The Role of Leaders. The mass media certainly play an important role in framing civil liberties disputes (e.g., Nelson, Clawson, and Oxley 1997). But in South Africa, the mass media are not universally accessible to ordinary people, in part due to illiteracy and in part due to language (and, of course, poverty). As a consequence, local political leaders play an uncommonly influential role in mediating disputes in many South African communities. Consequently, the "frames" that local leaders use to describe the controversy varied in the experiment from the leaders urging that the demonstration be banned (because it is dangerous and threatening) to urging that it be allowed to take place (because it is neither dangerous nor threatening).

Deliberation. We hypothesize that the views of leaders are important to most South Africans, but so too are the views and arguments put forth by ordinary people. In many civil liberties disputes, people do not know what to think, so they seek guidance from those whose views they trust. The deliberation that goes on is important for understanding the dispute since a tolerant outcome is unlikely without considered judgments (Stouffer 1955; Marcus et al. 1995; Gibson 1998a; but see Kuklinski et al. 1991, 1993). Consequently, we varied the discourse in the community from an argument favoring banning the group (because its speech will recruit more adherents) to an argument supporting the speech (because the speech will expose the foolishness of the group's ideas).

Summary

We hypothesize that tolerance depends upon the specific circumstances within which a civil liberties claim is asserted. Private speech is more likely to be tolerated than public speech; demonstrations likely to be controversial and disorderly are less likely to be tolerated than quiet, peaceful assemblies. As the history of constitutional litigation in the United States and elsewhere has taught us, whether one can exercise freedom depends largely on the circumstances.

Making Tolerance Judgments

The Dependent Variables

Tables 5.2 and 5.3 report the respondents' basic judgments of the vignettes. The first table describes the respondents' decisions on whether to tolerate the demonstration; Table 5.3 describes their estimates of the degree of threat posed by the demonstration.

Perhaps not surprisingly in light of earlier findings on the intolerance of South Africans (Gouws 1993, Gibson and Gouws 1997a), few respondents are willing to allow the rally to take place. Roughly two-thirds of the respondents (66.4 percent) favor prohibiting the demonstration. A large majority of Africans are intolerant, a significant proportion of Coloured South Africans is intolerant, as are a majority of South Africans of Asian origin, and a plurality of white South Africans (and, due to uncertainty, tolerance is fairly uncommon). Racial differences are substantial and statistically significant. The vignette was obviously fairly successful at generating intolerance.

A portion of the explanation for the intolerance can be found in Table 5.3. A substantial majority of South Africans (68.5 percent) perceived some degree of threat to the community arising from the details in the vignette, and many perceived the rally as very threatening. For instance, over two-thirds of the respondents viewed the rally as threatening to the community, and fully 35.0 percent rated the level of threat at the most

Table 5.2. *Should Political Enemies Be Allowed to Demonstrate?*

Group	Intolerant	Uncertain	Tolerant	Mean[b]	Std. Dev.	N
All South Africans	66.4	14.5	19.1	2.19	1.23	2,498
African	71.3	13.9	14.8	2.05	1.16	1,961
White	43.9	17.7	38.4	2.84	1.34	485
Coloured	61.3	13.3	25.4	2.28	1.33	248
Asian Origin	53.9	19.0	27.1	2.58	1.25	269

Vignette Judgments – Political Tolerance; Percentages[a]

Notes:
[a] These three columns total to 100 percent, except for rounding errors.
[b] Crossrace difference of means: $\eta = .24$; $p < .0000$.
The question read, "Do you think the rally ought to be allowed to take place?" The responses range from "1. Strongly believe it should not be allowed," to "5. Strongly believe it should be allowed." "Intolerant" responses are those that assert that the rally ought not to take place, whether the respondent felt strongly or not. Similar coding characterizes those described as giving "tolerant" responses. The means and standard deviations are based on the uncollapsed responses.

Table 5.3. *Perceptions of Group Threat*

| Group | Vignette Judgments – Perceived Threat | | | | | |
| | Percentages[a] | | | | | |
	Not Threatening	Uncertain	Threatening	Mean[b]	Std. Dev.	N
All South Africans	22.4	9.1	68.5	7.35	2.65	2,478
African	17.9	9.7	72.4	7.64	2.54	1,942
White	40.5	5.6	53.9	6.09	2.64	486
Coloured	27.8	8.9	63.3	7.10	2.93	248
Asian Origin	38.4	5.7	55.9	6.27	2.53	263

Notes:
[a] These three columns total to 100 percent, except for rounding errors.
[b] Cross-race difference of means: $\eta = .24$; $p < .0000$.
The question read, "First, think about how threatening such a rally would be *to the people in the community*. If 10 means that such a rally would be extremely threatening to the community and 1 means it would not be threatening at all, of all the numbers from 1 to 10, which best describes how threatening a rally would be? For example, you might answer with a 8 if you think the rally would be threatening but not extremely threatening, or a 3 if you think the rally would be just a little threatening to the members of the community." "Not Threatening" responses are those who answered with responses between 1 and 5; scores between 6 and 10 are counted as "threatening." The respondents were allowed to answer that they were "uncertain" about the level of threat posed. The means and standard deviations are based on the uncollapsed responses.

extreme point on the ten-point threat continuum. Again, racial/linguistic/ethnic differences are statistically and substantively significant, with Africans perceiving the largest threat and white South Africans (and those of Asian origin) perceiving the smallest threat to the people in the community.

These two variables are very closely connected. The correlations range from –.47 among the whites to –.72 among Coloured South Africans. This is powerful reconfirmation that one of the chief causes of intolerance is the threat posed by the group (see Sullivan, Pierson, and Marcus 1982; Duch and Gibson 1992; Marcus et al. 1995). For purposes of this analysis, we will attempt to determine whether the experimental manipulations affect intolerance directly or via their impact on threat perceptions.

The Direct Effect of the Manipulations

To what degree did the experimental manipulations affect the two primary judgment variables – the level of perceived threat and the

Table 5.4. *The Direct Effect of the Experimental Manipulations on Tolerance and Threat Perceptions*

Manipulation	Political Tolerance			Perceptions of Threat		
	Mean	Std. Dev.	N	Mean	Std. Dev.	N
Other Disliked Group						
Anticipated Lawlessness						
Will not follow	2.32	1.25	639	7.07	2.66	632
Promise to follow	2.30	1.27	600	7.00	2.79	594
Community Antipathy						
Won't care	2.35	1.24	605	6.89	2.70	600
Be angry	2.27	1.27	634	7.17	2.74	626
Role of Leaders						
Intolerant	2.31	1.27	626	6.99	2.72	620
Tolerant	2.30	1.25	613	7.08	2.73	606
Deliberation						
Pro-intolerance	2.29	1.27	611	7.07	2.71	607
Pro-tolerance	2.32	1.24	628	7.00	2.74	620
Most Disliked Group						
Anticipated Lawlessness						
Will not follow	2.07	1.18	667	7.66	2.56	662
Promise to follow	2.08	1.22	592	7.64	2.49	591
Community Antipathy						
Won't care	2.11	1.18	607	7.52	2.60	602
Be angry	2.04	1.21	652	7.77	2.45	650
Role of Leaders						
Intolerant	2.07	1.21	642	7.62	2.53	640
Tolerant	2.08	1.18	617	7.69	2.53	612
Deliberation						
Pro-intolerance	2.09	1.20	641	7.62	2.59	637
Pro-tolerance	2.06	1.20	617	7.69	2.46	615

Note: *None* of the within-manipulation difference of means tests is significant at .05.

willingness to allow the demonstration to take place? Table 5.4 reports the mean tolerance and threat responses for each of the experimental manipulations, divided by whether the stimulus employed was the most disliked group or another highly disliked group.

The overwhelming story of this table is that tolerance and threat perceptions are *not* dependent upon the context as represented in the vignettes. The strongest relationships are found with the community feelings manipulation; where the community was said to be angry, tolerance was less widespread, and perceptions of threat were higher (among both group stimuli). Even on this variable, however, the differences in means *do not* achieve statistical significance at conventional levels.

The failure of these contextual manipulations presents some interesting puzzles. For instance, whether the group promises to follow the law or not is irrelevant to perceptions of threat and willingness to tolerate. The explanation is surely simple: Promises made by hated political enemies may not be believed. This conjecture receives strong support from the manipulation check for this experimental treatment; there is no difference whatsoever in responses to the question, "How certain are you that [THE GROUP] will try to follow the law in holding this rally?" The promise was simply not credible to our subjects.

Similarly, the recommendations of community leaders had virtually no impact on the respondents. Since the stimulus directly concerns the level of threat posed by the group, we would have expected at least some influence on threat perceptions. None was observed. Again, the manipulation check revealed no differences in the certainty that "the leaders of the community say they support the right of [THE GROUP] to hold the rally." Our effort to convince the respondents that the leaders were tolerant failed.

Nor did the effort to encourage the respondents to deliberate succeed in influencing their positions on the demonstration. Earlier research has suggested that these arguments can be persuasive in certain contexts (Gibson 1998a); here, they had no effect whatsoever. It seems that by the time the respondents heard this portion of the vignette, their minds were firmly made up.

The community feelings experiment is the only manipulation that "passed" its manipulation check, with those told that the community was angry about the demonstration apparently believing it. Nonetheless, the direct effect of community anger on tolerance is, like the other direct effects, not statistically significant. Thus, neither the manipulations that were correctly nor incorrectly perceived had any impact on perceptions of threat and political tolerance.

These data reveal a remarkable degree of insensitivity to the context of civil liberties disputes. Indeed, a simple way to characterize these findings is that South Africans who are threatened by their political enemies would deny them the opportunity to participate in politics – period. Apparently, not much more need be said.[9]

---

9 Note that in 1997 the interview included a vignette on amnesty. Most of the manipulations in that experiment worked as expected (see Gibson and Gouws 1999), leading us to discount the possibility that the low level of education and literacy of the respondents had something to do with the failure of this tolerance vignette.

Table 5.5. *The Effects of Experimental and Perceptual Variables on Political Tolerance*

Variable	Model I				Model II			
	b	s.e.	Beta	r	b	s.e.	Beta	r
Experimental Treatment								
Community Antipathy:								
Apathetic v. Very Angry	−.07	.05	−.03	−.03	−.00	.04	−.00	−.03
Anticipated Lawlessness:								
High v. Low	−.01	.05	−.00	−.00	−.02	.04	−.01	−.00
Role of Leaders:								
Intolerant v. Tolerant	.00	.05	.00	.00	.00	.04	.00	.00
Deliberation: Intolerant								
v. Tolerant	.01	.05	.00	.00	.00	.04	.00	.00
Contextual Perceptions								
Certain Community Is								
Angry					−.08	.02	−.08*	−.38
Certain Group Will								
Try to Follow Law					.25	.02	.26*	.56
Likelihood of Violence					−.10	.02	−.11*	−.48
Certainty of Leader								
Tolerance					.14	.02	.15*	.43
Perceived Group Threat					−.15	.01	−.32*	−.58
Intercept (s.e.)	2.23	.06			3.11	.12		
Standard Error of								
Estimate	1.24				.89			
Standard Deviation	1.24				1.24			
R^2			.00				.48*	

Notes:
* Standardized regression coefficient (Beta) is significant at $p < .001$.
N = 2,463.

Perhaps not. Table 5.5 reports the results of regressing the tolerance judgment on both the objective and perceived characteristics of the experiment. That is, Model I reports the results of regressing tolerance on the four dummy variables representing the manipulations. Model II uses the same experimental variables but adds four perceptual variables (the items used as manipulation checks), as well as the perception-of-threat variable.[10] These data support several conclusions.

10 Note that once an equation includes the measure of threat perceptions, it is no longer necessary to control for whether the respondent was told a story about her or his most disliked or another highly disliked group.

First, confirming the preceding analysis, there is little direct effect of the experimental manipulations in either of the two models. Second, also as expected, perceived group threat has a moderate to strong direct influence on tolerance judgments ($\beta = -.32$; see Model II). In light of existing research findings, this is not at all surprising.

Several of the perceptual variables have significant influences on tolerance judgments. Especially important are perceptions of whether the group will follow the law. To the extent that the respondents perceived that the group would obey the law at the demonstration, they were tolerant. Conversely, an important justification for denying the group the right to demonstrate appears to be the fear that the group would break the law at the rally. Among those believing it very unlikely that the law would be followed, 91.6 percent were intolerant; among those believing law-abidingness very likely, only 38.9 percent were intolerant. And we further note that, somewhat unexpectedly, perceived lawfulness has a considerably stronger impact than perceptions that violence will occur at the demonstration. Irrespective of whether the respondents expected violence to occur, confidence that the group would follow the law substantially influences willingness to allow the demonstration.

It is noteworthy that violence has less impact on intolerance than law-abidingness. This result may be connected to the Marcus et al. (1995) arguments about "normative violations." They find, for instance, that the power or potential power of a group has little to do with tolerance. Instead, intolerance arises from the threat to the symbolic values of the community. (And this finding is similar to the conventional observation that sociotropic threat perceptions are more powerful predictors of intolerance than egocentric perceptions; see Gibson and Gouws 1997a, 2000; Feldman and Stenner 1997.) Breaking the law seems to be a more powerful transgression against community values than simply engaging in violence.

Although perceptions of community anger have a bivariate relationship with political tolerance, the multivariate effect is much weakened. This is to be expected in light of the influence of the more proximate variables concerning violence and following the law. Presumably, one of the reasons for community anger is the fear that the group will not follow the law at the demonstration. Once the effect of that variable is controlled, the influence of perceived community anger is slight.

Thus, we have an interesting paradox in these findings: *The actual context of the dispute has little impact on political tolerance, while the perceived context has a great deal of influence* (explaining nearly one-half of the variance in levels of political tolerance). This obviously implies that the variables measuring the actual context are weakly related to perceptions, and that is in fact the case.[11] What people perceive about civil liberties conflicts matters considerably, even if their perceptions are a function of their predispositions rather than reality.

The question naturally arising from these findings is, what accounts for variation in perceptions of the civil liberties context? It is beyond the scope of this chapter to consider a fully specified model of these perceptions. However, the finding that the strength of the group stimulus affects perceptions (see footnote 11) provides a clue to the origins of contextual perceptions. We hypothesize that those more threatened by the group are more likely to perceive the context as dangerous.

We have two independent measures of threat perceptions. The first is based on the threat of the group (most disliked or other greatly disliked) to the respondent and derives from questions asked independently of the vignette.[12] The second measure was the first question to follow the presentation of the story and it assesses threat to the community involved in the vignette. The correlation of these two measures is .41. Not surprisingly, since it is more proximate to the context, the latter is a better predictor of tolerance in the vignette ($r = -.58$ versus $-.38$), and vignette-based threat perceptions are strongly correlated with all other perceptions of the context of the story (correlations range from $-.35$ to .49). But the general perceptions of threat are also strongly related to the specific perceptions of the context. For instance, those who are more threatened by the group were less likely to believe it would follow the law ($r = -.37$), more likely to assert that the community would be angry ($r = .36$), and more likely to anticipate violence ($r = .39$). Clearly, generalized perceptions of threat have much to do with how people view the particular context of civil liberties controversies.

If we take a small step away from the data, we can see that the causal process involved here seems to be fairly simple. Most people are highly threatened by their political enemies, and they ascribe every manner of undesirable attributes to them. When faced with a civil liberties dispute,

---

11 We regressed each of the four perceptual variables on the five dichotomous manipulations (including whether the group was the most disliked or another highly disliked group). In every case, the type of group stimulus was significantly related to the perception. But in only a single instance did the experimental variables affect one of the perceptual variables: Those who were told the community would be angry in fact perceived the community as angrier, although the relationship is fairly weak ($\beta = .07$). In no other instance were perceptions grounded in the context of the vignette.

12 We measured threat perceptions in the conventional way using a set of semantic differential items to describe attitudes toward the groups; see Chapter 3. The measure employed in this analysis is the factor score from the unrotated solution.

most are prepared to believe the worst about the group, including that the group's promises cannot be believed, that the group will not follow the law, etc. These predispositions are not easily changed by reality, and indeed the actual details of the dispute have little impact on tolerance. In the scenario under consideration here, the respondents are prepared to believe that the rally is threatening to the community, and consequently that it should be banned. The variable that drives this entire process is the preexisting beliefs about the group. The reality of the circumstances has a very difficult time overriding the effect of these predispositions.[13]

These findings suggest a process of decision making that differs considerably from that which we originally envisaged. Instead of multidimensional processing, it appears that the judgments in this vignette were the product of fairly simple, unidimensional decision making. Because perceptions of these political groups are so strongly grounded in the reality of South African politics, a "satisficing" conclusion could be quite readily achieved for most respondents. Thus, it seems that the salience of civil liberties disputes has much to do with the psychological processes through which tolerance judgments are formed.

Our findings diverge somewhat from those of Marcus et al. (1995), who discovered a slightly stronger impact of contextual factors. There are several possible explanations for the differences in our findings. First, their analysis in fact reveals only modest effects of context on tolerance judgments (e.g., Table 5.4.2, page 77). Second, they employed a fictitious group and used (mainly) college students as their research subjects, and did so within the context of the United States. Our subjects are a representative sample of ordinary South Africans. The respondents named real political enemies, at a time when South African politics involved intense political rivalries and fairly common political violence. The realism of the vignette most likely contributed to our finding that predispositions toward the group overwhelmed all other contextual variance, under the hypothesis that the greater the significance of the group used, the weaker will be the influence of context. Marcus and his colleagues conducted their research on relatively insignificant groups, while our research was directed at relatively more significant groups. That difference probably accounts for our diverging conclusions about the role of context in tolerance disputes.[14]

---

13 Moving one step backward in the causal chain, earlier research has demonstrated that these general threat perceptions are linked to the social identities adopted by the various racial groups in South Africa. See Gibson and Gouws 2000.

14 Our argument here is that the judgments of people who perceive little threat will be more influenced by contextual factors than the judgments of those perceiving

At the same time, our analysis reinforces the view that "standing decisions" are extremely important for tolerance judgments. On this point, our findings comport well with those of Marcus et al.

A Note of Caution about Deliberation

The strongest contextual manipulation observed by Marcus et al. had to do with the "instruction set" advising the respondents on how to deliberate in making their decision: "Subjects who are told to pay attention to their feelings are significantly less tolerant than those who are told to pay attention to their thoughts. This finding is consistent with the notion that a 'sober second thought' leads people to reconsider their automatic response, which is a natural intolerance toward groups and ideas they find objectionable" (Marcus et al. 1995, 80). This finding is inconsistent with that of Kuklinski et al. (1991, 1993); it seems to be inconsistent with the findings we report here.

Our manipulation sought to influence the respondent's judgment by introducing arguments into the vignette that the respondent might not have otherwise considered. The manipulation had no effect whatsoever, despite the fact that similar arguments have been found in earlier work in Russia to have considerable influence (Gibson 1998a). We have some additional data, however, that perhaps clarify the role of "sober second thoughts" in this experiment (see also Chapter 7).

After the respondents had completed all questions connected to the vignette, we posed three additional counterarguments to determine whether they might be willing to alter their position:

more considerable threat. We contend that, in South Africa, political threats take on a more realistic character as compared to countries with more deeply institutionalized democratic institutions. Nonetheless, some South Africans do perceive relatively little threat from their enemies, so we can assess whether the contextual aspects of the vignette were more influential with them. To test the conditional hypothesis, we trichotomized the general measure of group threat, defining the categories as less than $-.5$, $-.5$ through $+.5$, and greater than $.5$ on the standardized factor score measuring threat perceptions. We then regressed the vignette tolerance measure on the four dichotomous manipulation variables within each of these threat levels. In the medium and high threat groups, none of the regression coefficients for the manipulation variables was significant at even $.05$. For the low threat group, the anticipated lawlessness manipulation coefficient is significant at $p < .05$, and the coefficient for the deliberation manipulation is significant at $p = .056$. Neither of the other two coefficients achieves statistical significance. This is, of course, a rather limited test, since few South Africans are entirely unthreatened by their political enemies (and the trichotomy indicates relative threat, not absolute levels of threat), but the findings are nonetheless compatible with our understanding of the process involved in the vignettes.

Table 5.6. *The Effects of Persuasive Communications on Political Tolerance*

| | Percentages[a] | | | | Std. | |
Argument	Intolerant	Uncertain	Tolerant	Mean	Dev.	N
Baseline	66.4	14.5	19.1	2.19	1.23	2,498
Promises Accepted						
by the Judge	55.0	20.3	24.7	2.44	1.26	2,495
Authorities Prevent						
Violence	52.3	18.6	29.1	2.52	1.31	2,494
Can't Trust the						
Authorities	54.5	20.2	25.4	2.47	1.26	2,490

Note:

[a] The rows total 100 percent, except for rounding errors. Note that this is a categorical variable created from the continuous tolerance judgments.

(1) Suppose that [THE GROUP], fearing it won't be allowed to hold the rally, promises to obey all laws during the rally, and it further promises not to attack the opposition party or its supporters. A local judge accepts these promises. Do you think the rally ought to be allowed to take place?
(2) Suppose that the local authorities promise that they will do whatever is necessary to insure that there is no violence at the rally. Do you think the rally ought to be allowed to take place?
(3) And finally suppose someone argued that you can't really trust the authorities to say who can and who cannot hold a rally and therefore all groups should be allowed to hold rallies. Do you think the rally ought to be allowed to take place?

It is instructive to note how those who gave intolerant or uncertain responses to the vignette reacted to these attempts at forcing further deliberation. Table 5.6 shows the results.

Each of these arguments increased the likelihood of tolerating the demonstration. While only 19.1 percent of the subjects were initially inclined to tolerate the rally, an additional 10.0 percent were persuaded to allow it under the condition that the local authorities would do their best to prevent violence. The other two manipulations had smaller effects. Nonetheless, the arguments were not entirely redundant – 33.1 percent of the respondents gave at least one tolerant response after hearing the three efforts to persuade them to support allowing the rally. Thus, these arguments had some effect on the respondents.

How is it that the arguments in the vignette were not persuasive, while the arguments after the vignette were? We wonder whether the respondents were making "satisficing" judgments as they were hearing the vignettes. That is, perhaps some respondents had enough information to form an opinion after the first sentence of the vignette – they hated the group, and did not want it to demonstrate. Perhaps most respondents had formed a judgment before hearing all of the statements that formed the vignette. The counterarguments were ineffective because the respondents ignored them. When presented as a separate question to which the respondents were explicitly asked to reply, the arguments had greater force. The point we wish to emphasize, however, is that the vignette evidence is perhaps not entirely incompatible with persuasibility research based on the "sober second thought" model. From a substantive point of view, this finding suggests that deliberation may be most effective when it is separated from the immediate context of the controversy itself and when people are forced to pay attention to contrary points of view.

DISCUSSION

Perhaps our most important conclusion is that context matters, but not in the way that we originally emphasized here. It is the *South African context* that matters, not the details of the particular civil liberties controversy. South Africans hold general views toward their political enemies; those views strongly flavor perceptions of the context, to the point of overwhelming objective information connected to a specific civil liberties dispute. The real context in South Africa is that people live in a political system in which violence is commonplace and group threat is real. Presenting these people a brief vignette, no matter how well-grounded in real-life situations, does not override what these people are experiencing just outside their doors. In this sense, the "perceived context" that is so influential in this analysis is more "real" than the "actual context" as described in the vignettes.

Results drawn from political systems in which questions of tolerance are central to the political process may well differ from results from political systems in which tolerance is more peripheral. In the United States, for instance, contextual factors seem to matter more (e.g., Marcus et al. 1995), probably because threat perceptions are less realistic and therefore do not dominate judgments. In South Africa, political tolerance is not a matter of whether "fringe" groups can compete for political power; instead, it is a crucial issue of how much freedom to extend to even the "loyal" political opposition. If ever there were a case in which issues of "applied" tolerance are important, it is South Africa. This basic reality surely influences all the findings of this research, accounting for the differences between our results and those reported in the U.S.-dominated literature.

This research was initiated in part by the suspicion that generalized tolerance attitudes were not particularly useful predictors of judgments within specific disputes. Our suspicions were entirely wrong. Instead, our principal finding is that these general attitudes are *extremely important* and that they shape reactions to specific disputes in virtually every fashion. The way people perceive contentious efforts to exercise civil liberties is heavily dependent on frames of reference provided by their predispositions. This makes further research on the origins of those predispositions – especially threat perceptions – all the more important.

Our research also demonstrates how useful it is to move beyond the American context when studying political tolerance. The United States is unusual in many respects, ranging from strong cultural individualism to powerful political institutions committed to protecting the rights of political minorities, and therefore the extent to which findings from the United States are generalizable is unclear. Political conflict in many parts of the world is far more severe than in the United States, rendering tolerance a precious and scarce commodity. The particular context of a demonstration seems not to matter in South Africa, most likely because the political stakes are so large. Thus, this research has identified a new contextual variable – the size of the stakes in the dispute – that can best be studied through crossnational research. It seems clear that if tolerance research is to make further progress, it must move beyond the boundaries of the American political system.

In the analysis reported in this chapter, we have focused on the context of civil liberties disputes. However, our research has given insufficient attention to one aspect of how actual civil liberties disputes unfold: deliberation. In real conflicts, people talk; they debate; they try to persuade each other of the rightness of their positions. It is this concern with *persuasion* that is the subject of the next chapter.

Part III South African Tolerance as It Might Be

6

The Persuasibility of Tolerance and Intolerance

The findings of the preceding chapters are not very encouraging for supporters of democratic tolerance. There is not much tolerance in South Africa, and intolerance is often directed at mainstream competitors for political power. Is effective political competition therefore doomed in South Africa?

Perhaps not. Perhaps there are ways in which intolerance can be converted to tolerance (or at least neutralized). After all, the answers people give us to questions during an interview are not necessarily immutable. The purpose of this chapter is therefore to determine whether South Africans can be "talked out of" their intolerance, whether they can be persuaded to adopt a more democratic position in disputes over civil liberties. This question of persuasibility is one that has attracted a variety of earlier inquiries from political psychologists.

THE MUTABILITY OF PUBLIC OPINION

Survey research is typically thought of as the art of providing respondents with stimuli that will provoke a report of the state of being of the person. Thus, when people are asked whether they approve of political groups, the traditional model envisages a process of recall: The respondent searches his or her memory to retrieve a thought that can serve as the basis for a reply. As Zaller and Feldman (1992, 579) characterize it, "The standard view is that when survey respondents say they favor X they are simply describing a pre-existing state of feeling favorably toward X."

This tradition in survey research is well established and provides important information about the properties of people. But especially in transitional societies, the store of information and experience on which people can rely in formulating their answers is not necessarily broad or stable. If few people in these regimes understand very much about democratic politics, and especially about complex topics like why one should put up with one's enemies,[1] looking up the answer in one's memory is not an altogether easy task.

If people do not hold firm and immutable attitudes, then it follows that their initial responses to our questions are not necessarily the only important aspect of their attitudes. After all, the respondents are often answering difficult and complex questions, and are doing so quickly, perhaps with relatively superficial processing of the stimuli. It would not be surprising, for instance, if respondents were more heavily influenced by the group mentioned in a tolerance question than by the political rights to which the questions refer. It is easier – and the attitude is more accessible – to know how one feels about the Inkatha Freedom Party than it is to know whether candidates should be allowed to stand for election. The initial responses to our questions are not unimportant, but nor are they the only important characteristic of the respondents and their attitudes.

Especially if the stimuli we present in interviews are not processed in the same way in which stimuli in the real political world are processed, these initial opinions are perhaps quite malleable. Initial responses, for instance, may well reflect the respondent's judgment of the *costs of tolerance* – bad things will be said by bad groups – and be little influenced by the costs of *intolerance* (other groups, saying good things, may have to be banned as well). Partial cognitive processing of our questions may therefore result in incomplete and perhaps even misleading answers, and may not reflect the processes through which citizens make judgments in actual disputes over civil liberties.

A quickly growing body of research in political psychology addresses this question of the *persuasibility* of attitudes.[2] Can respondents be per-

---

1 McClosky and Brill, for instance, argue that tolerance is a cognitively difficult position to adopt:

It is by no means self-evident . . . that the members of a white majority should have a right to make speeches that insult ethnic minorities; that revolutionaries should have a right to advocate the overthrow of the American political system. . . . Whether these and other liberties that exact a high price ought to be constitutionally protected raises highly vexing questions, and a fair amount of political sophistication is required to address them and make the case for freedom (McClosky and Brill 1983, 375).

2 See, for examples, Gibson 1998a; Cobb and Kuklinski 1997; Sniderman et al. 1996; Mutz, Sniderman, and Brody 1996a; Sniderman, Brody, and Tetlock 1991; Zaller 1992. There is a much broader literature on leadership and efforts of elites to manipulate mass opinion that also should be included under the rubric of persuasibility studies. See, for examples, Mutz 1998; McGraw 1991; Iyengar 1991; Iyengar and Kinder 1987.

suaded to change their initial views through additional deliberation? Persuasion is the essence of politics:

> Politics, at its core, is about persuasion. It hinges not just on whether citizens at any one moment in time tend to favor one side of an issue over another, but on the numbers of them that can be brought, when push comes to shove, from one side to the other. Politics is about turning the minorities of today into the majorities of tomorrow; and the risk as well as the strength of electorally contested politics lies precisely in its openness to change (Mutz, Sniderman, and Brody 1996b, 2).

Or, as Sniderman et al. (1996, 55) succinctly put it: "Where people start off politically matters, but what counts is where they wind up after the pushing and shoving of political argument."

Much of this literature has moved outside the laboratory, relying instead on survey research. One example is Donovan and Leivers' (1993) report on a systematic effort to reduce prejudice against Australian Aborigines via a media campaign. Sniderman et al. (1996) were extremely successful at getting Canadians to change their views about the regulation of "hate speech" through a single counterargument. Though there was somewhat less change, attitudes toward the regulation of pornography were also pliable (but asymmetrically so, with those favoring censorship being impervious to the counterarguments). Hibbing and Theiss-Morse (1995, 79–80) presented counterarguments to an American sample on the issue of term limits for members of the U.S. Congress. While only 13 percent of those favoring term limits changed their views in response to the arguments, fully 42 percent of the opponents of term limits changed their minds. This asymmetry in opinion is similar to Gibson's (1996d) finding on tolerance attitudes in the United States and Russia (Gibson 1998a). Jordan (1993) also considers the effects of media on mass preferences. Sniderman (1993, 234) comments on this sort of research as follows: "My sense of the initial stream of studies on political persuasion and attitude change is that they represent a new field of study in the making. Politics is about how you get people who start off in one corner of a room to move to another. What is necessary now is systematically to investigate who can be talked out of what political positions, and why."

Research on tolerance has not been entirely insensitive to this body of research. Since the beginning of modern empirical research on political tolerance, researchers have considered the possibility that one's initial opinion on civil liberties issues may not necessarily be one's final view. One of the insights from the earliest research on political tolerance (in the United States) was that tolerance requires considered judgment, not an emotional response. Indeed, the "natural" response to an idea that is disturbing and threatening may be to want to suppress it (Willhoite

1977). Stouffer (1955) argued that tolerance is most likely to emerge when people give political disputes a "sober second thought" – that is, when they reflect on the other values that are compromised or threatened by repression (Gibson 1998a). Since most people generally support the idea of freedom of speech (which is true in South Africa as well), this reconsideration often results in political tolerance. As Kuklinski et al. (1991, 3) describe it: "The logic . . . goes something like this: tolerance is always more reasonable than intolerance in democratic societies; since considered thought leads to more reasonable decisions than do emotions, a deliberative citizenry will be more tolerant than an emotionally reactive one . . . [W]ith deliberative thought (in contrast to emotions) comes increased political tolerance . . ." (see also Kuklinski et al. 1993).

This is just the process that Gibson and Bingham (1985) believe took place in Skokie, Illinois (United States), when a group of American Nazis applied for permission to hold a demonstration in a predominantly Jewish community. Initial reactions to the Nazis were decidedly hostile, and the community adopted three draconian ordinances restricting the civil liberties of Nazis and any other group seeking access to the streets for purposes of political demonstrations. The ordinances were initially widely supported, both in the community and throughout the country. But after a while, support faded. The change was caused by several things, but one important explanation was the intervention of an interest group, the American Civil Liberties Union. The ACLU was instrumental in developing a counterargument to the anti-Nazi sentiment, an argument that refocused and framed the dispute away from the rights of hated groups to the right of all citizens to express themselves politically, to fear of the government having control over who can give political speeches, etc.[3] The ACLU forced many people to give the issue a "sober second thought" – to examine the actual terms and text of the ordinances, for instance – and that thought caused many to realize the costs, not only the benefits, of repressing the Nazis. In real politics, as opposed to the circumstances of a survey, people are confronted with opposing arguments with which they have to deal. In real politics, people are often persuaded by argumentation.

Of course, not all arguments necessarily favor political tolerance. Kuklinski et al. (1991) quite rightly criticize the Stouffer formula for *assuming* that thinking a problem through will automatically result in greater political tolerance. It may very well be that, upon reflection, a group or a circumstance may be perceived as *more* threatening, *more* dangerous, and *more* worthy of repression (and this is just what Kuklinski

3 On framing in civil liberties disputes, see Nelson, Clawson, and Oxley 1997.

et al. discovered, 1991, 21). Giving a matter a "sober second thought" may well mean thinking about the possible violence that might erupt during a demonstration, thereby exacerbating intolerance.

Or perhaps a "negativity bias" exists in the initial responses to our tolerance questions. That is, when presented with a question about whether a hated political enemy should be allowed civil liberties, perhaps attitudes toward the hated group are far more accessible than attitudes toward civil liberties, and consequently group affect dominates the responses. If there is a differential in the accessibility of attitudes toward groups and attitudes toward civil liberties, then deliberation would in fact tend to generate more tolerant responses because the attitudes that were initially dormant would become activated.

Can people be taught to think about the *negative* consequences of *intolerance* and *repression*? In the first empirical effort to assess the persuasibility of tolerance in the United States, Gibson (1996d) was able to convince a number of respondents to reverse their initial intolerant response and approve of tolerance. Included in the survey was a series of items designed to force the respondent to give a "sober second thought" to the problem of political tolerance. All subjects were asked whether the government should allow a demonstration in their neighborhood by the group they identified as most disliked. Those who would allow the demonstration were presented with three pro–social order counterarguments and were then asked whether they would change their minds and oppose the demonstration. Those who would not allow the demonstration initially were presented with three counterarguments favoring individual liberty and were then asked whether they would change their minds and support the demonstration. Gibson had a fair amount of success at getting people to alter their views by this additional processing of the stimulus. Only 37 percent of those who were initially tolerant failed to change their views across the three counterarguments, while 62 percent of those initially intolerant did not change. Thus, the responses that subjects give with little reflection are not immutable. Attitudes may not be infinitely malleable, but they can be changed when citizens are encouraged to think through the implications of their replies to our questions. It seems clear that there are circumstances in which the attitudes expressed in response to simple survey stimuli can be altered under different sociopolitical contexts.

Marcus et al. (1995) also tried to manipulate their respondents by providing them with arguments favoring or opposing political tolerance. Unlike our work – in which we try to get respondents to change their initial response – Marcus et al. provide arguments supporting tolerance to half of their subjects and arguments opposing tolerance to the others. For instance, the cognitive argument against tolerance was:

The (WSF) [White Supremacist Faction] does not seem to respect the rights of others. In fact, it presents an outright danger to some law abiding citizens in our country. I think that groups like (WSF) which present a real threat to other people's civil rights and civil liberties, should not be given such rights themselves. If the (WSF) came into power, they would do away with freedom of speech and persecute those who disagree with them. People like that should not be given a chance to destroy the very rights that protect them. Our system is based on majority rule, and the majority objects so strongly to the (WSF's) notions they ought to be silenced. Furthermore, ideas like theirs can cause political disorder and affect the stability of society. So if we truly believe in free speech, we should not allow (WSF) to have free speech in this case.

Those given an argument favoring tolerance were told:

The right to political expression is established in our legal framework through the First Ten Amendments to the Constitution and through court cases. Minority groups like the (WSF) should, in a healthy society, have the right to persuade people that their views should be the majority view. Free speech in our system is supposed to invite dispute. In fact, free speech might be at its finest when it creates dissatisfaction or discomfort.

People should have access to a variety of ideas, so that they can make up their minds based on full information. After all, if people don't agree with an idea, they can always reject it. A lack of dissent in a society may indicate weakness, while dissent itself may point to a stronger society. All of these ideas lead me to conclude firmly that the (WSF) should be allowed to have their say.

They attempted to construct some arguments that were predominantly emotional in their focus and others that were predominantly cognitive, but their findings revealed few differences between subjects presented with arguments of different tones (1995, 126).

Unfortunately, the effect of offering the students these arguments was barely statistically significant ($p < .01$), and largely trivial in magnitude (1995, 127–8). Perhaps this is because college students at a prestigious (U.S.) state university were used as subjects. To the extent that issues of civil liberties and political freedom are more salient to college students (answering questions within a college environment), the students are surely less susceptible to change than are ordinary people. One would expect the impact of persuasive arguments to be greater within a less sophisticated sample. Marcus et al. are not insensitive to this sort of concern about their sample (and a few of their experiments are conducted on subjects who are not college students), but there can be little doubt that future work needs to move outside the college classroom.

We conceive of the process of persuasibility as something like the following. Information processing is an iterative process. Respondents receive a unit of information and consider it until they reach a satisfactory conclusion. In doing so, they are trading off additional processing time for confidence in the acceptability of the conclusion, and are thus in effect maximizing some utility function. When a satisficing solution is reached, further processing of the stimulus discontinues.

Just as in any iterative process, the process may stop when a local minimum is achieved. This is largely because the person does not evaluate the stimulus on all relevant dimensions. Thus, when asked whether a highly disliked group should be allowed to give a speech, most people evaluate only the group, quickly determine that the group would say undesirable things, and therefore become satisfied with a decision to ban the speech. If people can be persuaded to process the stimulus more thoroughly, considering not only the group but the civil liberties issues involved, then perhaps (but not inevitably) processing will continue and a different conclusion will result. Stouffer referred, intuitively, to this process as giving the matter of civil liberties "a sober second thought."

Conditional Influence – Individual Differences

A significant body of work has established that some people can be persuaded under some circumstances to change their political views. Progress has also been made in identifying the factors contributing to such changes, and the list of mediating variables is substantial. Researchers have concentrated on the attributes of the message source (e.g., Carmines and Kuklinski 1990, Iyengar and Kinder 1987, Kuklinski and Hurley 1996, Lupia 1995, and Mondak 1993), the particular mix of opinions among influential elites (e.g., Zaller 1992), the nature of the arguments (e.g., negative versus positive – Fiske 1980, Lau 1985, Skowronski and Carlston 1987, Cobb and Kuklinski 1997), whether the issues are "easy" or "hard" (Carmines and Stimson 1980, 1989; Cobb and Kuklinski 1997), whether the subjects are encouraged to think about the issue emotionally or cognitively (e.g., Kuklinski et al. 1991, Schwarz and Clore 1988, Lazarus 1982, Marcus et al. 1995), to the extent that cognitive processing is involved, the subject's cognitive abilities (Olson and Zanna 1993), the attentiveness of the respondent (Cobb and Kuklinski 1997), the degree of exposure to information (Zaller 1992), and several other attributes. Based on this literature, we have identified a number of factors that may account for variation in persuasibility in South Africa.

Attributes of the Stimulus. In this research, the respondents were presented with a scenario involving either the group they earlier indicated disliking the most or another highly disliked group. Even within these categories, the groups varied in terms of the degree of threat posed to the respondent. We therefore hypothesize that as the group is perceived as more threatening, intolerant respondents will be resistant to persuasion, but tolerant respondents will be susceptible to persuasion.

Attributes of the Source. As we noted previously, a considerable body of literature investigates the role of the message source in persuasibility. Here, we focus on the degree of trust the respondent places in the source, as well as on the degree to which the arguments of the source seem to be counterfactual. Trusted sources presenting arguments in line with the respondent's perceptions of the source are expected to be the most effective at persuasion.

Attributes of the Attitude Being Changed. Not all attitudes are equally susceptible to persuasion. Strongly held beliefs may be less manipulable than weakly held beliefs, for instance. More generally, it is likely that the degree to which a belief is embedded in a large, supportive belief system influences the mutability of the belief (see Converse 1964, 1970). Conversely, highly compartmentalized beliefs should be more readily changeable. Relatedly, the salience of the attitude should affect persuasibility – respondents who do not particularly care about an issue are expected to be more likely to respond to argumentation than respondents who do care.

There is an alternative possibility here. It may be easier to persuade individuals who hold conflicting values. To the extent that the message stimulates an alternative set of attitudes, also valued by the respondent, a means of inducing change becomes available. If, as we suggested previously, respondents often initially process tolerance questions primarily along the lines of group affect and threat, typically leading to an intolerant conclusion, then successful persuasion depends upon mobilizing an alternative attitude favoring tolerance. To the extent that a belief is compartmentalized, no alternative attitude is available. To the extent that beliefs are well integrated, then respondents may be able to see and make the connection to the alternative value and consequently attempt to adjudicate the conflict. Thus, this leads to the hypothesis that those with more highly articulated belief systems are more likely to be persuadable.

Attributes of the Individual. Beyond the specific attitudes being targeted in the persuasibility experiment, we hypothesize that individuals differ in the degree to which they are susceptible to change. A key variable here is closedmindedness – to the extent that respondents are dogmatic, we expect them in general to be resistant to change.[4]

Our persuasibility experiment is based on presenting the respondents with a set of arguments justifying a view contrary to t'heir initial

---

4 This hypothesis is contrary to Gibson's (1998a) findings in Russia. Despite that finding, the logic of dogmatism is that it should make respondents resistant to persuasion.

response. These arguments may be cognitively demanding for the respondents, and, although the respondents were not able to avoid exposure to the stimuli, there may well be variability in the degree to which they can assimilate and understand the reasoning to which they are exposed. Especially when a sizable number of respondents has a very low level of education (as is true in South Africa), then we cannot assume that the logic of these arguments is readily apparent to each person. It is therefore necessary to control for the cognitive abilities of the respondents.

We must also acknowledge that extraneous variables surely influence persuasion. For instance, the tendency to acquiesce most likely makes people more susceptible to exhortations to change their views. There may be effects associated with the order of the presentation of the arguments, or even with the characteristics of the interviewer. Although we cannot control for all possible extraneous influences on persuasibility, we do conduct a few tests to determine how serious this problem may be.

THE "POSSIBILITIES" FOR POLITICAL TOLERANCE: THE "SOBER SECOND THOUGHT" EXPERIMENT

The "sober second thought" experiment began with an invitation to the respondent to imagine that a highly disliked group was planning to make a speech in her or his community.[5] The respondents were then asked whether they would support a decision of the local authorities to ban the speech. Not surprisingly in light of the findings of Chapter 3, a majority of the subjects (58.3 percent) supported the efforts to prohibit the speech, while only 27.7 percent opposed the ban (13.9 percent were undecided). A follow-up question asked whether it mattered to the respondent one way or another whether the group actually gave its speech. For a plurality of respondents (41.0 percent), the issue mattered a great deal, with only 13.8 percent asserting that it would not matter at all whether such a speech were given.[6] For those strongly supporting the ban, 64.3 percent asserted that it would matter a great deal whether the speech were held, while only 33.3 percent of those strongly opposing the ban said that whether the speech were held made a great deal of

5 There will always be legitimate debate over the utility of asking respondents to imagine certain events and then to respond to them. For one of the most balanced defenses of this methodology, see Nagin and Paternoster 1993, especially pages 473–5. We agree heartily with the arguments made therein.

6 Racial differences on this variable are not trivial – 44.6 percent of the African respondents said it matters a great deal whether the demonstration is held, as did 42.4 percent of the Coloured respondents, but only 23.2 percent of the whites and 21.1 percent of the South Africans of Asian origin said it mattered a great deal.

difference to them. Thus, as we shall see throughout this analysis, there is a strong asymmetry in the intensity of intolerance and tolerance.[7]

The purpose of this question is not so much as a direct measure of intolerance, but rather as a means of beginning the persuasibility experiment. We treat this initial response as the respondent's "opening bid" – that is, as the opinion reached without a great deal of deliberation, and without much knowledge of the context of the dispute. It is this response that we attempted to manipulate.

All respondents answering the initial question on banning the speech were presented with a series of (randomly ordered) counterarguments. That is, we confronted the respondents with reasoned arguments why they should change their initial positions. If the respondent gave a tolerant answer initially, he or she was presented with three arguments in favor of banning the speech, and vice versa for those offering an intolerant answer as their initial reply. Those who were initially uncertain were presented with an argument in favor of tolerance and an argument against tolerance. Thus, we hoped to be able to talk the respondents out of their opening position on this controversy.

Three additional experiments were embedded in this research design. First, we varied the order in which the arguments were presented to the subjects. Second, we varied the source of the argument. One-half of the respondents were told that the argument was made by one of their friends, while the other half were told that the argument was made by the person whom the respondent named as "someone whom you know that you look up to and go to for advice when it comes to politics."[8] Finally, for one-half of the respondents, this whole series of questions referred to the most disliked group; for the other half, the questions referred to another highly disliked group. Before considering the results of these manipulations, we review the overall responses to this experiment.

How successful were these counterarguments?[9] As with earlier research using a similar research design (e.g., Gibson 1996d), there is a

---

7 Cobb and Kuklinski (1997) also found a strong asymmetry in change in responses to arguments regarding two issues (the North American Free Trade Agreement [NAFTA] and health care).

8 Actually, the design is somewhat more complicated than this, as will become clearer in the analysis that follows.

9 We should acknowledge that some have found that "con" arguments are more effective at generating attitude change than "pro" arguments (e.g., Cobb and Kuklinski 1997). In our research, all of these arguments are "con" – that is, they were designed to force the respondents to consider the negative consequences of their original position. Thus, the nature of the argument (but not its intensity or effectiveness) is controlled in this research.

basic and strong asymmetry in the ability to persuade the respondents to change their views. Of those who were initially intolerant, only 25.8 percent could be persuaded to accept a tolerant outcome to the dispute; of those initially tolerant, fully 57.7 percent changed their position to one of intolerance. Of those unable to form an opinion in response to the initial stimulus, 40.9 percent were persuaded to claim an opinion by at least one of the two counterarguments. Thus, overall, there is a considerable amount of change in opinions, but it is easier to convert the tolerant to intolerance than vice versa.

There were some important differences in the effectiveness of the various counterarguments (see the last column in Table 6.1).[10] Among those who were initially intolerant, 24.1 percent changed their view in response to the argument that allowing the speech would actually weaken the group because people would be able to see how wrong the group's views are.[11] On the other hand, only 12.7 percent were affected by the argument that the group should be allowed to give a speech because the authorities cannot be trusted to determine who can, and who cannot, give speeches. The fairness argument – that it is not fair to allow some to speak, but not others – persuaded 17.5 percent of the respondents who were initially intolerant.

The intolerance arguments varied even more in their effectiveness. Nearly one-half (49.4 percent) of those initially tolerant became intolerant when they heard the argument that, should the group achieve power in South Africa, it would do away with democracy. The least effective argument was that the speech of the group might hurt some people, but even this view converted 35.8 percent of the respondents to an

10 Note that the order in which these stimuli were presented to the respondents was randomly varied, and therefore we can investigate whether the effectiveness of the stimulus was dependent upon the order in which the respondent heard it. In only one of the eight tests were the responses significantly different across the order of presentation. The third pro-tolerance argument (allowing the group to express its views openly so that people can see they are wrong) was slightly (and significantly, at .004, N = 1450) more effective when it was presented last. However, the effect is extremely small – the percentage of respondents unpersuaded by this argument ranges from 71.7 percent to 65.8 percent, and the correlation between order and response is a mere .06 (nor is the curvilinear correlation any stronger). In light of the weakness of this effect, and the absence of order effects for the three anti-tolerance arguments, the two arguments presented to those who were initially uncertain about whether to allow the speech, and the two other pro-tolerance items, we conclude that the order of presentation is of little substantive significance and will ignore it as a variable in the analysis that follows.

11 All of these figures ignore those who were persuaded from intolerance to uncertainty. Across the three arguments, these percentages range from 6.0 to 7.3 percent of the respondents.

Table 6.1. *The Effects of Persuasive Communications on Political Intolerance*

	Initial Attitude		
Arguments	Strong	Not Strong	Total
Supporters of Banning Speeches – Initially Intolerant			
Can't trust authorities to decide who has rights			
Still ban speech	87.3	67.1	81.3
Don't know	4.2	10.1	6.0
Change, allow speech	8.5	22.8	12.7
TOTAL	100.0	100.0	100.0
N	1,024	426	1,450
Unfair to allow some and not others			
Still ban speech	81.4	60.6	75.3
Don't know	5.7	10.8	7.2
Change, allow speech	12.9	28.7	17.5
TOTAL	100.0	100.0	100.0
N	1,023	427	1,450
Express views openly so that people can see they are wrong			
Still ban speech	75.6	52.2	68.7
Don't know	5.5	11.4	7.3
Change, allow speech	18.9	36.4	24.1
TOTAL	100.0	100.0	100.0
N	1,023	427	1,450
Opponents of Banning Speeches – Initially Tolerant			
If came to power, would destroy democracy			
Still allow speech	30.2	49.0	42.1
Don't know	10.9	7.1	8.5
Change, ban speech	58.9	43.9	49.4
TOTAL	100.0	100.0	100.0
N	250	438	688
Ideas will hurt people			
Still allow speech	53.3	56.5	55.3
Don't know	7.1	9.9	8.9
Change, ban speech	39.7	33.5	35.8
TOTAL	100.0	100.0	100.0
N	251	438	689
Opposing audience might become violent			
Still allow speech	50.3	50.2	50.2
Don't know	8.0	10.2	9.4
Change, ban speech	41.7	39.6	40.3
TOTAL	100.0	100.0	100.0
N	251	436	687

Arguments	Initial Attitude		Total
	Strong	Not Strong	
"Uncertain" Whether to Ban Speeches – Initially Agnostic			
Can't trust authorities to decide			
Still uncertain	n/a	n/a	64.8
Change, ban speech	n/a	n/a	18.5
Change, allow speech	n/a	n/a	16.6
TOTAL			100.0
N			353
Ideas will hurt people			
Still uncertain	n/a	n/a	57.1
Change, ban speech	n/a	n/a	31.2
Change, allow speech	n/a	n/a	11.7
TOTAL			100.0
N			353

Note: n/a = not applicable.

intolerant position. The "heckler's veto" argument – that the opponents hearing the speech might become violent – resulted in a conversion to intolerance by 40.3 percent of the sample. Only a minority of these respondents (who are a fairly small minority of the total sample) maintained their tolerance in the face of these counterarguments.

Nearly 14 percent of the respondents were initially unable to express a judgment about whether the speech ought to be allowed. We attempted to convert these people to a substantive opinion with one pro-tolerance argument and one anti-tolerance argument. When we told the respondents that some argue that the government cannot be trusted to say who can and cannot be allowed to speak (the weakest of the pro-tolerance arguments), 16.6 percent became tolerant. However, 18.5 percent became *intolerant*. Although the numbers of respondents are small, this argument was equally effective at producing intolerance as it was in producing tolerance. On the other hand, 31.2 percent of those who heard that some might be hurt by the speech (the least powerful anti-tolerance argument) became intolerant, while only 11.7 percent switched to a tolerant view. Most of those who refused initially to assert a position were steadfast in their unwillingness to form a judgment about this dispute.[12]

12 Among those initially uncertain whether to allow the speech, some changed their views in contrary directions. A total of 52.7 percent of these respondents (N = 350) remained uncertain in response to *both* attempts to persuade them to express a view. Not many respondents were responsive to both arguments – only 5.9 percent became tolerant when presented with a pro-tolerance argument, but

Table 6.2. *The Macro-Level Consequences of Persuasive Communications*

Tolerance Intervals	Attitude after Tolerant Arguments	Initial Attitude	Attitude after Intolerant Arguments
All South Africans			
% Intolerant	42.6	58.3	75.9
% Tolerant	43.5	27.7	10.2
African			
% Intolerant	48.1	62.2	78.1
% Tolerant	39.0	24.9	9.0
White			
% Intolerant	23.3	44.0	66.7
% Tolerant	60.2	39.6	16.9
Coloured			
% Intolerant	27.8	47.8	73.5
% Tolerant	55.1	35.1	9.4
Asian Origin			
% Intolerant	28.6	54.3	71.0
% Tolerant	56.1	30.5	13.8

Note: Columns total to 100 percent, minus the percentage of respondents without an opinion.

It is important to understand these findings from the macro level as well, based on reconstituting the sample after our efforts at persuasion. If this hypothetical dispute over a political rally invoked uniformly pro-tolerance commentary, to which all South Africans were exposed, then we would expect a roughly even distribution of opinion after the arguments were made. Although 58.3 percent of South Africans would support banning the rally as their initial point of view, only 42.6 percent were intolerant after hearing the arguments (see Table 6.2). Conversely, the percentage of tolerant South Africans would rise from 27.7 percent to 43.5 percent. Thus, while South Africans initially divided roughly two to one in favor of intolerance, the effect of debating the issue is an evenly divided citizenry. One can readily imagine that the political consequences flowing from imbalanced opinion would be quite different from the consequences associated with symmetrical opinion.

intolerant when presented with the anti-tolerance argument. Perhaps inexplicably, 14.2 percent of the respondents were persuaded by both arguments to become intolerant, while 8.9 percent became tolerant in response to both arguments. A total of 10.9 percent were persuaded by the anti-tolerance argument but not by the pro-tolerance argument, while only 2.0 percent were persuaded to become tolerant but not to become intolerant. The remainder of the respondents (a very small percentage) gave answers that are even more difficult to understand.

On the other hand, if we assume that all commentary on the rally raised issues opposing tolerance, then South Africans would be very intolerant indeed. Under this circumstance, intolerance would balloon to 75.9 percent and tolerance would shrink to 10.2 percent. And if we add to this figure those who were initially undecided about the rally but who were persuaded to accept an intolerant position, this figure rises even further to 80.1 percent. This scenario would most likely lead to quite severe political repercussions since virtually no one would oppose banning the rally.

Table 6.2 also reports the *tolerance intervals* according to the race of the respondent. The table reveals a remarkable amount of variability in tolerance attitudes. Consider Coloured South Africans, for instance. If the attempt to demonstrate generated discussion favoring tolerance, then Coloured people would tend to be tolerant, by a ratio of about two to one. But if the dispute stimulated arguments in favor of intolerance, then the ratio of tolerant to intolerant Coloured people would be nearly one to eight. For every racial group, intolerant argumentation creates large majorities of intolerant citizens. But only among African South Africans does tolerant argumentation fail to bring about a tolerant majority.

How intolerant would South Africans be were they faced with the prospects of a political group attempting to hold a rally in an area where the group was quite disliked? The answer from conventional survey research would be 58.3 percent intolerant. But this figure depends heavily on the nature of the argumentation evoked by the dispute. Depending on the content of the arguments made, the percentage of South Africans who would be intolerant ranges from 42.6 percent to 75.9 percent, a sizable and politically significant interval indeed. These findings should give pause to those who place much credence in point estimates generated by surveys. The findings also document the importance of context; whether South Africans would support a rally like this one depends not only on the initial inclinations of the people but also on the nature of the debate generated by the dispute. The context of the dispute may well be crucial to the outcome of any controversy over the rights of a political minority.

We will address more completely the nature of these converted attitudes later in this chapter. For the moment, however, it may be useful to demonstrate that the structure of the variance in the converted attitudes has not been changed. Some might anticipate that persuasibility experiments are contaminated by a variety of extraneous factors, including random error. We have therefore investigated the degree to which the converted attitudes are connected to more general political tolerance and to perceptions of threat from the group used in the experiment.

The initial (trichotomized) responses to our tolerance item are strongly related to both general political tolerance (b = .31, standard error = .02) and to perceptions of threat from the group (b = −.13 standard error = .02). These relationships change only slightly when we examine the converted attitudes. When we use attitudes *after* being exposed only to pro-tolerance arguments, the unstandardized regression coefficients (with standard errors) are .29 (.02) and −.18 (.02), respectively; *after* being exposed exclusively to anti-tolerance arguments, the relationships are .22 (.02) and −.07 (.02); and when we allow exposure to both pro- and anti-tolerance arguments, the relationships are .20 (.02) and −.12 (.02). Thus, there is no clear evidence of a serious diminution of the coefficients, and we are therefore entitled to the conclusion that the responses emitted after hearing the persuasive arguments are not unduly contaminated with measurement error.

Table 6.1 also reports the results of our efforts to persuade according to the strength of the initial attitude. Among those who initially favored banning the speech, the strength of the original attitude had a substantial effect on persuasibility. For instance, on the first argument, 22.8 percent of those with moderate intolerance changed their views, while only 8.5 percent of those strongly intolerant were convinced. Across all three arguments, while 78.5 percent with a strongly intolerant attitude could not be persuaded to change their views, only 59.8 percent of those only moderately intolerant remained obdurate. This difference of nearly 20 percentage points is highly significant, even if it is entirely predictable.

Those who were initially tolerant, however, are not entirely predictable. Indeed, in response to the argument that the highly disliked group would destroy democracy, those more strongly tolerant were *more* likely to change than those only moderately tolerant. On the other two arguments, the differences between the two groups are trivial. Thus, we have a double conundrum with these data: Those who are tolerant are more easily persuaded to abandon their views than those who are intolerant, and the strength of the initial position is negatively related to change among those initially intolerant, but *positively* related (or unrelated) to change among those initially tolerant. Clearly, tolerance and intolerance are attitudes with quite different characteristics.

We should note in passing one more anomaly. Among those who are initially intolerant, strong attitudes outnumber moderate attitudes by about 2.5 to 1. But among those who are initially tolerant, the ratio of strong to moderate attitudes is very roughly .5 to 1, an exceptionally different ratio indeed. South Africans are likely to be intolerant, their intolerance is likely to be strongly felt, it is counterbalanced by a much smaller group with more democratic attitudes, and these attitudes are not strongly held. This is not a very encouraging mix for democratic politics.

As we noted previously, there are very substantial racial/linguistic differences in responsiveness to these arguments (see Table 6.2). Why are intolerant Africans so unresponsive to appeals to tolerate? We will explore several general possibilities more fully later in the chapter, but one simple answer may have to do with the groups about which the respondents were queried. Recall that the group named in the initial stimulus was either the most disliked group or another highly disliked group. Because subjects were randomly assigned to the treatment group, it is unlikely that Africans were disproportionately presented with the more disliked stimulus. It is possible, however, that different racial/linguistic groups perceive different levels of threat from the group with which they were presented, and that these differences account for the resistance of intolerant Africans to tolerant counterarguments. We must consider this possibility carefully before moving to further analysis.

In fact, the threat perceived by the African respondents from the group used in the persuasibility experiment (irrespective of whether it was the most disliked group or some other highly disliked group) was significantly higher than the threat perceived by whites, Coloured people, and South Africans of Asian origin. Moreover, there is a stronger relationship among Africans between threat perceptions and willingness to allow the group to make a speech than for non-Africans (i.e., high threat more readily materializes in intolerance). As a consequence of the higher perceived threat and the closer connection between threat and intolerance, one would predict that intolerant Africans are more resistant to appeals to become tolerant. Table 6.3 contains data with which the hypothesis can be tested. The table reports the relationships among perceptions of threat, the salience of the tolerance issue, and persuasibility.

Among those initially intolerant, perceptions of threat are indeed related to resistance to persuasibility. For three of the four racial groups, the degree of threat posed by the group mentioned in the tolerance question has a considerable influence on persuasibility: The greater the perceived threat, the more difficult it is to persuade the respondent to adopt a tolerant position. Consider the African South Africans first. The regression coefficient (Beta, the standardized regression coefficient) linking threat and persuasibility is a highly significant −.21 – as threat increases, persuasibility decreases. Roughly one-half of the respondents perceiving little threat could not be convinced to adopt a tolerant position, but very large majorities of the most threatened respondents resisted change (data not shown). Even the most threatened white, Coloured, and Asian

Table 6.3. *Determinants of Persuasibility*

Determinant	Race of Respondent			
	African	White	Coloured	Asian
Supporters of Banning Speeches – Initially Intolerant				
Perception of Group Threat				
b (s.e.)	−.17 (.02)	−.20 (.07)	.03 (.08)	−.27 (.08)
Beta	−.21*	−.19*	.04	−.26*
r	−.24	−.22	−.01	−.29
Concern over the Issue				
b (s.e.)	−.11 (.01)	−.11 (.04)	−.19 (.04)	−.08 (.16)
Beta	−.22*	−.19*	−.38*	−.14
r	−.25	−.22	−.38	−.19
Intercept	1.85 (.06)	2.05 (.14)	2.39 (.17)	1.92 (.16)
R^2	.11*	.08*	.15*	.10*
Standard error of estimate	.60	.75	.76	.75
Standard deviation	.63	.77	.81	.79
N	1,212	210	116	144
Opponents of Banning Speeches – Initially Tolerant				
Perception of Group Threat				
b (s.e.)	.13 (.04)	.03 (.06)	.08 (.07)	.06 (.09)
Beta	.15*	.03	.12	.08
r	.16	.06	.13	.06
Concern over the Issue				
b (s.e.)	.09 (.03)	.07 (.03)	.01 (.04)	−.04 (.06)
Beta	.17*	.15	.03	−.08
r	.18	.15	.05	−.06
Intercept	1.76 (.08)	1.55 (.10)	1.88 (.15)	2.05 (.09)
R^2	.06*	.03	.02	.01
Standard error of estimate	.79	.62	.61	.70
Standard deviation	.81	.63	.61	.69
N	486	189	83	82

Notes:
* Standardized regression coefficient is significant at $p < .01$.

respondents were not as resistant to change as the most threatened African respondents (although the numbers of respondents are small). The overall relationship among Africans, whites, and South Africans of Asian origin is similar.

Why is there no correlation between threat perceptions and persuasibility among Coloured South Africans? This is indeed a puzzling finding, one that requires additional analysis.

The Persuasibility of Tolerance and Intolerance

Although threat perceptions do not influence persuasibility among Coloured South Africans, the salience of the issue has a very strong effect indeed. Those to whom the proposed demonstration mattered more[13] were much less likely to be persuaded to become tolerant. The salience of the issue affected all respondents, but both the bivariate and multivariate relationships among Coloured people are uncharacteristically strong.

Among those who were initially tolerant, these relationships are considerable weaker, and *they are in the opposite direction*. That is, as perceptions of threat increase, the respondents are more, not less, likely to accept the intolerant counterargument. For example, the regression coefficient for the African respondents is +.15. The relationship is strongest among African and Coloured respondents, with sizable majorities of the most threatened respondents succumbing to intolerant argumentation.

Generally, then, the strength of the group stimulus (its degree of threat and salience to the respondent) affects processes of persuasibility. When the stimulus is highly threatening, it is difficult to persuade the intolerant to accept a tolerant outcome, while it is relatively easy to talk the tolerant South Africans out of their tolerance. Thus, the importance of perceived threat in the tolerance equation is strongly reinforced – not only are those who are threatened more likely to be intolerant initially, but they are also more likely to be intolerant even after hearing various arguments about tolerance, pro and con.

Among those initially tolerant, the findings are entirely different (see Table 6.3). Perceptions of threat from the group have only a slight impact on change in attitudes. Among Africans and Coloured people, greater perceived threat is associated with more, not less, change. Furthermore, the salience of the issue is positively (but weakly) related to change among Africans and whites, but is unrelated to change among Coloured people and South Africans of Asian origin.

Of course, these are only a few of the variables that might account for responsiveness to persuasive communication; a panoply of additional hypotheses requires investigation. In order for us to investigate these hypotheses, the dependent variable for the remainder of this analysis will be the degree to which the subject is responsive to persuasive

---

13 Instead of using the intensity of the initial response to the tolerance item, which is a dichotomy, we use as the measure of the salience of the issue the respondent's claim of how much a potential speech like this mattered. The item read, "Would it matter very much to you, one way or another if the group actually gave its speech?" This variable has five categories, and among all respondents is fairly strongly related to tolerance ($r = -.39$), the intensity of the initial attitude ($r = .34$), and to perceived threat ($r = .22$).

information. Some people were completely unresponsive, holding stead-fastly to their original view. Others, however, were fairly easily persuaded, changing their views in response to each of the counterarguments we presented to them. Still others were responsive to some counterarguments but not others; presumably, some of these arguments raised alternative considerations that were serious enough to "trump" their initial view, while others were brushed off as inconsequential. Thus, the dependent variable for our analysis of persuasibility is the ease with which the respondent is converted to the alternative position. "Ease" we measure by the number of arguments to which the subject responds. Because it appears that there are quite different dynamics to the persuasibility of tolerance and intolerance, we begin this analysis by considering the two dependent variables separately.

The Impact of Message Source

One aspect of the experiment involved varying the source of the arguments presented to the respondents. For half of the sample, the arguments were attributed to "a friend"; for the other half, the design is a bit more complicated. That portion of the sample able to name a local opinion leader was told that the arguments were made by the opinion leader. Among those respondents randomly assigned to the "leader" condition for the persuasibility experiment, but who were *unable* to name an opinion leader, we attributed the argument to Nelson Mandela. This is an important qualification to the experiment: Although respondents were randomly assigned to hear either the argument from a friend or an opinion leader, among the latter the split is systematically dependent upon whether the respondent could name a local opinion leader. The result then is a trichotomous variable indicating the source of the argument. Note further that this obviously is not a particularly strong manipulation (indeed, many respondents no doubt thought of the opinion leader they had identified in earlier questions when they were thinking about "a friend"), so we do not expect a great deal of variability in persuasibility according to message source. Nonetheless, our hypothesis is that leaders are more effective at changing opinions than friends.

Table 6.4 reports the simple effect of message source on persuasibility for each of the four main racial groups. The dependent variables reported here are dichotomies indicating whether there was any success in bringing about tolerance or intolerance in the respondent. Among those initially intolerant, the opinion leaders were most successful at persuading the respondents to allow the rally. For instance, over one-half of the white South Africans were persuaded by their opinion leader to become tolerant. For white and Coloured people (and perhaps people of Asian

Table 6.4. *The Effect of Message Source on Persuasibility*

	Message Source		
Percentage Persuaded	Friend	President Mandela	Opinion Leader
Initially Intolerant – Persuaded to Tolerance			
African	18.9 (630)	24.0 (262)	25.0 (372)
White	39.4 (99)	38.4 (86)	56.3 (48)
Coloured	33.3 (60)	32.4 (34)	52.9 (34)
Asian Origin	49.3 (69)	42.6 (47)	48.4 (31)
Initially Tolerant – Persuaded to Intolerance			
African	57.2 (264)	53.2 (111)	64.2 (159)
White	51.8 (114)	51.7 (60)	50.0 (38)
Coloured	66.0 (47)	62.5 (24)	65.4 (26)
Asian Origin	48.9 (45)	63.0 (27)	54.5 (11)

Note: The figures in parentheses are the numbers of cases on which the percentages are based. For instance, 18.9 percent of the 630 intolerant African respondents in the sample were persuaded to a tolerant viewpoint by the arguments of a friend.

origin as well), the opinion leaders were more effective than Mandela (president at the time of the survey) in creating political tolerance. Among whites, only 38.4 percent were persuaded by an argument attributed to President Mandela, in contrast to the 56.3 percent who were persuaded by an opinion leader. For Africans, however, attributing the argument to Mandela was no more or less effective at attitude change than attributing the argument to a friend. This is a somewhat surprising finding. Message source has little effect on the South Africans of Asian origin, but the other three groups responded somewhat differently according to the source of the argument.

Among those who were initially tolerant, the effect of message source is less clear. Africans were somewhat more persuaded by an argument made by an opinion leader, but whites and Coloured people were not, and among those of Asian origin, the most effective source was President Mandela, not the opinion leader. Since the number of cases on which many of these percentages are based is relatively small, we resist trying to interpret the findings for South Africans who are Coloured or of Asian origin.

Perhaps these relationships signal an important flaw in the experiment. In some instances, it is possible that attributing the counterarguments to one's opinion leader seems counterfactual to the respondents, and therefore the manipulation is not effective. Most South Africans agree quite a bit with the person they named as their opinion leader (at least according to the perceptions of the respondents), with about one-third of the respondents claiming to agree completely with the political views of the opinion leader and another one-third claiming to agree somewhat. More-over, as the frequency of political discussion increases, so too does perceived agreement. If most South Africans have friends and opinion leaders with similar views, then it may well be that our counterargument strategy was simply not believable to some since we told the respondents that the leader was making an argument that was out of character with the respondents' perceptions of the views of the leader. The nature of the experiment was such that the leader was always said to be arguing a position contrary to the views of the respondent. This problem may be especially serious with that portion of the sample hearing that their opinion leader – a specific named individual – was making the counter-argument, as well as for those hearing that President Mandela was making the argument. In these cases, the believability of, for instance, our claim that President Mandela argued in favor of intolerance may have been strained.

Another reason that the different types of leaders have such slight and confused effects on the respondents may be the wide variability in the types of connections between the respondents and the opinion leaders. For instance, the degree of politicization of the relationship with the opinion leader varies considerably. While 34.8 percent of the respondents reported that they had at least weekly conversations about politics with their opinion leader, 17.3 percent reported that they never discussed politics with the opinion leader and another 17.2 percent only rarely dis-cussed politics. Further, there is considerable difference in the degree to which the different sources are trusted, ranging from only 44.5 percent who claim to trust their opinion leaders a great deal to 26.9 percent who do not trust them very much. Finally, the political homogeneity of the dyads differs considerably, ranging from 39.5 percent who claim com-plete political agreement with their opinion leader to 9.1 percent who claim disagreement with their leader and another 12.8 percent who are uncertain about the level of agreement. In light of this variability, it seems prudent to substitute the *perceived* attributes of the relationship with the opinion leader for the nominal association between the respondent and the leader in considering the effect of message source on persuasi-bility. Because of the dwindling cell sizes for Coloured and Asian South Africans, we exclude them from this portion of the analysis.

Among Africans, levels of trust in Mandela did indeed have some influence on persuasability. Among those trusting Mandela very much, about one-third changed their expressed opinion on whether the demonstration ought to be banned by accepting one of his arguments in favor of tolerance, and, generally, increases in trust are associated with increases in persuasability $(r = .20)$. Among those who heard *intolerant* arguments attributed to Mandela, nearly two-thirds adopted an intolerant position. Overall, the relationship between levels of trust in Mandela and conversion to intolerance is also moderately strong among Africans ($r = .23$). When Nelson Mandela speaks, African South Africans seem to listen.

Among white South Africans, the persuasibility of President Mandela is largely independent of how much the respondent claims to trust the president. Levels of trust are very weakly related to conversion to tolerance ($r = .09$) and are independent of conversion to intolerance ($r = .04$). A portion of the explanation of the effectiveness of this variable has to do with the fact that whites are considerably less likely to express the highest levels of trust in the president, and it is at these highest levels that persuasibility seems to be most effective. In general, we conclude that *Mandela has little capacity to change the views of white South Africans when it comes to disputes over civil liberties.*

A similar sort of analysis can be conducted for those for whom we used the opinion leader as the source of the argument, since the respondents were asked to indicate their degree of trust in their opinion leaders. Among the African respondents, even the most trusted opinion leaders were not terribly successful at persuading the respondents to adopt a tolerant position; only one-fourth of the respondents became tolerant after hearing the arguments attributed to their opinion leader. There is no statistical relationship between the degree of trust in the opinion leader and the effectiveness of the persuasion ($r = .02$).

The opinion leaders were, however, somewhat more effective at producing intolerance. Three-fourths of those hearing the arguments from a very trusted opinion leader changed their views, while only about one-half of those trusting their opinion leaders less succumbed to the intolerant arguments. Trust and conversion are at least weakly related ($r = .14$). Perhaps one reason why trust in the opinion leader has a greater effect on persuasion to intolerance is that initial tolerance is a weaker attitude. This possibility will be investigated in the multivariate analysis we present in the next section.

With many fewer white South Africans to analyze, the data reveal a number of anomalies. For instance, trust is *negatively* related to conversion to tolerance ($r = -.18$) among the forty-eight whites in this portion of the analysis, meaning that less trusted leaders were more effective at bringing about opinion change. Surely this is an artifact of the small number of cases available for analysis. And although trust is strongly related to conversion to intolerance ($r = .38$, N = 37), we have little confidence in the stability of this relationship. Generally, the most reasonable conclusion is that black and white South Africans do not differ a great deal when it comes to the role of trust in persuasion. Leaders who are trusted more are more likely to be effective at persuasion.

Although we do not have a direct measure of trust in the respondents' friends, we do have a measure of the degree to which the respondent trusts people in general. Generally, South Africans are not very trusting of people and this lack of variance surely depresses these relationships. Nonetheless, there is some slight tendency for trust to be correlated with persuasion to tolerance among both blacks and whites, although there is no similar relationship between trust and conversion to intolerance. Perhaps these relationships, weak in the first place, are largely spurious, with more trusting people being more likely to be tolerant initially (or less likely to be strongly intolerant), so we reserve our final conclusions about these relationships for the multivariate analysis.

The Impact of Attitude Structure

We hypothesize that compartmentalized attitudes are more readily changed than are more integrated or "crystallized" attitudes. According to Sniderman, Brody, and Tetlock (1991, 210), the crystallization concept

... has three aspects relevant to an analysis of persuasibility. In general, the more crystallized an opinion, the more ego-involving and well rehearsed it is; the more deeply it is embedded in supportive information; and the more thoroughly it is enmeshed in a network of supportive beliefs. For each, and all, of these reasons, it should be expected that the less crystallized a person's political beliefs, the more amenable they are to persuasion, other things equal.

To test this hypothesis, it is necessary to develop a measure of attitude integration for each respondent.

Political tolerance is but one of several attitudes comprising a democratic belief system (see Gibson, Duch, and Tedin 1992; Gibson and Duch 1993b; Gibson 1995a). Indeed, earlier research has demonstrated that in some cultures political tolerance is only very weakly related to the other elements of the democratic belief system (e.g., Russia – see Gibson and Duch 1993a; Gibson 1996c), while in other cultures there is a fairly strong relationship between other democratic values and political tolerance (e.g., the United States – Sullivan, Piereson, and Marcus 1982; Sullivan et al. 1985). At the level of the political system, the degree to which tolerance is closely connected to other democratic beliefs may be dependent upon the extent of experience with democratic governance. At the level of the individual citizen in a new democracy, the degree of integration of these attitudes surely varies widely.

Integration may be indexed by predictability. That is, the degree to which attitudes toward the demonstration are integrated within a democratic belief system can be indicated by the extent to which the demonstration attitudes are predictable from these more general democratic values. Consequently, we have regressed attitudes toward the demonstration on a democratic values factor score (see the appendix to this chapter, where the construction of this measure is discussed). To reiterate, this is a composite index derived from four subindices measuring: (1) support for a multiparty system; (2) support for competitive elections; (3) support for the rule of law; and (4) support for individual liberty in contrast to social order.

There is a highly significant relationship between attitudes toward the proposed rally and support for democratic norms. The factor score does not account for much of the variance in attitudes toward the rally, but the standardized regression coefficient is .10, indicating at least a weak relationship between general attitudes toward democratic institutions and processes and political tolerance in this applied case.

We have measured attitude crystallization for each respondent as the squared residual derived from this equation. The residuals indicate the degree of difference between the observed opinion and the opinion predicted on the basis of the other democratic values. Since we are unconcerned in this portion of the analysis about whether the observed view is more or less tolerant than predicted, we eliminated the sign of the residual by squaring all of the values. Large scores therefore indicate that attitudes toward the rally are less predictable (deviate more from the expected value), while small scores indicate closer integration between the more general democratic attitudes and specific opinions. To reiterate, our hypothesis is that more closely integrated attitudes are more resistant to change than are more compartmentalized attitudes.

Among those initially intolerant, persuasion was more likely to take place among those with *better* integrated attitudes. The correlation is significant and substantial for Africans ($r = -.22$), whites ($r = -.21$), and South Africans of Asian origin ($r = -.22$), but is trivial for Coloured South Africans ($r = -.02$). Thus, for most South Africans, persuasion is more likely to be successful when the initial response is *well integrated* with other democratic values.

We expected quite the contrary, based on the assumption that compartmentalized attitudes result in less belief system dissonance when they change. That is, a change in the primary attitudes requires no complementary change in other attitudes because the various attitudes in the system are not connected. Instead, we have discovered that attitude change comes *least* readily among those with compartmentalized beliefs.

The basic idea behind Stouffer's sober second thought intuition was that some people would be capable of thinking about the civil liberties issues in multidimensional terms if given the time and incentives to do so. Rather than processing the stimulus in strict isolation from other values, multidimensional processing implicates multiple values in evaluating the stimulus. But other values must be connected to the primary value in order for this supplementary processing to take place. If some people simply cannot imagine how a stimulus can be thought of in a different light, then it is unlikely that they will be capable of changing their views. Persuasion involves the mobilization of supplementary attitudes; to be mobilized, these attitudes must be connected to the initial way of viewing the stimulus. Those with better integrated belief systems are more likely to be able to make connections to supplementary attitudes, and hence to change their initial views. In this instance, those who support myriad democratic institutions and processes are those with alternative attitudes to which appeals via persuasive argumentation can connect.[14]

On the other hand, the degree of compartmentalization of the initial response is *positively* related to conversion to intolerance among Africans and South Africans of Asian origin ($r = .20$ and $.23$, respectively), is unrelated to change among initially tolerant whites ($r = .01$), and is negatively related to change among Coloured South Africans ($r = -.24$). These findings certainly complicate our understanding of the processes involved.

Stouffer did not originally posit that the process of attitude change was symmetrical. Instead, his was a theory about conversion to tolerance among the intolerant. He argued that the initial reaction to political enemies was intolerance, largely because the stimulus was perceived as threatening. He suggested no mechanisms through which those who are initially tolerant could be persuaded to become intolerant.

Among black South Africans, integrated tolerance is more resistant to change; integrated intolerance is more susceptible to change. This finding can probably be ascribed to the nature of the belief system we are examining here. It is most likely the case that our measure of support for democratic institutions and processes is not entirely symmetrical. That is, one end of the continuum is surely marked by highly integrated beliefs about majority rule and minority rights. The other end of the continuum, however, is most likely characterized by the *lack of integration*, not by integration within an *antidemocratic* belief system. When we speak of integrated tolerance, we are referring to tolerance that is supported by a variety of other democratic attitudes. We doubt that intolerance is similarly bolstered by antidemocratic attitudes among many respondents. Instead, the intolerance is most likely surrounded by a mixture of democratic and antidemocratic attitudes. Thus, our

---

14 Sniderman et al. (1991, Chapter 11) report a similar finding using level of education as a surrogate for attitude crystallization.

finding seems to be that tolerance connected to other democratic values resists conversion to intolerance; but intolerance that is surrounded by a mixture of democratic and antidemocratic values is prone to being converted to tolerance.

Multivariate Analysis

To this point, we have investigated a series of essentially bivariate relationships. Bivariate findings are not entirely uninformative since they depict the *total* effect of one variable on another. But rigorous hypothesis testing requires multivariate analysis in order to isolate the *independent* effects of the various predictors. Consequently, Tables 6.5 and 6.6 report the full equations predicting responsiveness to our efforts at inducing tolerance and intolerance.

Before considering the results of this analysis, it may be useful to restate our basic hypotheses:

- H_1: Those who are especially trustful of the source of persuasive communication are more likely to heed messages and change their views.
- H_2: Those to whom the issue of demonstrations is more salient are less likely to respond to persuasive communications.
- H_3: Similarly, those who are more threatened by the group used in the experiment are less likely to change their views.
- H_4: Those with more integrated belief systems are more likely to respond to attempts at persuasive communications since it is more likely that the counterarguments will mobilize an alternative belief.

Table 6.5 reports the regression results for those who were intolerant in their initial reaction to the demonstration.

This analysis reveals several significant predictors of persuasibility, confirming most of the bivariate analyses. Those for whom the group is threatening and/or the issue is salient are quite unlikely to respond to the pro-tolerance arguments.[15] To the extent that people are engaged by the issue and are fearful of the group claiming the civil liberty, not only will

---

15 Note that there are substantial differences in the levels of statistical significance of these relationships across the various groups. The conclusions we draw in this analysis are based mainly on the unstandardized and standardized regression coefficients. Within an equation, the standardized coefficients are most useful, and we typically impose a minimum coefficient of .10 to be considered substantively significant. Our analyses across the groups rely on the unstandardized coefficients, which must be interpreted with regard to the metrics upon which the variables are measured.

Table 6.5. *Multivariate Analysis of Persuasibility – Persuasion to Tolerance*

Persuasion to Tolerance	b	s.e.	Beta	r	Equation Statistics a	s.e.	R^2	N
African					1.91	.06	.14*	1,184
White					2.11	.14	.10*	208
Coloured					2.30	.20	.16*	112
Asian Origin					2.02	.18	.12*	137
Attitude Compartmentalization								
African	−.11	.02	−.15*	−.22				
White	−.10	.06	−.13	−.22				
Coloured	.05	.09	.05	.02				
Asian Origin	−.13	.08	−.15	−.22				
Salience of the Issue								
African	−.10	.01	−.19*	−.25				
White	−.08	.04	−.15	−.22				
Coloured	−.19	.04	−.39*	−.39				
Asian Origin	−.06	.05	−.12	−.18				
Perception of Group Threat								
African	−.16	.02	−.20*	−.24				
White	−.18	.07	−.17*	−.22				
Coloured	.00	.09	.00	−.04				
Asian Origin	−.23	.09	−.23*	−.29				
Trust in Message Source								
African	.18	.04	.13*	.09				
White	−.06	.16	−.02	−.03				
Coloured	.13	.18	.07	.06				
Asian Origin	.07	.19	.03	.01				

Note:
* Standardized regression coefficient is significant, $p < .01$.

they adopt an initial opinion of intolerance, but they will be intransigent in their views. With the exception of the salience/threat anomaly among Coloured people (discussed previously), this finding pertains to each of the racial groups.

The multivariate analysis weakens but does not eliminate the effect of attitude crystallization on persuasibility, at least for three of the four groups. Better integrated attitudes are more, not less, likely to be changed by argumentation. This is an important finding – the people most likely to be converted to political tolerance are those who hold related values conducive to individual liberty. When these people give the issue a "sober second thought," they are likely to come up with tolerant views.

Finally, the effect of trust in the message source remains significant (but only weakly so) only for Africans.[16] In the multivariate equation, when a more trusted source makes the counterargument, Africans are more likely to be persuaded. For white, Coloured, and Asian South Africans, who presents the argument makes little difference for its effectiveness.

Generally, this simple equation is fairly effective at identifying those who can be persuaded to change their views, with the amount of explained variance ranging from 10 to 16 percent.

Conversion to intolerance is not quite as predictable; the equation is able to account for roughly half as much variance as the persuasion to tolerance equation (see Table 6.6). This is an important finding because it indicates that the inducement toward political tolerance results in more systematic attitudes than the attitudes induced by appeals to intolerance. The contribution of each of the independent variables is also a bit more confused.

Those who view the issue as salient and who are threatened by the group are more likely to abandon their initial tolerance. This is the mirror image of the finding for conversion to tolerance – high threat and salience make the intolerant more resistant to change, and the tolerant more receptive to change. The effects are not especially strong, and do not pertain to South Africans of Asian origin, but generally threat and salience undermine political tolerance.

As with the findings for persuasion to tolerance, there is a weak effect of trust in the message source, and it is confined to Africans. Those who trust the source more are more likely to be persuaded to become intolerant. The slightly weaker effect here may be associated with attributing counterfactual arguments to the message source.

Attitude crystallization has several different effects on persuasibility to intolerance. Among African and Asian South Africans, greater compartmentalization is associated with more attitude change. Among whites, there is no effect, and among Coloured people, greater compartmentalization is associated with greater resistance to change. These findings mirror the bivariate relations, and generate no reasons to alter our speculations presented in that context.[17]

---

16 The trust variable characterizes several different sources of the argument (friends, Mandela, opinion leaders), and therefore one should not expect its statistical effect to be particularly strong.

17 We should also reiterate that the number of cases upon which some of these findings are based is quite small (e.g., only eighty Asian origin respondents), and this may account for some of the instability in the coefficients.

Table 6.6. *Multivariate Analysis of Persuasibility – Persuasion to Intolerance*

Persuasion to Intolerance	b	s.e.	Beta	r	Equation Statistics			
					a	s.e.	R^2	N
African					1.52	.10	.09*	473
White					1.57	.12	.04	185
Coloured					2.20	.20	.08	83
Asian Origin					1.74	.28	.06	80
Attitude Compartmentalization								
African	.06	.02	.16*	.20				
White	−.02	.03	−.07	.01				
Coloured	−.07	.03	−.26*	−.24				
Asian Origin	.07	.04	.22	.23				
Salience of the Issue								
African	.08	.03	.14*	.18				
White	.08	.04	.19*	.17				
Coloured	.03	.04	.07	.05				
Asian Origin	−.03	.06	−.06	−.08				
Perception of Group Threat								
African	.11	.04	.13*	.16				
White	.03	.06	.03	.05				
Coloured	.09	.07	.15	.13				
Asian Origin	.02	.09	.02	.05				
Trust in Message Source								
African	.19	.08	.11*	.11				
White	.12	.14	.06	.04				
Coloured	−.04	.16	−.03	−.05				
Asian Origin	−.09	.24	−.04	−.03				

Note:
* Standardized regression coefficient is significant, $p < .01$.

Among the African and Asian origin respondents, we find quite different effects of attitude crystallization, depending upon whether the persuasion attempt is directed toward tolerance or intolerance. When respondents who were generally supportive of democratic institutions and processes gave an intolerant (inconsistent) reply to our question about a demonstration, that answer was manipulable via the counterarguments. However, when a democratic respondent gave an initial reply that was tolerant (consistent), the attitude was unresponsive to the efforts to change it. Thus, to the extent that the initial response is consistent with the larger set of beliefs, it is resistant to persuasion. Among white South Africans, inconsistent attitudes are susceptible to change, but whether tolerant attitudes are consistent or not has no consequence for persuasibility. For Coloured South Africans, compartmentalized tolerance is *resistant* to change, while integrated tolerance is susceptible to change, a finding difficult to explain (and this is even true of more highly educated Coloured people). We do not at present understand the dynamics of these different processes, but clearly the relationship between the target attitude and surrounding values is an important determinant of persuasibility.

This chapter was motivated in part by a concern about the ability to neutralize the high levels of South African intolerance, especially among African South Africans. According to our results, intolerance can best be converted by lowering the threat and salience of the issue, and appealing to collateral democratic values, especially if trusted elites make such appeals. If these conditions could be fulfilled, intolerance would decline markedly.

CONCLUSIONS

We should perhaps begin summing up our discussion of receptiveness to persuasive deliberation by noting that some portion of the change in reported attitudes is nothing more than that – *reported* change. We are not under any illusion that we have brought about long-term attitudinal change by providing the respondents with a different way of thinking about this dispute over the rights of a hated political minority. Our more modest goal was merely to try to model one important aspect of politics: the fact that people argue with one another, and that they try to convince one another to change their views. Opinion formation and political judgment do not take place within a sterile vacuum; instead, they are part of a contextual, dynamic, and interactive process. We suspect that the next time these people are interviewed, those who were initially intolerant but persuadable may very well give intolerant initial answers again. But we also expect that they will be responsive to counterarguments again, and that they may well change their positions again. Politics is, fortunately or unfortunately, a dynamic process.

This analysis has captured a portion of that dynamism. By forcing the respondents to give this political controversy a "sober second thought," we have brought about change in the stated positions of a large proportion of our sample. Many people changed their minds when asked to consider additional aspects of the civil liberties dispute. To this extent, the survey was able to replicate at least a portion of the dynamics of real politics within the interview.

Attitudes after considering our arguments were different, but no less systematic. That is, our statistical analysis makes clear that the new attitudes are not simply the old attitudes plus some additional random component. Since the factors that accounted for initial views also accounted for subsequent views, we have considerable confidence that our manipulations were more than a sophistry.

We also suggested that the differences between initial attitudes and attitudes following deliberation have important implications for the manner in which civil liberties disputes are resolved. "Tolerance intervals" are the range of possible positions of the mass public, and, in this case, the interval ranged from a sharp division of opinion to nearly consensual intolerance. The enormous variation here indicates just how contextual real politics can be. Depending on the nature of the argumentation that ensues, public opinion can wind up at many different points along the interval. This amply documents the pliability of mass opinion, without deprecating the mass public for being fickle or possessing "non-attitudes."

We have also made some inroads into discovering the factors that affect public opinion. Different arguments had different degrees of effectiveness. More important, persuasion seems to be most likely when people hold alternative, but connected, values to which counterarguments can appeal. The conventional view that compartmentalized attitudes are most malleable because they are unanchored receives little support in this research. Instead, value conflict produces change. And value conflict requires that an issue stimulates more than a single value. Those who have poorly articulated belief systems are intransigent in part because no auxiliary value can be brought to bear on the dispute.

Very much in keeping with existing research, our research finds that threat perceptions play a central role in undermining political tolerance. But unlike most earlier work, our research also demonstrates that those who are threatened are not only more intolerant initially, but they are also more resistant to appeals to tolerate, and more accepting of arguments to abandon their tolerance. Reducing the threat presented by one's political enemies is thus a crucial condition for increasing tolerance, and efforts to explain why some are threatened and others are not ought to be redoubled.

Apathy also plays an important role here. Though we do not wish to argue that apathy among the mass public is necessarily beneficial for democracy, our findings indicate that those more concerned about this civil liberties issue are more likely to be intolerant, and to be resistant to efforts to convert them to tolerance. The greater the salience of the issue, the more likely are those who are tolerant to abandon their tolerance. And it is important to note that the effects are independent of the degree to which the group is perceived as threatening. Those who become engaged in civil liberties disputes are not those likely to foster a democratic outcome. To the extent that ordinary people are disengaged from disputes such as these, tolerance is more likely to prevail.

The Persuasibility of Tolerance and Intolerance

Despite our utilization of a research design that is not particularly strong, we nonetheless find some effect of leaders on the mass public. The most effective leaders are not necessarily those holding high office, and it appears that different segments of the South African population seek their political cues from different sources. Certainly Mandela does not have a uniform influence among all South Africans. Leaders who are trusted are more effective at persuasion, and that is true of persuasion to intolerance as well as to tolerance. Africans are more likely to be influenced by leaders than non-African South Africans.

Finally, many of the findings of this chapter vary by the racial/linguistic/ethnic group of the respondent. We frankly do not yet understand in all instances exactly why and how. In analyses not reported here, we have investigated a variety of variables (e.g., level of education) that we considered as potential explanations of the differences across groups. None of these proved to be particularly enlightening. Perhaps some of the intergroup differences have to do with the specific political enemies named as among the most disliked, but these must be differences *not* associated with the level of threat or antipathy posed by the group since these are variables that are explicitly represented in our equations. We simply do not know, for instance, why Africans are more likely to be persuaded by trusted leaders than are whites, Coloured South Africans, or South Africans of Asian origin.

Even though we have tried to be sensitive to contextual factors in this chapter, we have ignored one central aspect of civil liberties disputes: the role of institutions, and especially the intervention of courts. That topic consumes our attention in Chapter 7.

APPENDIX: THE MEASUREMENT OF SUPPORT FOR DEMOCRATIC INSTITUTIONS AND PROCESSES

The index we employ in this chapter to indicate support for democratic institutions and processes is composed for four subscales: (1) support for a multiparty system; (2) support for competitive elections; (3) support for the rule of law; and (4) support for individual liberty in contrast to social order. The items making up these scales are:

- *Support for Competitive Elections*
  There are better ways to choose our political leaders than elections amongst candidates from several parties. (Disagree)
  If the leaders we elect cannot improve the situation in the country, then it is better not to have competitive elections in the future. (Disagree)
  Those supporting multiparty elections are doing harm to the country. (Disagree)

- *Support for a Multiparty System*
  All this country really needs is a single political party to rule the country. (Disagree)
  A country made up of many ethnic groups should be ruled by only one party to prevent too much ethnic conflict from occurring. (Disagree)
  Democracy in South Africa is too fragile to allow many political parties to compete with each other. (Disagree)
- *Support for the Rule of Law*
  Sometimes it might be better to ignore the law and solve problems immediately rather than wait for a legal solution. (Disagree)
  It's all right to get around the law as long as you don't actually break it. (Disagree)
  In times of emergency, the government ought to be able to suspend the law in order to solve pressing social problems. (Disagree)
  It is not necessary to obey the laws of a government that I did not vote for. (Disagree)
- *Support for Liberty over Order*
  It is better to live in an orderly society than to allow people so much freedom that they can become disruptive. (Disagree)
  Free speech is just not worth it if it means that we have to put up with the danger to society of radical political views. (Disagree)
  Society shouldn't have to put up with political views that are fundamentally different from the views of the majority. (Disagree)
  Because demonstrations frequently become disorderly and disruptive, radical and extremist political groups shouldn't be allowed to demonstrate. (Disagree)

When factor analyzed, these items generate the expected four-dimensional structure, with moderate to strong correlations among the factors.[18] All of the statements designed to measure support for a multiparty system load on the first factor; the political tolerance items define the second factor; the propositions measuring the relative value of individual liberty load on the third factor; and, with one exception, the items indicating attitudes toward competitive elections define the last factor. Generally, the factor structure provides fairly strong support for the hypothesized multidimensionality of support for democratic institutions and processes.

Since these four factors are themselves fairly strongly intercorrelated, we conducted a second-order factor analysis. This produced a single dominant factor, the scores on which will serve as our primary measure

---

18 The eigvenvalues of the first five factors extracted are 2.63, 1.61, 1.39, 1.19, and .87.

of support for democratic institutions and processes. Those scoring high on this index tend to support competitive elections and a multiparty system, are committed to the rule of law, and attach more value to individual liberty than to social order. In short, they attribute more legitimacy to the key institutions and processes of democratic governance in South Africa.[19]

19 This measure of support for democratic institutions and processes is fairly reliable. Cronbach's α for the set of thirteen items is .66, indicating acceptable reliability (by the standards of survey data). However, considerable variability across subsets of the data exists in the reliability of the scale. For instance, among the least educated South Africans, α is .41; among the best educated, α exceeds .70. It is perhaps not surprising that the reliability of the scale would vary by the level of education of the respondent, but this does confound the data analysis.

7

The Law and Legal Institutions as Agents of Persuasion

The preceding chapter dealt primarily with two specific aspects of persuasion: getting the respondents to change their minds and to adopt a new substantive position, and doing so through the use of deliberative argumentation. We have demonstrated some success at changing opinions (although we are better at creating intolerance than creating tolerance), and have gone some distance toward explaining why some people are persuadable and others are not. In general, we have found that the initial positions people take on issues of political tolerance are not necessarily the same as the positions they take after giving considered thought to the matter.

However, another form of persuasion is equally important for democratic politics. It is not always necessary to get citizens to change their own views in political disputes (see Franklin and Kosaki 1989); often it is sufficient to get citizens simply to desist their opposition to democratic policy outcomes, to acquiesce to tolerant decisions made elsewhere. Especially if either elites or political institutions are more strongly committed to democratic processes,[1] then persuading people to "go along with" a democratic outcome may be just about as valuable as persuading them to change their minds.

Indeed, democratic cultures typically sanctify acquiescence without attitude change. Citizens in a democracy may be told how to behave, but not what to think. The right to think one's own thoughts is perhaps the dearest democratic value. Thus, citizens in democracies often reserve the right to disagree even when they agree to acquiesce to decisions that are disagreeable.

---

1 There is a voluminous literature on elite and mass differences in the degree of commitment to civil liberties for unpopular political minorities. See, for examples, Nunn, Crockett, and Williams 1978; McClosky and Brill 1983; Sullivan et al. 1993; Sniderman et al. 1996; Rohrschneider 1999; Guth and Green 1991.

Thus, the purpose of this chapter is to consider a different form of persuasion. Rather than attempting to get the respondents to change their minds, here we direct our attention to whether they are willing to acquiesce to an institutional decision allowing a highly disliked group to exercise its civil liberties. Our primary concern is with the role of law and courts in processes of democratic persuasion. A substantial literature precedes and informs our efforts.

COURTS, LAW, AND COMPLIANCE

One of the most widely held conventional hypotheses in the literature on law and politics is that courts have a special and unusual ability to generate compliance among ordinary citizens. Some refer to this as a "legitimacy-conferring capacity," which means that citizens are predisposed to accept decisions made by judicial institutions, even decisions that are unpopular (see Dahl 1957). In the context of the United States, Adamany (1973, 807) describes this as "an evaluative perception by the people that Supreme Court mandates should be accepted because the justices, as guardians of the Constitution, act by legal right, because they exercise a traditional authority, and because they constitute an appropriate societal institution." This special legitimacy of courts is often thought to be an essential component of the democratic rule of law.

This theory of institutional legitimacy is widely accepted among those studying judicial institutions in the United States, and numerous studies of the legitimacy of the U.S. Supreme Court have been conducted (e.g., Murphy and Tanenhaus 1968, 1990; Tyler and Mitchell 1994; Caldeira and Gibson 1992). Most relevant for our purposes here, Gibson (1989c) found that the Supreme Court has some ability to generate acquiescence to unpopular decisions, although the effects are not as great as many might have supposed. Gibson and Caldeira (1995) extended this research to a transnational context, examining the legitimacy of the European Court of Justice (see also Caldeira and Gibson 1995). Though the European Court of Justice has a limited store of legitimacy, Gibson and Caldeira found it to be effective at converting that legitimacy into compliance with its decisions, even its unpopular decisions. Thus, some empirical research does indeed support the conventional wisdom that, "The greater the perceived legitimacy of the Court, the greater the probability that its policies will be accepted and faithfully implemented" (Johnson and Canon 1984, 194; see also Marshall 1989; Mondak 1991, 1992, 1994; Hoekstra 1995, 2000; Hoekstra and Segal 1996; Franklin and Kosaki 1989). There is something about law, courts, and judges that seems to hold uncommon sway over ordinary citizens.

This process has also been investigated using experimental methods. For instance, Sniderman, Brody, and Tetlock (1991, Chapter 11) report an interesting experiment in the United States addressing the degree to which law operates as a persuasive symbol. The hypothesis they test (and support) is that, "so far as citizens attach a positive value to a law and perceive in the process of making a law the making of an authoritative decision as to what is right and proper, they should be inclined to view positively a policy that has become a law" (1991, 209). They discover that law does indeed affect citizens' attitudes, with the legitimacy of law making encouraging acceptance of public policies (see also Gibson 1989c). Most interesting, the effect of law was greatest upon those with the *highest* levels of education, so the effectiveness of legal symbols is not limited to the least informed citizens. And indeed, law seems able to engender acceptance of public policies even on the issue of race relations and even among those holding the most anti-black opinions. The process driving persuasibility is value conflict[2] – the coexistence of seemingly conflicting beliefs (e.g., belief in equality in the presence of anti-black beliefs) provides the opportunity for law to have an influence. While their analysis is only suggestive, support for the rule of law (as well as the logical inconsistency of claiming rights for oneself while denying them to others) may serve as a powerful impediment to putting pernicious schemes of repression into effect.[3] Thus, as Sniderman and his colleagues assert with regard to the United States, "It is a premise of our culture that law can serve as a persuasive symbol, that the law can instruct us, as citizens, not only with respect to our rights but also with respect to our obligations" (Sniderman, Brody, and Tetlock 1991, 206). At least in the Western context, courts seem to be effective at getting people to accept unpopular court decisions.[4]

Not all research is in agreement that courts have the ability to persuade citizens. Franklin and Kosaki (1989), for instance, argue that a court decision may actually polarize the mass public. "When the Court rules on politically controversial cases, it may establish the law of the

---

2 For an explication of the psychodynamics of this process, see Abelson et al. 1968; see also Gibson 1998a.

3 Gibson and Caldeira (1996) have shown that support for the rule of law as an attribute of polities' legal cultures is associated with the degree to which member states comply with the directives of the European Union. See also Gibson and Gouws 1997b.

4 We realize that the legitimacy of the rule of law in South Africa has been considerably undermined by the arbitrary government that has so long dominated politics. Yet we expect that there is widespread agreement that the new democratic state must be based on the rule of law. Gibson and Gouws (1997b) address more fully South Africans' attitudes toward the rule of law. See also Ellmann 1995.

land, but it does not put an end to debate. . . . A satisfactory theory of Supreme Court impact must recognize that Court decisions do not necessarily bring about agreement and may instead sow the seeds of dissension" (1989, 753–4; see also Murphy and Tanenhaus 1990; Hoekstra 2000; Rosenberg 1991; Marshall 1989; Gibson and Caldeira 2000). A court ruling can, under some conditions, *begin* the process of discussion and debate, not end it. If court decisions increase the salience and intensity of attitudes, then they may also mobilize people to political action, since holding intense attitudes often gives rise to political behavior. Thus, we must be mindful not to assume that courts always have the last say on the matters on which they rule.

Furthermore, though we have learned much in the last few decades of research on mass perceptions of judicial institutions and their consequences for compliance with court decisions, many questions remain unanswered. For instance, to what degree are the findings from long-established democratic polities generalizable to the emerging democracies throughout the world (see Brown 1998)? Courts like the U.S. Supreme Court and the German Federal Constitutional Court have enormous stores of legitimacy, developed over a long period of time.[5] How do courts in fledgling democracies acquire the ability to elicit compliance, to make their decisions "stick"? Do, and how do, people in political systems with little history or tradition of democratic governance come to accept, for instance, granting countermajoritarian powers such as judicial review to relatively unaccountable political institutions?[6] Though scholars widely accept the legitimacy-conferring capacity of courts, the generalizability of the theory must be more thoroughly investigated.

Moreover, culture surely matters. Many Western courts are able to capitalize on deep-seated support for the rule of law, individual liberty and liberalism, limited government, and political tolerance (through respect of minority rights; see Gibson and Caldeira 1996). But many new democracies tend toward the "illiberal democratic" model, and systems in which minority rights are not much respected are increasingly commonplace, even among nominally democratic regimes (e.g., Zakaria

---

5 Gibson, Caldeira, and Baird (1998) have shown that the length of time a court is in operation is in fact an important contributor to the legitimacy of the institution.

6 Research on the development of a democratic political culture within nondemocratic regimes has shown that support for the majoritarian aspects of democracy is more readily established than support for the minoritiarian democratic principles (e.g., Gibson 1995). People in nondemocratic regimes want democracy for themselves, the majority, and are often reticent to establish institutions extending those same rights to hated political minorities.

1997; but see Karatnycky 1999). Courts are fundamentally liberal institutions, so how do such institutions establish this power to induce acquiescence in "illiberal democracies"?[7] How do illiberal cultural values get squared with minoritarianism and respect for the rights of minorities, including hated minorities? These are questions much in need of answers.

Thus, the purpose of this chapter is to investigate whether courts can contribute to a tolerant outcome in civil liberties disputes. After all, public policy rarely directly reflects the preferences of mass publics. Institutions matter, especially courts, since they are typically insulated from direct influence from political majorities. Can South Africans be persuaded to put their intolerance aside and acquiesce to a court decision protecting the civil liberties of an unpopular political minority?

THE ACQUIESCENCE EXPERIMENT

Legitimacy is a concept that takes on importance primarily in the presence of an "objection precondition": When people approve of a decision, the legitimacy of the decision maker is of little consequence; when the decision is unpopular, the efficacy of the decision hinges upon the degree to which the decision-making process and institution are perceived as legitimate. Thus, the acquiescence experiment was structured so that all respondents were faced with an institutional decision with which they disagreed.[8]

---

7 We suspect that the Western tendency to extend legitimacy to courts and to accept their decisions does not characterize large parts of the world. For instance, Brown gives "acts of sovereignty" as an example of judicial impotence in dealing with Islamic executives and parliaments. Such legislation falls outside the jurisdiction of the courts in many Islamic states (1998, 93). Furthermore, reports from Central and Eastern Europe and the former Soviet Union (with several important exceptions) indicate that confidence in legal and judicial institutions is often as low as any other political institutions. Courts in many countries have been unable to distinguish themselves from ordinary politics, and consequently their legitimacy has not been established. Murphy and Tanenhaus (1990, 992) put forth the hypothesis that, "If neither the general culture nor the specific cultures of professional political elites endowed judges with much respect, citizens would feel small compulsion to obey judicial decisions." On legal cultures, see also Gibson and Caldeira 1996.
8 The research literature disagrees on whether a research design without random assignment of subjects to treatment conditions can properly be termed an "experiment." For one who believes that random assignment is necessary to experiments, see McGraw 1996 (although note that she acknowledges that, "Using random assignment as the defining criterion of experiments is not always held in the political science literature. Many studies that do not include random assignment would be considered experiments by many political scientists" (1996, 771)). A contrary

Legal Institutions as Agents of Persuasion

Our analysis of institutional legitimacy began with the scenario that opened the block of questions related to persuasibility (see Chapter 6). To reiterate, we asked the respondents:

Now we would like to ask you to imagine that the [HATED POLITICAL ENEMY] were planning to make a public speech in your community. How would you feel about a decision of the local authorities to ban them from giving a speech here? Would you strongly support banning the speech, support banning the speech, oppose banning the speech, or strongly oppose banning the speech?

Since such speeches are a common part of political life in South Africa, we doubt that many of the respondents had any difficulty conjuring up an image of such an event. As we have noted, a strategy often used by political parties in South Africa is to make recruiting speeches in "enemy" territory (including the no-go areas).

The initial responses of the South Africans to a proposed speech by a hated political enemy are, in general, fairly intolerant. Indeed, over 41 percent of the respondents strongly support banning the speech, with another 17 percent supporting the ban but not strongly. Since 14 percent of the respondents were uncertain of their own position, only 28 percent of the South Africans gave a tolerant reply when asked about an opponent's desire to express its views. To reiterate the experiment, 58 percent of the sample was presented with institutional decisions allowing the speech to take place, while the tolerant 28 percent were confronted with a court decision banning the speech.[9]

opinion is held by Kinder and Palfrey, who assert, "... experiments need not include control groups and need not include random assignment" (1993, 7). Though some of the stratified analysis that follows satisfies the requirement of random assignment, we ultimately agree with Kinder and Palfrey when they assert, "For the moment, the main point is to avoid paralyzing squabbles over exactly what is, and exactly what is not, an experiment. Experiments are preoccupied with control and with ruling out alternative interpretations, and, to these ends, control groups and random assignment are often, but not always, essential" (1993, 10). Random assignment is not essential in this case because theory dictates the need to present a stimulus with which the respondent disagrees.

9 Since the number of respondents with no initial view is a nontrivial portion of the sample, we cannot entirely ignore them. However, it makes little sense to ask respondents without an opinion whether they would challenge an institution's decision on the issue. We assume that citizens always accept decisions about which they do not care, so whether they perceive an institution as legitimate or not has no relevance (no "objection precondition" is present). Thus, institutions usually begin with a bedrock of acquiescent citizens – those who approve of the outcome and those who do not care. Whether those citizens who do not care about the issue are politically valuable for an institution is doubtful, however.

South African Tolerance as It Might Be

The South Africans were then told that what they did not want to happen in the dispute was about to happen, and were asked whether they would do anything about it. The next question posited that the local political authorities had made a decision on the controversy that was contrary to the respondent's own preferences.[10] For instance, those who would *allow* the speech to take place were told that the local authorities had decided to *ban* the speech. They were then asked whether they would accept or contest the decision of the local authorities. Finally, the subjects were told that the South African Constitutional Court had made a decision contrary to the respondent's own view. Thus, for each of the South Africans in the survey, we measured (a) the preference prior to any institutional intervention; (b) the respondent's initial behavioral propensity; (c) willingness to accept a contrary decision of the local authorities; and (d) willingness to accept a contrary decision of the South African Constitutional Court.[11] Table 7.1 reports their responses to these questions.[12]

10 For instance, intolerant South Africans were told, "Now suppose the speech was scheduled to take place next. Using these categories, how likely is it that you would try to get the authorities to stop the speech?" This approach has been used in several earlier studies of acquiescence, including Gibson 1989c; Murphy and Tanenhaus 1990; Gibson and Caldeira 1995.

11 There is little doubt that a considerable chasm exists between simulated or hypothetical behavior and actual action within a real civil liberties dispute. Nonetheless, there are important reasons for studying hypothetical behavior. First, hypothetical behavior may be thought of as a behavioral propensity. Reactions to any given dispute may diverge from the behavioral propensity due to contextual factors, but the propensity nonetheless represents the central tendency (or most likely response, on average) of a larger distribution of actual behaviors. Second, it is exceedingly difficult to study actual repressive political behavior. It is difficult because opportunities to repress one's fellow citizens do not emerge with the periodicity of elections, court appearances, and other opportunities for political activism. Consequently, researchers rarely can mobilize a field study of these sporadic events. (For examples of studies that examine particular civil liberties disputes, see Gibson and Bingham 1985; Gibson 1987; Gibson and Tedin 1988.) Although hypothetical behavior is not the same as actual behavior, it is useful to try to take a step beyond the simple focus on attitudes to determine whether respondents themselves foresee behavioral consequences of their beliefs. For an excellent study of hypothetical behavior in a related area, see Muller 1979 and Marcus et al. 1995. On the use of hypothetical, or "role-playing," measures more generally, see Cooper 1976, and Forward, Canter, and Kirsch 1976. For convincing evidence that attitudes are indeed related to actual behavior, see Kraus 1995.

12 We investigated whether the responses varied according to the order in which we presented these two behavioral options to the respondents. The results of this investigation are conclusive: Order of presentation makes no difference whatsoever.

Table 7.1. *Initial Behavioral Reactions in a Civil Liberties Dispute*

Dispute	Percentage[a]			Mean	Std. Dev.	N
	Likely	Uncertain	Unlikely			
Among the Tolerant						
Try to get the speech allowed[b]						
South Africans	32.1	9.9	58.1	2.54	1.52	688
African	34.6	11.3	54.1	2.67	1.51	486
White	22.6	4.2	73.2	2.09	1.41	190
Coloured	31.4	8.1	60.5	2.37	1.57	86
Asian Origin	35.8	19.8	44.4	2.84	1.49	81
Accept decision/do nothing[c]						
South Africans	42.5	9.7	47.8	3.06	1.54	688
African	38.4	12.1	49.5	3.15	1.48	487
White	59.5	2.1	38.4	2.60	1.61	190
Coloured	40.0	5.9	54.1	3.29	1.66	85
Asian Origin	37.0	14.8	48.1	3.19	1.50	81
Among the Intolerant						
Try to get the speech banned[d]						
South Africans	53.5	7.3	39.2	3.26	1.62	1,451
African	57.4	8.3	34.3	3.42	1.59	1,215
White	25.6	1.4	73.0	2.18	1.44	211
Coloured	54.7	3.4	41.9	3.22	1.66	117
Asian Origin	43.2	6.2	50.7	2.77	1.58	146
Accept decision/do nothing[e]						
South Africans	40.1	7.7	52.2	3.25	1.61	1,450
African	36.9	8.6	54.5	3.35	1.59	1,215
White	61.9	1.4	36.7	2.61	1.61	210
Coloured	45.3	4.3	50.4	3.07	1.65	117
Asian Origin	41.8	8.2	50.0	3.15	1.56	146

Notes:
[a] The three percentage columns total to 100 percent, across the rows, except for rounding errors.
The significance tests for differences in means across the racial groups follow.
[b] $\eta = .17, p < .0000.$ [c] $\eta = .16, p < .0001.$
[d] $\eta = .26, p < .0000.$ [e] $\eta = .15, p < .0000.$

Among the initially tolerant respondents, action in defense of tolerance was not particularly likely. Over 58 percent of the respondents said they would be unlikely to take action to try to get the speech permitted, with another 9.9 percent being uncertain whether they would do something to try to get the speech allowed (and were thus unlikely to act). Only one-third (32.1 percent) report being likely to act to defend the civil liberties of their political enemy. Conversely, 42.5 percent said they would be likely to do nothing (with another 9.7 percent claiming uncertainty). Some crossrace variability on these behavioral propensities exists; tolerant whites are considerably more acquiescent (i.e., the 73.2 percent likely to remain inactive).

Among the intolerant respondents, action was more likely. For instance, 53.5 percent of the South Africans claimed to be likely ("somewhat" or "very") to do something to try to get the speech banned, and 52.2 percent of the respondents said they were unlikely to do nothing at all. Again, intolerant whites are significantly more likely to be passive (e.g., 61.9 percent of the whites would do nothing, compared to 36.9 percent of the Africans). Generally, intolerance is substantially more likely to result in political behavior than tolerance.

Earlier research has also demonstrated a similar strong asymmetry in the behavioral consequences of tolerance and intolerance. For instance, Marcus et al. (1995, 190) discovered that the intolerant were significantly more likely than the tolerant to assert an intention to take action. After testing several hypotheses about the origins of behavioral intentions, they concluded that attitudinal intensity is the main explanation of the difference in behavioral propensities. Their results are not entirely unambiguous, however, since some interaction between attitudinal substance (tolerant versus intolerant) and intensity exists (Marcus et al. 1995, 199), and, generally, behavioral intentions are not well predicted by their model. Some attitudes, more strongly held, apparently lead to action, but others do not.

As noted, we also asked the respondents about their behavioral intentions after the intervention of political institutions. The respondents were first told that the "local authorities" made a decision contrary to the respondent's preference (e.g., intolerant respondents were told that the authorities decided to allow the speech to take place), and were then queried about their likely behavior. They were next told that the Constitutional Court had intervened and made a contrary decision, and were asked how they would react. Thus, the series of questions closely mirrors the reality of civil liberties conflicts.[13] Local authorities make

---

13 Though the experiment is complex owing to its various manipulations, the questions asked any given respondent are actually quite simple. Consider someone who says she does not want the group to give a speech. The acquiescence questions are:

Now suppose the speech was scheduled to take place next week. (SHOW RESPONDENT SHOWCARD 15) Using these categories, how likely is it that you would try to get the authorities to stop the speech?

Suppose the local authorities decided to allow the speech to take place. How likely is it that you would try to get the authorities' decision reversed by another government department?

Table 7.2. *Behavioral Reactions after Local Authorities Intervene in a Civil Liberties Dispute*

	Percentage[a]					
Reactions	Likely	Uncertain	Unlikely	Mean	Std. Dev.	N
Among the Tolerant						
Try to get the speech allowed[b]						
South Africans	28.2	9.8	61.9	2.41	1.51	690
African	33.6	10.9	55.5	2.63	1.54	488
White	12.1	3.2	84.7	1.66	1.14	190
Coloured	20.9	11.6	67.4	2.17	1.46	86
Asian Origin	25.9	21.0	53.1	2.49	1.33	81
Accept decision/do nothing[c]						
South Africans	52.8	8.6	38.6	2.72	1.60	689
African	49.9	9.7	40.5	2.79	1.58	487
White	68.9	3.2	27.9	2.28	1.50	190
Coloured	44.2	8.1	47.7	3.00	1.76	86
Asian Origin	40.7	17.3	42.0	2.96	1.48	81
Among the Intolerant						
Try to get the speech banned[d]						
South Africans	44.8	9.6	45.6	2.97	1.61	1,450
African	48.4	10.4	41.3	3.11	1.60	1,214
White	22.3	2.4	75.4	2.02	1.45	211
Coloured	42.7	8.5	48.7	2.89	1.59	117
Asian Origin	33.6	11.0	55.5	2.61	1.46	146
Accept decision/do nothing[e]						
South Africans	34.1	8.7	57.2	3.50	1.56	1,450
African	28.5	8.7	62.8	3.70	1.49	1,214
White	66.8	4.7	28.4	2.36	1.46	211
Coloured	45.3	12.0	42.7	3.01	1.59	117
Asian Origin	45.9	13.7	40.4	3.01	1.41	146

Notes:
[a] The three percentage columns total to 100 percent, across the rows, except for rounding errors.
The significance tests for differences in means across the racial groups follow.
[b] $\eta = .27$; $p < .000$.   [c] $\eta = .15$; $p < .000$.
[d] $\eta = .23$; $p < .000$.   [e] $\eta = .30$; $p < .000$.

decisions about whether demonstrations can proceed, and those decisions are often appealed to courts. Table 7.2 reports the likelihood of acting after the local authorities have made a decision contrary to the wishes of the respondent.

> And finally suppose that the Constitutional Court ruled that the speech should be allowed to take place. How likely is it that you would try to get the Court's decision reversed by another government department or court?

Even a cursory comparison of Tables 7.1 and 7.2 reveals that the intervention of the authorities decreases the (already low) likelihood that tolerant South Africans would act in favor of their tolerance. For instance, across all South Africans, the percentage likely to do nothing rose by 10 percentage points from 42.5 percent to 52.8 percent. For each racial group, the likelihood of inaction increased. The effects are not particularly great, but the decision of the local authorities tends to reduce the chance that the tolerant would try to get the group's civil liberties respected.

A different, more confused pattern characterizes the intolerant. Generally, the reaction to the decision of the authorities *seems to be to spur intolerant South Africans to action*. For instance, the percentage likely to do nothing declines from 40.1 percent to 34.1 percent. However, the proportion likely to challenge the decision also declines from 53.5 percent to 44.8 percent, and this decrease in the likelihood of challenging the decision characterizes each racial group. These data seem to indicate that, while the authorities might not be challenged, many South Africans would take some other course of action to express their displeasure with the decision. Generally, the effect of the local authorities on acquiescence to the decision is weak and variable across the groups.

Table 7.3 reports levels of acceptance and acquiescence after the Constitutional Court has made an unwelcome decision on the demonstration. Among the tolerant, a majority would do nothing – 56.6 percent claim it is somewhat or very likely that they would accept the decision of the Court and do nothing. Similarly, only 28.0 percent of the sample would take political action to challenge the Court's decision. Tolerant whites are again distinctive, with fully 75.7 percent asserting that they could accept a contrary Court decision. African South Africans are most likely to challenge a decision by the Court (33.7 percent).

Among the intolerant, a tolerant Constitutional Court decision would not be so widely accepted. A majority of South Africans (51.9 percent) assert that they would be unlikely to accept the decision; 39.2 percent would take action to challenge the Court's policy to let the demonstration go forward. Racial differences are again quite substantial, with, for instance, only 31.6 percent of the Africans willing to accept the decision, while 73.9 percent of the whites are so inclined. Coloureds and South Africans of Asian origin are less similar to Africans than they are to whites in the sense that a majority would accept the decision.

The most direct summary evidence of the effect of the institutional intervention can be found in Table 7.4, which reports change in the behavioral propensity measures. Three change scores are reported: (1) the difference in behavioral propensities prior to the intervention (the

Table 7.3. *Behavioral Reactions after the Constitutional Court Intervenes in a Civil Liberties Dispute*

Reaction	Percentage[a]			Mean	Std. Dev.	N
	Likely	Uncertain	Unlikely			
Among the Tolerant						
Try to get the speech allowed[b]						
South Africans	28.0	11.9	60.0	2.39	1.51	688
African	33.7	13.6	52.8	2.64	1.53	487
White	13.2	2.6	84.1	1.65	1.14	189
Coloured	20.9	14.0	65.1	2.13	1.57	86
Asian Origin	21.0	19.8	59.3	2.27	1.33	81
Accept decision/do nothing[c]						
South Africans	56.6	9.8	33.6	2.60	1.58	687
African	52.1	10.7	37.2	2.75	1.58	486
White	75.7	3.7	20.6	2.05	1.40	189
Coloured	54.7	11.6	33.7	2.55	1.66	86
Asian Origin	46.9	17.3	35.8	2.86	1.55	81
Among the Intolerant						
Try to get the speech banned[d]						
South Africans	39.2	11.1	49.7	2.80	1.62	1,448
African	43.0	12.4	44.7	2.95	1.62	1,213
White	10.9	1.4	87.7	1.64	1.16	211
Coloured	37.6	7.7	54.7	2.77	1.60	117
Asian Origin	33.8	13.8	52.4	2.59	1.44	145
Accept decision/do nothing[e]						
South Africans	37.8	10.3	51.9	3.33	1.61	1,447
African	31.6	11.4	57.0	3.54	1.55	1,212
White	73.9	2.8	23.2	2.14	1.44	211
Coloured	51.3	5.1	43.6	2.94	1.63	117
Asian Origin	52.1	13.9	34.0	2.80	1.47	144

Notes:
[a] The three percentage columns total to 100 percent, across the rows, except for rounding errors.
The significance tests for differences in means across the racial groups follow.
[b] $\eta = .27$; $p < .000$.   [c] $\eta = .19$; $p < .000$.
[d] $\eta = .27$; $p < .000$.   [e] $\eta = .30$; $p < .000$.

baseline) and after the local authorities made a decision; (2) the difference between the baseline and the decision of the Constitutional Court; and (3) the difference in propensities between the decisions of the local authorities and the high court. We hypothesize that the intervention of the institutions will decrease the likelihood of action (and increase rates of acquiescence), and that the Constitutional Court will be more powerful than the local authorities.

Table 7.4. *Change in Behavioral Propensities as a Result of*
Institutional Intervention

	Change in Likelihood of Acting – Percentages				
Institutional Interventions	Less Likely	No Change	More Likely	Total	N
Among the Tolerant					
Baseline – Local Authorities	25.8	37.4	36.7	100.0	685
Baseline – Constitutional Court	28.3	33.6	38.1	100.0	683
Local Authorities –					
Constitutional Court	24.6	47.7	27.6	100.0	685
Among the Intolerant					
Baseline – Local Authorities	23.8	45.4	30.8	100.0	1,444
Baseline – Constitutional Court	23.0	40.0	37.0	100.0	1,442
Local Authorities –					
Constitutional Court	17.5	53.9	28.6	100.0	1,440

The effects of the institutional interventions do not differ greatly between the tolerant and the intolerant. For instance, the intervention of the Constitutional Court made action less likely among 28.3 percent of the tolerant South Africans; the comparable figure for intolerant respondents is 23.0 percent.

Perhaps the most unexpected aspect of Table 7.4 is the tendency of the institutional intervention to *increase* the likelihood of acting. Consider for instance the relative effect of a decision by the Constitutional Court. Among the tolerant, roughly one-fourth (24.6 percent) accepted the Court decision and desisted opposition; among the intolerant, the percentage is somewhat lower (17.5 percent). However, more respondents were spurred to action by the Court decision than became acquiescent. Among the intolerant, the effect is greater, with 28.6 percent becoming more likely to act compared to 17.5 percent becoming less likely to act. The modal response is clearly not to change one's behavioral intentions, but there is nonetheless a great deal of variability in how South Africans respond to a decision of their Constitutional Court.

Comparison of the changes from the baseline is also revealing. Roughly, about one-fourth of the respondents were more likely to acquiesce as a result of the institutional decisions. More important, there appears to be little significant difference between the intervention of the local authorities and of the Constitutional Court. For instance, among the tolerant, a Court decision generates more acceptance among 28.3 percent of the South Africans, compared to a figure of 25.8 percent accepting the decision of the local authorities. Similar results

Table 7.5. *Behavioral Reactions to an Adverse Institutional Decision*

Institutional Interventions	Initial Behavioral Inclination toward Decision		
	No Action	Uncertain	Some Action
Among the Tolerant			
Decision by Local Authorities			
Accept	70.5	35.8	40.5
Uncertain	3.4	43.3	5.8
Not Accept	26.0	20.9	53.7
Total	100.0	100.0	100.0
N	292	67	328
Decision by the Constitutional Court			
Accept	72.9	40.0	45.6
Uncertain	5.5	38.5	7.6
Not Accept	21.6	21.5	46.8
Total	100.0	100.0	100.0
N	292	65	329
Among the Intolerant			
Decision by Local Authorities			
Accept	60.6	15.2	16.7
Uncertain	7.8	43.8	4.1
Not Accept	31.6	41.1	79.2
Total	100.0	100.0	100.0
N	579	112	756
Decision by the Constitutional Court			
Accept	59.7	30.3	22.1
Uncertain	9.3	37.6	7.0
Not Accept	31.0	32.1	70.9
Total	100.0	100.0	100.0
N	580	109	756

characterize the intolerant. The Court seems to have little comparative advantage in South Africa in generating acquiescence.

Table 7.5 reports a slightly different way of looking at the question of change. In this table, we report the behavioral propensities controlling for the initial likelihood of acting against the decision of the institution. For instance, of those who were tolerant but who initially claimed they would take no action in favor of the civil liberties of their hated political enemy (thereby accepting the decision), 70.5 percent said they would do nothing if the local authorities banned the demonstration. Conversely, of those who would not initially accept the decision to ban the demonstration, 53.7 percent vowed they would challenge a decision of the local authorities. The most interesting respondents are those mobilized to action by the local decision (26.0 percent) and those who desisted their opposition as a result of the decision (40.5 percent). The former group was galvanized by the state's action; the latter acquiesced to the unpopular decision. These percentages are shaded in Table 7.5.

The data in this table indicate that the mobilizing effects of the institutional interventions are considerably smaller than the acquiescence effects. For the local authorities, the two figures are 26.0 percent and 40.5 percent. For the Constitutional Court intervention, the percentages are 21.6 percent and 45.6 percent. Thus, the difference in the effectiveness of the two institutions is quite small. A Court decision is more likely than a decision by the local authorities to generate acquiescence, but only by 5.0 percentage points. Before a state institution intervened, 42.5 percent of the tolerant South Africans would acquiesce to an intolerant outcome to the civil liberties dispute. After the local authorities endorse the intolerance, this figure rises to 52.8 percent. After the Constitutional Court sanctions the intolerance, the percentage climbs to 56.6 percent.[14] Most important, nearly one-half of those inclined to challenge an intolerant outcome acquiesced in the end. Tolerant South Africans can clearly be convinced to accept intolerant public policy.

But can intolerant South Africans be convinced to accept a tolerant outcome? The second portion of Table 7.5 reports the data necessary to answer this question.

First, we note that those who are intolerant are considerably *less likely to acquiesce* to a tolerant decision by the authorities. For the local authorities, only 16.7 percent could be persuaded to desist opposition; after the intervention of a tolerant Constitutional Court, only 22.1 percent said they would accept the decision and do nothing. This represents less than half the effect of the institutional interventions on those who are tolerant.

Moreover, the unpopular governmental decision is more likely to mobilize the intolerant to action (31.6 percent and 31.0 percent respectively for the local authorities and the Constitutional Court). The figure for mobilization after a Constitutional Court decision among the intolerant is about 9 percentage points higher than for the tolerant. Indeed, on balance, a tolerant government decision generates *more resistance than it does acceptance*. Only a very small proportion of the intolerant activists is willing to desist and acquiesce. Intolerant South Africans

---

14 This is a conservative test of the effectiveness of the Constitutional Court since in every instance the respondents heard of the decision of the local authorities first. Though the experiment has the virtue of verisimilitude, we have no doubt that were the Constitutional Court stimulus read to the respondents first, the estimates of the Court's effectiveness at generating acquiescence would be much higher.

Table 7.6. *Summary of Effects of Institutional Intervention*

Institutional Interventions	Acquiescence Advantage[a]	
	Among the Tolerant	Among the Intolerant
African		
Local Authorities	9.8	−23.9
Constitutional Court	15.4	−17.9
White		
Local Authorities	34.3	32.2
Constitutional Court	53.7	46.7
Coloured		
Local Authorities	−2.1	3.7
Constitutional Court	25.1	6.5
Asian Origin		
Local Authorities	9.2	3.9
Constitutional Court	25.4	17.5
All South Africans		
Local Authorities	14.4	−14.9
Constitutional Court	24.1	−8.9

[handwritten margin note: why the diff.? b/c apartheid gave law a bad name]

Note:
[a] The "acquiescence advantage" is the difference between the percentage of the activists persuaded to accept the institutional decision and the percentage of the inactives mobilized to action by the decision. High scores indicate greater net acceptance of the decision.

[handwritten note: Tolerant can be persuaded to accept intolerant institution intervention. Intolerant can't be persuaded to accept tolerant institution intervention]

are influenced somewhat by government action in defense of the civil liberties of their enemies, but *they are mainly influenced to mobilize their intolerance.*

The two most important types of people we have considered here are those mobilized to action by the institutional decision and those who desist their opposition as a result of the institutional decision. We have calculated an "acquiescence advantage" index as the difference between these two percentages. Positive numbers indicate that the institutional decision generated more acquiescence than mobilization; negative numbers indicate that more were mobilized than "demobilized." Table 7.6 reports the acquiescence advantage scores for both the tolerant and the intolerant, according to the respondent's race and the specific institution intervening. Some care must be exercised in considering the figures in Table 7.6 since, in some instances, they are based on fairly small numbers of respondents. Nonetheless, the broad contours in the data are fairly easily summarized.

African South Africans (who obviously dominate in the "All South Africans" figures) illustrate the most extreme difference between initial tolerance and intolerance. Among tolerant Africans, an institutional intervention generates a modest degree of acquiescence to intolerance. The differences between a decision by the local authorities and the Constitutional Court (9.8 versus 15.4 percent) are small but significant. On the other hand, among intolerant Africans, a tolerant institutional decision results in intolerant mobilization. The differences here are fairly substantial. A Constitutional Court decision results in slightly less mobilization than a decision by the local authorities (−17.9 versus −23.9 percent, respectively).

White South Africans are *entirely* different. First, their initial tolerance or intolerance is of little consequence; both groups are likely to acquiesce to an institutional intervention. Second, white South Africans acquiesce considerably more to a Constitutional Court decision than to a decision of the local authorities. Finally, a very substantial acquiescence advantage can be found among whites.

The patterns among Coloured people and South Africans of Asian origin are a bit more complicated. First, the intervention of the local authorities has little net impact on either the tolerant or the intolerant. Second, among the tolerant, the intervention of the Constitutional Court has a substantial effect in producing an acquiescence advantage. Among intolerant Coloured people, the Court has little impact, although it does seem to influence intolerant South Africans of Asian origin. Thus, the picture emerging from these data is fairly complicated, with only whites (and perhaps those of Asian origin) behaving entirely as hypothesized.

Perhaps the most interesting contrast in these data is between Africans and whites, and especially between intolerant Africans and intolerant whites. White intolerance can be tamed by an institutional intervention; the acquiescence advantage is 46.7. African intolerance cannot be similarly neutralized. Indeed, only among intolerant Africans is there a strongly negative acquiescence advantage (indicating that intolerant mobilization is much more widespread than tolerant acquiescence). This is a finding replete with consequences for democratization in South Africa.

The Total Effect of the Court's Intervention

How successful would the Constitutional Court be in getting acquiescence to an unpopular decision? With the aid of a few simple assumptions, we can simulate the effects on the South African mass public of a court ruling.

Before the intervention of the Constitutional Court, 58.3 percent of the respondents were intolerant; 27.7 percent were tolerant. Let us assume that:

- A Court decision with which the respondent agrees does not affect her or his initial opinion. Thus, those who are tolerant remain tolerant after the Constitutional Court makes a tolerant decision.[15]
- A Court decision has no effect on those without an opinion on the civil liberties dispute. Those who are agnostic about whether a speech ought to be allowed remain agnostic after the Constitutional Court decides the case.[16]

With these two assumptions, we need only examine the reactions of those who are opposed to the Court decision in order to estimate public opinion as it would exist after the Constitutional Court intervened in the dispute.

Let us assume that the Court makes a tolerant decision. The 27.7 percent who are tolerant would not change their views; neither would the 13.9 percent who are agnostic. Among the 58.3 percent who are initially intolerant, the Court decision converts some to grudging tolerance, converts others to uncertainty, and does not influence the views of yet another portion of the sample. Applying the calculations, a tolerant Court decision would result in 56.8 percent of the South Africans accepting the decision, 20.4 percent being uncertain, and 22.8 percent persisting in their intolerance. Thus, the Court is able to boost tolerance from 27.7 to 56.8 percent – an increase of 29.1 percent.

Assume the Court makes an intolerant decision. Then, the tolerant segment of society shrinks to 7.7 percent, while intolerance (real or grudging) balloons to 75.0 percent. Thus, the effect of the Court is to diminish political tolerance by 20.0 percentage points.

These simulations demonstrate that the effect of a Constitutional Court decision can be rather dramatic. Indeed, the "tolerance interval" – the range of opinion depending on what the Court decides – varies from 7.7 to 56.8 percent, a sizable and politically meaningful interval. Thus, the intervention of the Constitutional Court makes an important difference.

15 No empirical test of this proposition is possible, since by the design of the experiment, all respondents were presented only with a Court decision contrary to their own preferences. It is not unreasonable to assume, however, that when a court decides the way someone wants it to decide, the decision does little to change the opinion of the person (except perhaps to reinforce and strengthen it).

16 Neither is this assumption testable, since those with no opinion were not told anything about a decision by the Court.

Table 7.7. *Political Tolerance before and after*
Constitutional Court Intervention

Tolerance	All South Africans	African	White	Coloured	Asian Origin
Initial View					
Intolerant	58.3	62.2	44.0	47.8	54.3
Uncertain	13.9	12.9	16.5	17.1	15.2
Tolerant	27.7	24.9	39.6	35.1	30.5
Total	100.0	100.0	100.0	100.0	100.0
N	2,493	1,961	480	245	269
Final View – Court Rules in Favor of Tolerance					
Intolerant	22.8	26.6	4.8	18.0	18.3
Uncertain	20.4	20.6	17.1	20.8	22.8
Tolerant	56.8	52.7	78.1	61.2	59.0
Total	100.0	100.0	100.0	100.0	100.0
N	2,487	1,955	480	245	268
Final View – Court Rules in Favor of Intolerance					
Intolerant	75.0	75.3	77.2	70.6	72.4
Uncertain	17.2	16.3	17.5	22.0	21.3
Tolerant	7.7	8.4	5.2	7.3	6.3
Total	100.0	100.0	100.0	100.0	100.0
N	2,490	1,959	479	245	268

Table 7.7 reports these effects for the different racial groups. Consider whites first. Though initially fairly evenly divided, whites acquiesce to a Court decision in great numbers, producing large majorities accepting a Court decision, whatever position the institution takes. Similar, but not as dramatic effects are seen among Coloured and Asian South Africans. Among Africans, however, an important asymmetry exists: The Court can contribute to an *intolerant* consensus (75.3 percent agreement), but still can convince only a bare majority of blacks (52.7 percent) to accept a *tolerant* outcome to the dispute. The Court has some power of persuasion within the black community, but not nearly as much as it seems to have among all other racial groups in South Africa. Thus, the Constitutional Court is least effective with the majority in South Africa – blacks.

DISCUSSION: THE EFFECTIVENESS OF SOUTH AFRICAN INSTITUTIONS AS PROTECTORS OF CIVIL LIBERTIES

Though our findings are not simple, a host of general conclusions emerge from this analysis. Our results have implications for the Constitutional Court, the institutional persuasibility of tolerance and intolerance, and the likelihood that an unpopular political minority would be able to exercise its civil liberties in South Africa.

The South African Constitutional Court enjoys neither a deep or broad reservoir of good will within the South African mass public (see Gibson and Caldeira 2000). Only relatively small proportions of the mass public are willing to put aside their own preferences and accept a decision of the Court, although the efficacy of the Court varies significantly with the race of the citizen. The Court is particularly impotent when it comes to influence over the vast majority of the South African population – Africans. The Constitutional Court has some ability to influence white South Africans, but limited ability to influence blacks.

The Court's powers of persuasion also vary depending upon the position the judges adopt. A tolerant Court is relatively ineffective at convincing South Africans to tolerate; an intolerant Court has a much greater likelihood of convincing the tolerant to accept a repressive outcome. Thus, the Court is considerably more likely to be effective at undermining civil liberties than at protecting them. This is not the role that democratic theorists usually expect courts to perform.

South Africans can be persuaded to change their views on a civil liberties dispute, even if tolerant people are more susceptible to argumentation than the intolerant. In a sense, our experiment worked quite well since we were able to get a reasonably large proportion of South Africans to alter its views in response to decisions by political institutions. These findings remind us once more that one's initial position in a political dispute need not be one's final position. People change their opinions over the course of a controversy, and they sometimes change in response to what political institutions are doing.

Understanding the politics of civil liberties in South Africa must begin with the simple fact that intolerance outnumbers tolerance within the mass public by at least a ratio of three to one. Tolerant South Africans are a lonely few. Perhaps one reason for their ready pliability is that they are often confronted with contrary views and arguments from the intolerant majority. An intolerant South African may not even have contact with one who is tolerant; a tolerant South African surely experiences daily those who hold the opposite view about whether to put up with despised political minorities. It is perhaps not very surprising that those holding such a minority viewpoint are readily persuaded by the actions of political institutions.

Though we cannot directly address actual political behavior with the available survey data, our measures of behavioral propensities suggest that attitudes may well have consequences for real political action. Especially when people are threatened and when the issue is important to them, South Africans seem prepared to act on the basis of their general predispositions toward the civil liberties of unpopular political minorities.

We discover once more, however, an important asymmetry: Those with intolerant attitudes are far more likely to act in opposition to civil liberties than those with tolerant attitudes are likely to try to defend the rights of a group they strongly oppose. The behavioral gap between tolerant and intolerant South Africans is substantial, and, we might add, ominous.

These findings reinforce the view that tolerance and intolerance are not mirror images of each other. The psychological significance of intolerance seems to be stronger, with intolerant attitudes less susceptible to change and more compelling for actual political behavior. The research literature has slowly accumulated findings of this nature – and this chapter contributes to that body of evidence – but little progress has been made in understanding differences in the psychodynamics of tolerance and intolerance. Additional research must address this important asymmetry.

When the Constitutional Court sides with intolerance, virtually the entire population accepts that viewpoint. Under such a circumstance, it would be difficult to imagine an effective roadblock to the suspension of civil liberties and the implementation of political repression.[17] Further, should the Court come down in favor of protecting the civil liberties of an unpopular minority, there is little guarantee that its decision would be respected and implemented. Such is the asymmetry of institutional persuasion in South Africa.

These findings are indeed ominous for those favoring minority rights in South Africa. Tolerant South Africans can be persuaded to abandon their tolerance when the government sanctions intolerance. But intolerant South Africans are mobilized to action by a tolerant government decision. This asymmetry poses a serious threat to democracy in South Africa. The ability of the Court to perform a "countermajoritarian" role in a time of political crisis appears to be limited. Whether the Constitutional Court can serve as a "protector of democracy" against a determined majority is unclear.

South Africa is much in need of a strong, legitimate (and independent) Constitutional Court. The country is badly divided by race and class,

---

17 At the time of this writing (August 2000), there was a growing fear in South Africa that a large majority of the population would support the suspension of due process as a means of dealing with what is perceived to be rampant crime and growing terrorism. We predict that this concern for social order will unfold similarly to political tolerance and intolerance, perhaps producing a serious threat to human rights in South Africa.

and politics currently provides little hope of bridging that gap. Law and the civil religion of constitutionalism – offers one possibility for constraining the intense conflict characterizing South African politics. Moreover, a serious potential threat to the country's fledgling democracy is unchecked majoritarianism. The hegemony of the ANC – with its as-yet-unused ability to mobilize its super-majority to modify the Constitution – frightens many, including those who support the substantive (as opposed to procedural) goals of the party. A strong Constitutional Court may be essential to "veto" popularly supported governmental excesses (e.g., government efforts to combat the recent escalation of urban terrorism); indeed, if ever there were a need for a veto player, it is in South Africa. Without a Constitutional Court that is willing and able to stand up effectively for democracy – both in its commitment to majoritarianism and to minoritarianism – the consolidation of democratic reform in South Africa may be an arduous and ultimately unsuccessful process.

This and the previous chapter have addressed attitude change within the context of the interview itself. But what of change over a longer period of time? What role does the larger political environment in South Africa play in attitude change? Because our study is based on a panel design, with data collected in 1996 and 1997, the next chapter analyzes the dynamics of change in tolerance and intolerance over a period of about a year and a half.

8

Becoming Tolerant? Short-Term Changes in South African Political Culture

Political analysts will long remember the decade of the 1990s as a period of intense change. Consider the recent political history of South Africa. During the 1990s, the old apartheid regime dissolved, democratic reform swept the land, the ANC consolidated its power, and the economy rode a roller coaster of change. South Africa is perhaps an extreme example, but fundamental change swept countries as diverse as Indonesia, Russia, and East Germany.

How do citizens cope with change in their political, social, and economic systems? Do they – and how do they – adjust their attitudes, change their values? Unfortunately, with few exceptions (e.g., Rohrschneider 1999), we know little about the processes of change at the level of the individual citizen. This is in part because change is difficult to study, requiring longitudinal, panel data and necessitating statistical techniques that can distinguish between true change and the ever-present and thundering noise of unreliability. Further, theories of attitude and value change are not well developed, especially theories predicting relatively short-term change within individuals. Consequently, we know more about how institutions evolve than we do about how individuals cope with and adjust to changing institutions and systems.

The purpose of this chapter is to investigate attitude change within the South African mass public. For several reasons, our main concern is with political tolerance. Tolerance is of course a crucial element in the matrix of democratic values. But it is also the most paradoxical attitude in the set, since earlier research (e.g., Gibson 1995) has demonstrated that tolerance may be the most difficult democratic value to learn. If we can understand what causes South Africans to come to tolerate their political enemies, then we will gain better purchase on the chances for a successful consolidation of the South African attempt at democratization.

Our analysis to this point has produced at least a limited understanding of the dynamics of short-term change in tolerance attitudes. Relying upon the persuasibility experiment, we discovered that short-term attitude change can be induced by exposing South Africans to argumentation – that is, to arguments favoring a contrary position on a dispute over political tolerance (see Chapter 6, and Gibson 1996c). These arguments were more successful at generating intolerance than tolerance, but they provide some insight into the processes through which these attitudes are formed and therefore how they might be altered. We have also discovered that legal institutions have some abilities to change opinions, at least in the very short term.

Change in response to persuasive argumentation within an interview tells us something about the nature of tolerance attitudes, but it does not capture many of the processes involved in short-term attitude change. In particular, the growing literature on the political economy of attitudes – the ways attitudes are shaped by the performance of the political and economic systems – yields valuable hypotheses about short-term attitude change. Especially when coupled with theories of the political implications of economic distress, these models may be useful in predicting change in political tolerance.

Thus, the purpose of this chapter is to determine the nature of attitude change over the course of a two-year period. Relying on our panel survey of South Africans, this analysis first describes changes in political tolerance, and then tests several hypotheses about the origins of such change. The hypotheses derive from both the conventional crosssectional determinants of tolerance as well as from theories of how citizens react to the performance of the political and economic systems, especially during times of political distress. We conclude by speculating about how changes in levels of tolerance differ across South Africa's various racial communities. The origins of intolerance do vary across groups, and understanding these origins may provide some useful tools for making South Africa a more tolerant country.

UNDERSTANDING THE ETIOLOGY OF POLITICAL TOLERANCE

To account for how attitudes change, one must first understand the basic origins of the attitude. If we know what causes political tolerance in the first place, then it is a fairly simple matter to hypothesize that change in tolerance stems from changes in the primary determinants of tolerance. Of course, explaining why the determinants themselves change may not be so easy, but any analysis of change must begin with a basic model of the etiology of political tolerance.

Relying upon Sullivan, Piereson, and Marcus (1982), Figure 8.1 depicts the most widely accepted view of the origins of tolerance. Tolerance

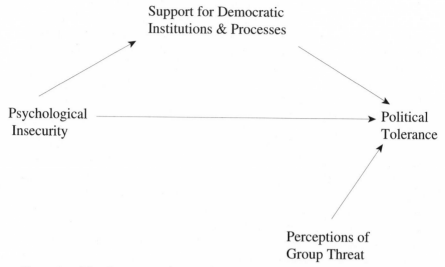

Figure 8.1. The Conventional, Crosssectional Model of the Origins of Political Tolerance

stems from three primary sources. First, those who are more threatened by their political enemies are less likely to tolerate them. Second, tolerance is typically connected to a larger set of beliefs about democratic institutions and processes. Those who believe in the basic institutions of majority rule, with institutionalized protections of minority rights, are more likely to tolerate even their most hated political enemies.[1] Finally, psychological insecurity contributes directly to intolerance. Those who are insecure tolerate less, and not because they are more threatened by their enemies (i.e., the effect is direct, and is not mediated through threat perceptions). These three variables provide a powerful explanation of the variance among citizens in levels of political tolerance.[2]

The first step in considering how tolerance forms and dissolves, then, is to examine the influence of these three conventional predictors. However, these variables are drawn from a model that is largely static. To predict *change in attitudes*, we must consider a different body of theory as well.

---

1 However, this relationship may be fairly weak in transitional regimes, and in fact earlier research on the connections between tolerance and other democratic values in Russia indicates that only a modest correlation exists between these two values (Gibson 1998b; Gibson and Duch 1993a; Gibson, Duch, and Tedin 1992).

2 There have been other important attempts to account for the variance in tolerance (e.g., Bobo and Licari 1989), but extant research identifies no other predictors with a strong theoretical grounding and consistent predictive capacity.

Becoming Tolerant?

THEORIES OF SHORT-TERM ATTITUDE CHANGE

Much of the debate within the comparative politics field about attitude change has been primarily concerned with the relative primacy of culture and institutions (see, for example, Crawford and Lijphart 1995). Culture – the aggregation of beliefs, values, and attitudes toward politics – is often said to change quite slowly, with generational replacement being the primary engine of change (e.g., Almond and Verba 1963; Putnam 1993; Inglehart 1997). Because theories of short-term attitude change are so underdeveloped, many analysts cannot imagine that culture can change relatively quickly.

However, considerable research has been conducted on one source of short-term change: perceptions of the performance of the economy. Indeed, a vast literature has arisen, with some authors directly concerned about the implications of economic evaluations for support for democracy (e.g., Anderson and Guillory 1997; Przeworski et al. 1996). That literature teaches us that at least support for incumbents is dependent to some degree on perceptions of the performance of the economy.[3] Those perceiving a deterioration in either their own or their country's economic condition are likely to punish incumbents with their votes, and may ultimately reject the political system for its failure to manage the economy, even if the system is democratic (e.g., Weimar Germany).

Little of this research considers directly evaluations of the performance of the *political* system, as distinct from the economy (but see Diamond 1999; Mishler and Rose 2001; Feldman and Stenner 1997; and especially Evans and Whitefield 1995). The assumption is typically made that citizens hold the government responsible for the performance of the economy, but it is rare that the performance of the larger political system is examined, especially in terms of non-economic issues such as crime control.[4] Particularly in political systems in which non-economic issues such as crime are extremely salient, this is an unfortunate oversight.

Though the connection is rarely made, theories of institutional legitimacy provide a heuristic for understanding short-term change in support for democratic institutions and processes. Dissatisfaction with system outputs may not directly undermine basic commitments to democratic

---

3 It is not entirely clear what attitude is being measured when people are asked about how democracy is working in their country. We are especially doubtful that those asserting that democracy is not working well necessarily reject democratic institutions and processes, even though that is a common assumption among many scholars.

4 There is surprisingly little attention in the literature to the implications of crime for politics, especially in transitional regimes. For a most useful exception, see Winer 1997.

governance, just as economic success does not directly create democratic values. But over the long term, the accumulation of experiences may well contribute to more basic and enduring allegiances to the fundamental institutions and processes of the political system. Some refer to this as a "running tally," in the sense that people keep a counter in their heads that summarizes their experiences with economic and political institutions (e.g., Lodge and Taber 2000). Pleasurable experiences result in increments in the counter; unpleasant experiences decrement the ticker. Even when people forget *why* they feel the way they do toward an institution, the tally captures the residue of their experiences. Running tallies summarize people's experiences with the major political and economic institutions in a country, and may be shaped by perceptions of the performance of both the economy and the political system.[5]

In transitional regimes, running tallies are volatile since people have limited experiences with the new and evolving political and economic institutions.[6] No *reservoir of good will* exists. Consequently, many analysts are concerned that economic failure will undermine the new democracies of Central and Eastern Europe (e.g., Diamond 1996; Haggard and Kaufman 1995) and Africa (Mattes and Thiel 1998). From a microtheoretical perspective, this means that we should expect the influence of environmental factors on how much support people extend to the major political and economic institutions of a country to be more substantial in transitional regimes like South Africa than in established and stable democracies (but see Remmer 1991, who argues the contrary).

How, specifically, do economic and political perceptions contribute to intolerance? In particular, is there a connection between these perceptions and the three primary predictors of political tolerance: threat perceptions, support for democratic institutions and processes, and psychological insecurity?

---

5 Rohrschneider (1999) strongly emphasizes the importance of experience and practice in shaping durable commitments to democratic institutions and processes.

6 In many respects, the process of attitude change among citizens in newly emerging democracies is akin to processes of change associated with becoming an adult in a stable democracy. Jennings (1989) refers to the latter process as one of "crystallization." As one moves from adolescence to adulthood, attitudes acquire "affective mass," largely through learning and habituation. The young hold unstable attitudes due to their weak experiential base. "Not yet having reaped the benefits of extensive reality testing, reassessment, reinforcement, and a growing familiarity with the political terrain, the orientations of the young are especially susceptible to influence" (Jennings 1989, 315). The acquisition of experience, reinforcement, etc., results in relative attitude stability among adults. Many attitudes of citizens in newly emergent democracies are unlikely to have this "affective mass."

A vast literature exists linking economic and political distress with increasing perceptions of threat.[7] During times of turmoil, political conflict is exacerbated, the stakes of politics rise, and citizens become frustrated and often seek explanations for their unhappiness (e.g., LeVine and Campbell 1971). These explanations typically point to those on the fringes of the political system. *Scapegoat theories* predict that threat perceptions will increase during times of economic and political turmoil (e.g., Lauderdale et al. 1984; see generally Douglas 1995), and consequently that political intolerance will rise as well.[8]

The literature on support for democratic institutions and processes also points to some linkage to economic perceptions, although measurement difficulties confound that literature (e.g., Duch 1999). The speculation in some new democracies is that democracy will be turned out in favor of a traditional preference for social order – that an "iron hand" will restore stability, at the expense of democracy (e.g., Wyman 1994; Grey et al. 1995; Whitefield and Evans 1994; Obolonsky 1995). Little literature addresses this question rigorously, however (but see Gibson 1997b; Miller, Hesli, and Reisinger 1997; see also Kliamkin 1994). Generally, though, many believe that social disorder exacerbates feelings of threat, which in turn undermine political tolerance and support for democratic institutions.

Thus, our plan here is to consider first the etiology of intolerance using the conventional static model, and then to determine whether change in tolerance is associated with change in the three primary predictors of tolerance. The final step in the analysis involves connecting the three predictors to environmental change in South Africa, and especially to perceptions of the performance of the economic and political systems.

---

7 See, for example, Tajfel 1981. The scapegoating process is fairly simple: "when there is tension and social problems seem insurmountable, find an innocent, weak, and distinctive group to blame and victimize" (Babad, Birnbaum, and Benne 1983, 103). An interesting literature exists at the macro level linking environmental conditions with perceptions of threat and authoritarianism. On the role of environmental conditions in exacerbating threat perceptions, see Sales 1973; Doty, Peterson, and Winter 1991. For an excellent micro-level study on perceptions of the environment and threat and authoritarianism, see Feldman and Stenner 1997.

8 Examples of such arguments are the research on the increased lynching of American blacks during times of economic distress (e.g., Hovland and Sears 1940) and the rise of fascism and anti-Semitism in Germany during the interwar years (e.g., Dollard et al. 1939). Many theories of anti-Semitism rely on a basic scapegoating model (e.g., Levin and Levin 1982; Billig 1978).

South African Tolerance as It Might Be

As we have noted, tolerance means putting up with that with which one disagrees. It means allowing one's political enemies to compete openly for political power. A tolerant citizen is one who would not support unreasonable or discriminatory governmental restrictions on the rights of groups to participate in politics.

In the first-wave survey in 1996, we asked our survey respondents to express their views toward a variety of competitors for political power in contemporary South Africa. The primary purpose of the group affect questions is to set up the selection of target groups for the consideration of political intolerance. Consequently, after the respondents rated each group, they were asked to indicate which group they disliked the most, second most, third most, and fourth most. These results are discussed in Chapter 3. From these questions, we identified for each respondent the "most disliked" group, and what we have termed "another highly disliked" group. It is these groups that provide the "objection precondition" for the respondents, a necessary condition for valid measurement of political intolerance.

The structure of the tolerance questions in the second-wave interview in 1997 was somewhat more complicated. First, the questions were designed so that the tolerance items did not necessarily ask about the group named as most disliked *in* 1997. We did this for several reasons. First, for some portion of the respondents, the questions would in fact ask about the most disliked 1997 group, but via a different rationale and selection method. Second, intolerance is so widespread in South Africa that to ask all respondents about their most disliked group is a waste of items; there is virtually a consensus in the country that extremely hated groups such as the AWB should not be allowed basic civil liberties. Third, we felt it necessary to hold the nominal group identity constant for the battery of tolerance questions assessing change (which of course also affects the persuasibility experiment). Failure to do so would introduce a rival hypothesis – connected to the specific identity of the group – to account for observed change. Consequently, in 1997, the respondents were asked about the group used in the tolerance persuasibility questions in 1996. Even this, however, is complicated because the 1996 instrument used a split ballot, asking half of the respondents about the group named as most disliked in 1996 and the other half about another highly disliked group. Table 8.1 summarizes the structure of the groups used in both the 1996 and 1997 surveys. The first column indicates the ranking of the group asked about in 1996. For instance, for 49.5 percent of the respondents, our questions concerned the group rated as most disliked. The "1st 1997 Group Asked About" is the group used in this analysis of

Table 8.1. *The Nature of the Groups Used to Measure*
South African Intolerance

Group, 1997	Rank	1996 Group Rating – Percentage	1997 Group Rating – Percentage
1st 1997 Group Asked About	Most Disliked	49.5	21.0
	2nd Most	7.9	10.8
	3rd Most	12.8	15.1
	4th Most	28.5	35.3
	Other	1.3	17.9
	Total	100.0	100.0
	N	1,277	1,277
2nd 1997 Group Asked About	Most Disliked	4.4	0.0
	2nd Most	12.2	8.7
	3rd Most	7.7	22.0
	4th Most	28.5	69.3
	Other	47.2	0.0
	Total	100.0	100.0
	N	1,277	1,277

change, since that is the group asked about in 1996. As a result, in 1997, 49.5 percent of the respondents were queried about the group named as most disliked in 1996 (since the 1996 experiment assigned half of the respondents to the most disliked condition, the other half to the other highly disliked group condition). As the data indicate, for about one-fifth (21.0 percent) of the respondents, this meant they were asked about the group they named as most disliked in 1997; that is, the 1996 group turned out to be the most disliked group in 1997 for 21.0 percent of the respondents. The table also reports that in 1997 17.9 percent were asked about a group not among those named as the four most disliked groups in 1997. Still, the respondents highly disliked all groups used to measure change in tolerance, and the group asked about in 1996 and 1997 is exactly the same (and we therefore refer to this as "constant group" analysis).[9]

9 Over the relatively short period of time between the two surveys, we concluded that it was unwise to investigate change in tolerance of the "least-liked" group, since the identity of that group changed between the two surveys for many respondents. Were we to analyze change over a longer period of time, perhaps tolerance of the least-liked group would indeed be the most useful dependent variable. Any differences in the perceived threat from the group between 1996 and 1997 are controlled for in the analysis that follows. Note that the second group asked about in 1997 plays no role in this analysis of change.

Table 8.2. *Political Tolerance, 1996–7 (Constant Group)*

Tolerance Items	1996				1997			
	Mean[a]	Std. Dev.	N	% Tolerant	Mean[a]	Std. Dev.	N	% Tolerant
Prohibit Candidates	2.49	1.36	1,257	30.0	2.35	1.38	1,274	28.9
Allow Demonstration	2.03	1.18	1,259	17.4	1.95	1.21	1,273	17.1
Ban the Group	2.38	1.33	1,258	27.3	2.41	1.39	1,269	27.7
Tolerance Index[b]	2.30	1.30	1,259	42.0[c]	2.24	1.11	1,274	41.5[c]

Notes:

[a] Higher scores indicate more tolerance.

[b] The index is simply the mean of the three items.

[c] This is the percentage of respondents who gave at least one tolerant response to the three tolerance questions.

How tolerant are the South Africans? As Sullivan, Pierson, and Marcus (1979, 1982) have taught us, this is not necessarily an easy question to answer. We begin consideration of the issue by examining tolerance in 1996 and 1997 of the group used in the persuasibility experiment in 1996. This is a "constant group" analysis since the questions referred to exactly the same group.

In both 1996 and 1997, the answer is the same: South Africans are not very tolerant (see Table 8.2). The means for each of the tolerance items is below the midpoint on the scale (2.5). In 1996, only 17.4 percent of the South Africans would allow their political enemy to hold a demonstration; only 42.0 percent expressed any tolerance at all toward the group. Tolerance was not any more common in 1997, with only 41.5 percent expressing some tolerance toward their political foe. Intolerance is the preferred position of a majority of South Africans.

In Table 8.3, we report the percentage of respondents who would not tolerate their political enemies in both 1996 and 1997. This table differs from Table 8.2; the former addresses aggregate levels of tolerance, while this table addresses individual-level change (analysis possible only with panel data). Bear in mind that the groups used in the tolerance queries are nominally the same, although the degree of antipathy the respondent holds toward the groups may not be identical. Nonetheless, for most, the group is one of the respondent's most hated political enemies at both points in time.

In 1996, fully 57.8 percent of the South Africans would not tolerate their political enemy; in 1997, this figure increased to 59.8 percent, a

Table 8.3. *Change in Political Tolerance, 1996–7*

Constant Group (1997)	1996		1997 Marginals
	No Tolerance	Some Tolerance	
No Tolerance	64.2%	53.7%	59.8%
Some Tolerance	35.8	46.3	40.2
Total	100.0%	100.0%	100.0%
N	726	529	1,255
1996 Marginals	57.8%	42.2%	100.0%

statistically insignificant change (see the marginals in the table). Thus, at the aggregate level, tolerance seems to be fairly stable in South Africa.

As Table 8.3 shows, there is considerable asymmetry in the temporal stability of those who were tolerant in 1996 versus those who were intolerant. Intolerance was relatively stable; 64.2 percent of those giving no tolerant responses in 1996 gave no tolerant responses in 1997 (see Table 8.3). But of those giving any tolerant responses in 1996, only 46.3 percent gave at least one tolerant response in 1997; 53.7 percent offered no tolerant responses. Thus, the propensity toward intolerance is more temporally stable than the propensity toward tolerance. Obviously, opinion change was common, with a substantial asymmetry between tolerant and intolerant South Africans.[10] Considering the index of tolerant responses (but using the total sample – 1255 – as the denominator, data not shown), 37.1 percent of the South Africans expressed complete intolerance in 1996 and 1997, 19.5 percent were tolerant at both interviews, and the tolerance of 43.3 percent changed over the course of the year-and-a-half period between the two surveys.

Regression analysis also reveals that political tolerance was not very stable during the 1996–7 period. The correlation between the two indices is only .22 and the regression equation[11] (with the standard errors of the coefficients) linking the two variables is:

$$\text{Tolerance}_{1997} = 1.70 + .23 * \text{Tolerance}_{1996} + e$$
$$(.07) \quad (.03)$$

10 This asymmetry in the pliability of tolerance and intolerance is a familiar finding. In earlier research on persuasibility in the United States, South Africa, and Russia, Gibson (1996c, 1998a) discovered a similar difference between the tolerant and the intolerant.

11 These coefficients are highly significant statistically. In the bivariate case, $r = \beta = .22$.

Thus, there is a considerable amount of variability in attitudes – roughly 94.7 percent of the variance in tolerance scores in 1997 is not predictable from the tolerance scores in 1996.[12]

These data indicate that at the macro level, South Africans in 1997 became little more tolerant of the groups they would not tolerate in 1996. At the level of the individual South African, it is also clear from these data that some amount of change occurred in political tolerance between these two surveys. Even ignoring changes in intensity, 43 percent of the South Africans changed their basic tolerance or intolerance. Is that change random or systematic? More important, to what degree can the change be accounted for via conventional theories of the etiology of intolerance?

THE ORIGINS OF INTOLERANCE

Figure 8.2 reports the basic model of the origins of political tolerance within each of the survey crosssections. These data support several conclusions.

First, perceptions of threat are strongly related to political tolerance. This is an entirely conventional finding from the tolerance literature, although the strength of the relationship (especially in 1997) is unusual. Most likely, this can be ascribed to the use of groups of varying degrees of dislike (and hence threat) in this analysis (as well as the realism of the threat posed by the groups). Recall that the group about whom the tolerance questions were asked vary in terms of the degree of antipathy. Analysis focusing only upon the most disliked group – the conventional approach – typically produces degenerate variance in threat perceptions, resulting in attenuating the correlation between threat and tolerance. Though we cannot yet determine why the relationship increased in strength from 1996 to 1997,[13] the magnitude of the coefficients is considerable in both years.

Political tolerance is also a function of more general support for democratic institutions and processes, although the relationships are not particularly strong. This finding also parallels earlier work on the structure of democratic values in the former Soviet Union and Russia (e.g., Gibson, Duch, and Tedin 1992; Gibson and Duch 1993b; Gibson 1995, 1998a)

---

12 Note that Gibson (1992a, 566) reports that the correlation between tolerance measures in a short-term U.S. panel is .72, which is considerably higher than the .22 reported here. Further, Gibson (2002) reports a similar correlation of .40 in a two-year Russian panel.

13 Note, however, that the 1996 estimates are based on those respondents interviewed in both 1996 and 1997, and therefore these results are not a function of panel attrition.

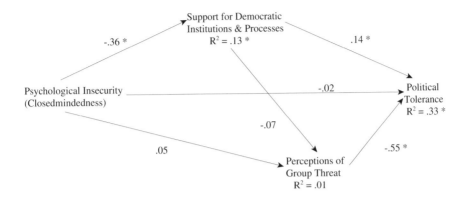

1997

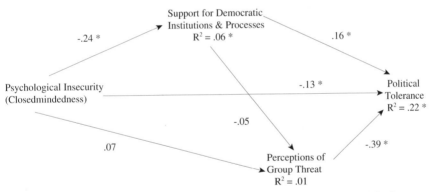

1996

Figure 8.2. The Origins of South African Intolerance, 1996–7 (Maximum Likelihood Estimates).
Note: N ≈ 1,250, * $p < .000$.

in showing that political tolerance is *not* highly integrated within a broader democratic belief system. This may be due in part to the difficulty of South Africans learning the liberal aspects of democratic thought, especially in a system dominated since World War II by apartheid.

Finally, psychological insecurity contributes significantly to support for democratic institutions and processes, but not at all to threat perceptions, and only weakly and inconsistently to political tolerance. The

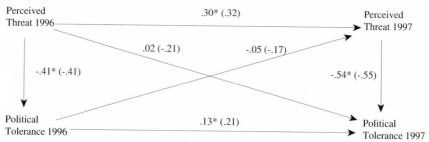

Figure 8.3. Tolerance and Threat, 1996–7 (Constant Group).
Note: The coefficients shown are the standardized regression coefficients and, in paren-theses, the bivariate correlation coefficients. * $p < .000$, for standardized regression coefficients. N = 1,245.

significant direct effect on tolerance in 1996 is most likely connected to the relative failure of threat perceptions to explain more variance. The strong relationships between closedmindedness and support for democratic institutions and processes reminds us once more that democratic politics involves ambiguity, shifting coalitions of friends and enemies, and a strong willingness to compromise.

The findings in Figure 8.2 are compatible with most earlier research on the origins of intolerance. Some of the relationships are stronger than is typical, but that is largely a function of using more diverse targets of intolerance in the questions. Next, we consider whether these cross-sectional findings are sustained through longitudinal analysis.

BASIC PANEL RESULTS

The conclusion that emerges from the analysis in Figure 8.2 is that tolerance is overwhelmingly determined by threat perceptions. Con-sequently, we begin consideration of the panel data with a simple two-variable model at each time point. Figure 8.3 reports this analysis. The coefficients are based on the regressions of tolerance and threat in 1996 and 1997. We report both standardized regression coefficients and bivariate correlation coefficients. The similarity of the coefficients in this figure linking threat and tolerance to those in Figure 8.2 is a function of the exogeneity of threat perceptions.

Threat perceptions are reasonably stable over time; the cross-time cor-relation coefficient is .32, which is not diminished by controlling for 1996 tolerance. For survey data, this coefficient indicates a moderate degree of stability; those threatened in 1996 tended to be threatened as well in 1997.

Political tolerance is considerably less stable, with the independent effect of 1996 tolerance on 1997 tolerance limited to a regression coef-ficient of .13. Note that this effect is independent of threat perceptions, meaning that there is at least some stability in the generalized propensity to tolerate. Thus, being threatened in the past is associated with being threatened in the present, which in turn strongly contributes to political intolerance. From this analysis, tolerance seems to be less of a generalized, stable attitude than a response to the state of the respondent's political environment.

The direct crosssurvey coefficients linking threat and tolerance are also interesting. Both of the crosssurvey bivariate correlations are moderate (−.17 and −.21), indicating that threat in 1996 is associated with tolerance in 1997, and tolerance in 1996 is associated with threat perceptions in 1997. Yet both of these relationships are reduced to insignificance in the multivariate equation; the bivariate relationship between perceived threat in 1996 and tolerance in 1997 is entirely filtered through perceived threat in 1997. Those threatened in 1996 tended to be threatened in 1997, and perceptions of threat in 1997 tended to produce contemporaneous intolerance. Were the bivariate effect not to flow through 1997 threat perceptions, the process would be difficult to explain substantively.

Similar findings characterize the tolerance – threat crosssurvey correlation. Once threat perceptions in 1996 are controlled, the independent effect of tolerance on threat in 1997 is reduced to insignificance. The bivariate relationship appears to be spurious.

In sum, perhaps the most important finding from this analysis is that threat perceptions are more stable over time than is political tolerance itself.

The data in Figure 8.3 depict a highly simplified view of the dynamics of political tolerance. A more complete model must incorporate a variety of sources of change, including analysis of change in the variables directly influencing political tolerance.

CHANGING POLITICAL TOLERANCE

Why would tolerance change in a relatively short period of time? The most obvious answer has to do with changes in perceptions of the group, especially the degree of threat posed. But it is also important to consider the degree to which threat perceptions are shaped by changes in the social, economic, and political conditions in the country. We consider first the simplest possibility – that change in the level of perceived threat from the group causes changes in political tolerance.

Changing Perceptions of Group Threat

Table 8.4 reports the means for the various measures of group threat as measured in 1996 and 1997. Also reported are the percentages of

Table 8.4. *Perceived Threat, Highly Disliked Group*
(Constant Group), 1996–7

Perception	% at Most Extreme Score	Mean[a]	Std. Dev.	N
Dangerous to Society				
1996	55.1	5.66	1.91	1,257
1997	48.1	5.54	1.86	1,275
Unpredictable				
1996	49.1	5.48	1.92	1,257
1997	45.9	5.51	1.89	1,275
Not Committed to Having Democracy in South Africa				
1996	54.7	5.68	1.80	1,257
1997	45.8	5.51	1.81	1,275
Dangerous to the Normal Lives of People				
1996	43.7	5.27	2.03	1,257
1997	37.6	5.15	1.99	1,273
Likely to Gain a Lot of Power in South Africa				
1996	5.1	2.49	1.80	1,256
1997	3.9	2.46	1.73	1,273
Likely to Affect How Well My Family and I Live				
1996	27.4	4.34	2.25	1,258
1997	21.2	4.38	2.08	1,274
Angry toward the Group				
1996	45.5	5.14	2.17	1,257
1997	42.6	5.09	2.16	1,271
Unwilling to Follow the Rules of Democracy				
1996	53.4	5.71	1.75	1,257
1997	43.4	5.50	1.75	1,273
Powerful				
1996	11.5	3.06	2.10	1,257
1997	7.1	2.99	1.93	1,275

Notes:
[a] High scores in every instance indicate greater degrees of perceived threat.
None of the between-year differences in means is statistically significant at $p \leq .001$.

respondents giving the group the most extreme rating on each of the dimensions. For instance, in 1996, 55.1 percent of the respondents rated their political enemy at 7 on a 1 through 7 continuum measuring the degree of danger of the group to South African society.

On most of the measures, these groups are rated as quite threatening. Nearly all of the items have means exceeding 5.0 (on a scale with a maximum of 7). Most South Africans perceived their political enemy as dangerous to society and not committed to democratic governance. However, there is little consensus that the group is powerful, or likely to gain power in South Africa. Thus, virtually all respondents view the group as quite threatening, even if they disagree about whether the group has the power to implement its ideas (for further analysis of threat perceptions, see Chapter 3).

Generally, threat perceptions changed little in the aggregate over the interval between the two interviews; not a single test of the difference in means across the two surveys is statistically significant at $p \leq .001$. Table 8.5 reports a more detailed analysis of change in threat perceptions. The last column in the table reports the standardized regression coefficient resulting from regressing the threat perception in 1997 on the perception in 1996. Most of the crosssurvey coefficients hover around .2, and most difference scores (the first column in the table) are indistinguishable from zero, indicating little change between the two surveys.

However, two exceptions to this general conclusion are necessary. First, in 1997, the group is less likely to be perceived as unwilling to follow the rules of democracy – the decline is 10 percentage points (as reported in Table 8.4). This may indicate a growing acceptance of legitimate competition for political power in South Africa. Second, there is perhaps also a decline in the tendency to see the group as not committed to a democratic South Africa (mean difference = −.16 – see Table 8.5). These no doubt reflect something of the growing stability and legitimacy of democracy in South Africa. On most dimensions of threat perceptions, however, there seem to be slight differences over time. These aggregate distributions are compatible with the previous finding of a moderate degree of micro-level stability in perceptions of threat.

Environmental Origins of Threat Perceptions

To what degree does the nature of the sociopolitical environment in South Africa affect threat perceptions? Here we consider first three types of environmental factors as possible influences on threat perceptions: (a) evaluations of the performance of the economy; (b) evaluations of the performance of the political system; and (c) perceptions of social problems, and especially of crime. In each instance, we hypothesize that those who see social, political, and economic conditions as worsening will feel more threatened by their political enemies.

The general hypothesis that undergirds this analysis is that any political context generating anxiety among people will be associated with higher perceived threats from their political enemies. Economic distress, for instance, often makes politics more salient, exacerbates intergroup

Table 8.5. *Change in Perceptions of Threat, 1996–7*

Threat Perception	Difference Scores			Percentage			Regression Results: $t_2 = f(t_1)$			
	Mean	Std. Dev.	N	Less Threatening	No Change	More Threatening	Intercept	b	s.e.	β
Dangerous to Society	−.12	2.30	1,254	33.2	40.0	26.8	4.16	.25	.03	.25***
Unpredictable	.04	2.48	1,254	34.2	32.3	33.4	4.73	.15	.03	.15***
Not Committed to Democracy	−.16	2.24	1,254	35.4	36.9	27.7	4.20	.23	.03	.23***
Dangerous to People	−.11	2.48	1,252	37.9	29.5	32.6	3.93	.23	.03	.24***
Likely to Gain Power in South Africa	−.05	2.22	1,252	34.6	30.6	34.9	1.95	.20	.03	.21***
Likely to Affect How Well My Family and I Live	.05	2.84	1,254	40.9	20.3	38.7	3.85	.13	.03	.14***
Angry toward the Group	−.05	2.75	1,250	35.8	31.4	32.8	4.14	.19	.03	.19***
Unwilling to Follow the Rules of Democracy	−.19	2.22	1,252	37.0	34.5	28.6	4.42	.19	.03	.19***
Powerful	−.08	2.68	1,254	37.9	24.2	37.9	2.67	.11	.03	.12***

Note: Difference scores are the differences between the threat perceptions in 1997 and 1996. The percentages are calculated on the basis of collapsed difference scores (although the difference scores are based on the uncollapsed responses). The percentages sum to 100 percent, across the three rows.

*** $p \leq .001$, β = standardized regression coefficient.

Table 8.6. *The Impact of Economic Evaluations on Perceptions of Group Threat and Political Tolerance*

	Threat Perceptions		Political Tolerance	
Contemporaneous Perceptions	1996	1997	1996	1997
Retrospective Sociotropic – Economic	.07*	−.05	−.07*	−.01
Retrospective Egocentric (Pocketbook) – Economic	.04	−.09*	−.01	.00
Prospective Sociotropic – Economic	.11*	−.05	−.04	.01
Prospective Egocentric (Pocketbook) – Economic	.09*	−.04	−.07*	.01

Note: Entries are bivariate Pearson correlation coefficients. * $p < .01$.

tensions, favors extremism, and contributes to the perception of threat. We test this hypothesis first using perceptions of the economic and political conditions in South Africa.

We measured the respondent's perceptions, both retrospective and prospective, of the performance of the economy. Following conventions, we asked for evaluations of how the system is performing in general (sociotropic judgments) and specifically how the respondent was faring (egocentric judgments). Several conclusions emerge from a variety of analyses, including the bivariate correlation coefficients reported in Table 8.6.

First, many of these relationships are in the wrong direction. The expected relationships with threat perceptions are negative (greater optimism should be associated with less threat) and with tolerance are positive (greater optimism should be associated with more tolerance). Thus, all of the correlations between economic perceptions and political tolerance are negligible or in the wrong direction. Only in 1997 do we see a correctly signed significant relationship – those who perceive their own economic circumstances to have recently improved are likely to be less threatened by their political enemies ($r = -.09$, $p < .01$). Still, though significant, this relationship borders on being trivial. Economic perceptions simply do not seem to have much to do with perceptions of threat and political intolerance.

Table 8.7 considers in more detail the impact of economic evaluations on threat perceptions within each racial group. The table reports the results of regressing both threat perceptions and tolerance on the economic perceptions variables (measured contemporaneously). The overwhelming conclusion supported by the data in this table is that economic evaluations have little impact on perceptions of group threat. Though some of the coefficients seem somewhat larger than zero (e.g.,

Table 8.7. *The Impact of Economic Evaluations on Threat Perceptions*

Perceptions of the Economy	Threat Perceptions – 1996				Threat Perceptions – 1997			
	b	s.e.	β	r	b	s.e.	β	r
All South Africans (N ≈ 1,260)								
Retrospective Sociotropic	−.00	.03	−.00	.07	−.00	.03	−.00	−.05
Retrospective Egocentric	−.00	.03	−.04	.04	−.01	.03	−.10	−.09
Prospective Sociotropic	.01	.03	.09	.11	−.00	.03	−.02	−.05
Prospective Egocentric	.01	.03	.06	.09	.00	.03	.03	−.04
African South Africans (N ≈ 1,027)								
Retrospective Sociotropic	−.00	.03	−.04	.00	−.00	.04	−.03	−.12
Retrospective Egocentric	−.01	.04	−.05	−.01	−.01	.04	−.09*	−.12
Prospective Sociotropic	.01	.03	.08	.06	−.01	.03	−.10*	−.13
Prospective Egocentric	.00	.04	.04	.04	.00	.03	.04	−.08
White South Africans (N ≈ 194)								
Retrospective Sociotropic	−.14	.08	−.15	−.18	−.01	.07	−.08	−.13
Retrospective Egocentric	−.01	.08	−.12	−.16	.01	.08	.08	−.05
Prospective Sociotropic	.00	.06	.02	−.07	−.01	.06	−.10	−.16
Prospective Egocentric	.00	.08	.05	−.11	−.01	.07	−.13	−.14
Coloured South Africans (N ≈ 115)								
Retrospective Sociotropic	.00	.09	.00	.09	−.01	.10	−.08	−.05
Retrospective Egocentric	.13	.09	.15	.19	−.00	.10	−.02	−.03
Prospective Sociotropic	−.00	.10	−.06	.08	.00	.11	.07	.01
Prospective Egocentric	.12	.12	.13	.16	−.00	.11	−.03	−.02
South Africans of Asian Origin (N ≈ 153)								
Retrospective Sociotropic	−.00	.07	−.14	−.14	−.00	.09	−.03	−.02
Retrospective Egocentric	.01	.07	.11	.03	.01	.10	.08	.06
Prospective Sociotropic	−.00	.07	−.04	−.10	−.00	.08	−.02	−.03
Prospective Egocentric	−.00	.07	−.06	−.06	−.00	.09	−.01	.02

Note: * $p < .05$; ** $p < .01$; *** $p < .001$.

retrospective sociotropic evaluations among whites in 1996), virtually none of the coefficients achieves statistical significance at even the .05 level. Moreover, all variables in the table are expected to have a negative relationship with threat perceptions (i.e., as economic optimism increases, threat perceptions should decrease), but many of the coefficients are improperly signed (e.g., among all South Africans, as expectations of greater future economic prosperity for the country increase, threat perceptions *increase* as well – $r = .09$). Further, few of the relationships are consistent over time, most likely reflecting the influences of chance variation driving some coefficients slightly above zero, others slightly below zero. Across racial groups, there are few consistent patterns. For instance, retrospective sociotropic evaluations influence the threat per-

Table 8.8. *The Impact of Political Evaluations on Perceptions of Group Threat and Political Tolerance*

Judgment of How Well Democracy Works	Threat Perceptions		Political Tolerance	
	1996	1997	1996	1997
All South Africans (N ≈ 1,250)	.00	−.07**	−.00	.07**
African South Africans (N ≈ 1,020)	.00	−.09**	.01	.08**
White South Africans (N ≈ 193)	−.07	−.10	.03	.14*
Coloured South Africans (N ≈ 113)	−.08	−.04	−.04	.09
South Africans of Asian Origin (N ≈ 150)	−.04	−.02	.13	.10

Note: Entries are bivariate Pearson correlation coefficients. * $p < .05$; ** $p < .01$.

ceived by whites and South Africans of Asian origin, but not of Africans and Coloured South Africans. The most reasonable conclusion to draw from the coefficients in this table is that how South Africans rate the threat posed by their political enemies has very little to do with the performance of the personal or national economy.

Thus evaluations of the South African economy do little to shape threat perceptions. How do political evaluations fare? That is, do those who perceive the political situation in the country as deteriorating perceive greater threat from their political enemies? We first consider overall evaluations of political performance, and then specifically the impact of concerns about the rising crime rate in South Africa.

We have measured perceptions of performance of the political system using a standard measure of political perceptions: "All in all, how well or badly do you think the system of democracy in South Africa works these days?" Most South Africans are reasonably optimistic about their political system, with over 54 percent asserting that the system works pretty well. Table 8.8 reports the relationship between these political judgments and perceptions of threat and political tolerance.

Only one of the coefficients in 1996 exceeds .10: South Africans of Asian origin who judged democracy to be working well in South Africa tended to be slightly more tolerant in 1996 ($r = .13$). In 1997, a similar relationship holds among those of Asian origin ($r = .10$). Generally, in 1997, the coefficients are all in the expected direction (negative for threat perceptions and positive for tolerance), although few substantial relationships are revealed in this table. The hypotheses are supported most strongly among whites; in 1997, those who viewed democracy as working well tended to see less threat from their political enemies ($r = -.10$), and were consequently more tolerant ($r = .14$). Though the correlations are all weak, in 1997, South Africans of every race who judged democracy to be successful tended to be less threatened and more tolerant.[14]

This analysis indicates that the perceived performance of the *political* system has only some direct impact on threat perceptions. But one aspect of the political process may be especially relevant in South Africa: the success (or lack thereof) at coping with the crime problem. Rightly or wrongly, South Africans perceive a tremendous increase in crime in their country. Those fearful about crime may well also be fearful of their political enemies.[15]

Not surprisingly, the results indicate that most South Africans believe that crime has indeed gotten worse – 46.4 percent asserted it got a great deal worse, 30.8 percent claimed it had not changed in the last year, and only 10.4 percent told us that the crime problem had actually gotten better. Racial differences in these perceptions are dramatic. Nearly four out of five whites asserted that crime had gotten a great deal worse, while only two of five Africans gave the same rating. Coloured and Asian-origin South Africans are closer to whites in their perceptions than they are to Africans. A majority of each racial group rates the crime problem at the most extreme point on the scale.

Table 8.9 reports the relationship between perceived increases in crime and the threat and tolerance variables. Our expectation is that those perceiving an increase in crime will be more threatened (positive correlation) and less tolerant (negative correlation). Note that perceptions of crime were measured only in the 1997 interview, so that the correlations with 1996 threat and tolerance are surely attenuated substantially by the eighteen months elapsing between the two surveys.

Table 8.9 contains a number of surprises. First, the threat hypothesis is only clearly supported among white South Africans. Whites who view the crime problem as having gotten worse are more threatened by their political enemies (and the relationship is stronger in 1997 than it was in 1996, as it should be). Within no other group are the correlations substantively significant, and among Coloured South Africans, though

---

14 We cannot entirely rule out the opposite direction of causality, although it makes more sense that general judgments of democracy would cause rather specific perceptions of threat, rather than vice versa.

15 We have measured crime perceptions using the following item: "There has been some talk recently about crime in South Africa. In terms of how it affects you personally, would you say that in the last year the level of crime has got worse, has not changed, or has got better?"

Table 8.9. *The Impact of Crime Evaluations on Perceptions of Group Threat and Political Tolerance*

Perceptions of Change in Crime	Threat Perceptions		Political Tolerance	
	1996	1997	1996	1997
All South Africans (N ≈ 1,254)	−.04	−.01	.05	.05*
African South Africans (N ≈ 1,023)	.02	.05	−.00	.00
White South Africans (N ≈ 192)	.10	.19**	−.14*	−.17**
Coloured South Africans (N ≈ 116)	−.16*	−.06	.12	.01
South Africans of Asian Origin (N ≈ 150)	.01	.05	.08	.06

Note: Entries are bivariate Pearson correlation coefficients. * $p < .05$; ** $p < .01$.

barely statistically significant, the coefficients are wrongly signed (more concern over crime is associated with less threat). Only for whites does crime seem to have clear political implications.[16]

The results for the tolerance hypothesis are similar. Among whites, more concern with crime is associated with less political tolerance, and the relationship is stronger when both variables are measured in the same interview. The coefficients for no other groups achieve statistical and substantive significance.

These findings are puzzling from a somewhat different viewpoint as well. Whites are quite united in their views that crime has increased significantly, yet variation in crime perceptions still predicts threat and political tolerance.[17] Still, for most South Africans, perceived increases in crime have few implications for political tolerance.

16 We do not contend that political intolerance is necessarily connected to beliefs about criminal activity on the part of the disliked group. It seems more likely that this relationship is to some degree spurious, reflecting a common origin of threat perceptions and crime concern in the political psychology of the individual. Earlier studies of threat have found that a "predictability versus unpredictability" continuum is one of the strongest determinants of intolerance (e.g., Sullivan, Piereson, and Marcus 1982). In some respects, fear of the unknown is a more potent stimulus to intolerance than certainty about the obvious "badness" of the group. Those who do not know what to expect are the most threatened. Such people are also likely to be fearful of becoming a victim of crime, and that probably accounts for the relationship depicted in Table 8.9.

17 Whites and South Africans of Asian origin have significantly smaller standard deviations on the crime perceptions variable than do black and Coloured South Africans.

Thus, threat perceptions are only slightly related to perceptions of stress in the political and economic situation in the country. Environmental factors do not explain a great deal of the variance in threat perception. However, in light of the failure of earlier research to account for any variability in threat perceptions, these findings take on added significance.

A DYNAMIC MODEL OF TOLERANCE

The preceding analysis has considered bits and pieces of the overall model of change in political tolerance. In Figure 8.4, we have put the pieces together within a single integrated, dynamic model. The model hypothesizes that the two primary exogenous variables accounting for change in 1997 are perceptions of changes in crime and satisfaction with the performance of democracy in South Africa. We have added a third exogenous variable, measured in the 1996 survey only, representing judgments of how the respondent's life has changed since the fall of apartheid.[18] We hypothesize that these judgments influence not only attitudes in 1996, but change in attitudes between 1996 and 1997. These equations were estimated using Structural Equation Modeling (with maximum likelihood estimates).

The coefficients in Table 8.10 address several different aspects of the results of the modeling.[19] Before considering these coefficients, however,

---

18 It is perhaps counterintuitive that not all African respondents look back on apartheid unfavorably. Although a large plurality reported that their lives were a lot worse under apartheid, and a majority say their lives were at least a little worse, perhaps surprisingly, about one-fourth of the blacks claimed to have lived better under apartheid than they do now (1996), and another 19.6 percent have experienced little difference. Coloured and Asian respondents also answered this question similarly, with about a third of each group claiming to have been better off under apartheid. While we are certain that few black respondents would welcome a return of apartheid to South Africa, it is obvious that the old system treated some better than others.

On the other hand, nearly one-half of the white respondents reported living better under the old regime (and over half of these claimed to have lived "a lot better"). Another large proportion of the whites asserted that life has neither improved nor gotten worse since the change in regime. Generally, whites see their fortunes as having declined under the new system of majority rule. Obviously, changes in the political system, as important as they may be, do not automatically result in improvements in the lives of ordinary people.

19 Since the variances of these variables may differ across the various groups, we have analyzed the covariance matrices rather than the correlation matrices.

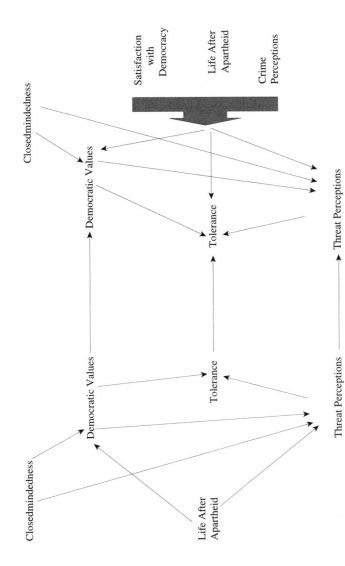

Figure 8.4. Hypothesized Model of the Dynamics of Political Tolerance

we should examine the goodness of fit of this effort to model change in tolerance.[20]

For the overall model, across all groups, χ^2 is 134, with 80 degrees of freedom.[21] The probability associated with this χ^2 is .0002. Thus, the model should be judged not to fit the data particularly well. However, when complex models are analyzed, χ^2 often achieves statistical significance, rendering statistical significance a not very useful criterion for judging the model. The statistic is less than three times the degrees of freedom, so the model should not necessarily be rejected. Indeed, the Root Mean Squared Error of Approximation (RMSEA) is .04, which indicates a close fit between the model and the data. Thus, we conclude that the model is appropriate for these data.

The Goodness of Fit Indices (GFIs) for the four groups are .995, .948, .972, and .968, for blacks, whites, Coloureds, and South Africans of Asian origin, respectively. All of these indicate good fit, although clearly the model fits the white subsample least well. This can also be seen in the contribution of each group to the overall χ^2 – 28.4, 60.0, 18.6, and 27.2 percent for each group, respectively. In general, though, the set of equations are reasonably consistent with the data from each group. We now turn to the statistical and substantive findings.

Table 8.10 first provides evidence on the stability of each of the major attitudes in the model. For instance, the first row in the table reports that levels of tolerance in 1997 are moderately related to tolerance in 1996

---

20 A variety of measures of the overall goodness of fit of the model is available. We rely on three indices. First, the χ^2 test is a measure of the overall fit of the model to all groups. As Jöreskog notes, "In practice it is more useful to regard chi-square as a *measure* of fit rather than as a *test statistic*" (1993, 308, emphasis in original). By this he meant that χ^2 should be understood as a relative measure. Of course, χ^2 is really a "badness-of-fit" index in the sense that a small χ^2 indicates a good fit and a large χ^2 corresponds to a bad fit. χ^2 is also a very important statistic since many (if not most) measures of goodness of fit derive from it (Jöreskog 1993, 309). χ^2 is also valuable in this particular case since the total value of the measure can be decomposed into components associated with each of the racial groups under consideration.

Jöreskog also recommends the GFI (Goodness-of-Fit Index) since it is not dependent upon sample size, and because the index indicates "how much *better* the model fits compared with no model at all" (1993, 309, emphasis in original).

Finally, the Root Mean Squared Error of Approximation (RMSEA) is also a useful index. An RMSEA of .05 indicates a close fit, with values up to .08 representing "reasonable errors of approximation in the population" (Jöreskog 1993, 310).

21 Researchers can always improve the goodness of fit of a model by making idiosyncratic (and largely atheoretical) modifications to the model, especially by allowing correlations among error terms. We have resisted this tack since no theory is available to guide us in selecting among the numerous modifications possible.

Table 8.10. *Summary Results of Comprehensive Model of Change in Tolerance, 1996–7, Structural Equation Modeling*

Hypotheses and Variables	Race of Respondent			
	African	White	Coloured	Asian Origin
Stability of Attitudes – 1996–7				
Political Tolerance	.05	.19	.22	.20
Threat Perceptions	.28	.31	.35	.39
Democratic Values	.08	.29	.04	.43
Closedmindedness	.02	.37	−.03	.18
Basic Hypotheses				
Threat → Tolerance				
1997	−.53	−.37	−.24	−.57
1996	−.38	−.29	−.31	−.49
Democratic Values → Tolerance				
1997	.10	.11	.13	.25
1996	.10	.29	.17	.12
Closedmindedness → Democratic Values				
1997	−.35	−.22	−.17	−.36
1996	−.21	−.29	−.15	−.36
Predictors of Threat Perceptions[a] 1997				
Democratic Values$_{1997}$		.07	−.12	.06
Closedmindedness$_{1997}$	.06	.13	−.08	−.06
Democratic Values$_{1996}$	−.05	−.07		
Closedmindedness$_{1996}$	−.05		.09	
Predictors of Threat Perceptions[a] 1996				
Democratic Values$_{1996}$			−.16	
Closedmindedness$_{1996}$	.07	.11		.09

Notes:
[a] Coefficients greater than .05 are reported.
The coefficients shown are from the Common Metric Standardized Solution, based on Maximum Likelihood Analysis of the group-based covariance matrices.

for whites, Coloured people, and South Africans of Asian origin, but that little relationship exists among Africans (β = .05). The data in the table also reveal that the most stable attitude in this model is threat perceptions, confirming the preceding analysis. For each group, a moderately strong relationship exists: Those who were threatened in 1996 tended to be threatened in 1997 as well. Not a great deal of variability across the groups exists in the magnitude of this relationship.

On each of the other attitudes, stable relationships can be found for most of the groups except Africans. The weakness of the coefficients for tolerance, democratic values, and closedmindedness among Africans stands out starkly in the table. This no doubt reflects the lack of crystallization of attitudes (and perhaps that many of our questions were too demanding, with measurement error compounded by difficulties in translation). That threat perceptions are stable, however, suggests that this is not entirely a measurement error problem; on issues that are apparently salient to the Africans – such as knowing how threatening one's enemies are – some attitude stability exists.

Whites are exactly the opposite. On each of the four attitudes, considerable stability exists, although tolerance is the least stable attitude. South Africans of Asian origin are similar to whites in the stability of their attitudes. For Coloured South Africans, tolerance and threat perceptions are stable, while support for democratic institutions and processes and closedmindedness are not at all stable. Thus, as in most of our analyses, considerable differences exist across the major racial groups in South Africa.

The second portion of Table 8.10 reports the results of testing three hypotheses central to the model. In each instance, the hypothesis is supported, and differences across the groups are *not* great. For instance, we find that threat perceptions are associated with low levels of tolerance in both 1997 and 1996, for each of the groups. Support for democratic institutions and processes predicts tolerance, but not strongly, for all races. And closedmindedness uniformly predicts democratic values. That each of these hypotheses is supported, especially among Africans, revives confidence in the quality of the measurement of the variables in this model.[22] Further, the coefficients testify to the generalizability of the basic tolerance model developed in the West, since these conventional hypotheses are supported within all four of the groups.

It is tempting to evaluate change in the strength of the coefficients shown under the "Basic Hypotheses" section of the table. For instance, among Africans and Coloured South Africans, tolerance is weakly connected to more general support for democratic institutions and processes, and that relationship changed little between the 1996 and 1997 surveys. Among those of Asian origin, the connection between tolerance and democratic values increases, while among whites, the relationship decreased somewhat. Perhaps this weakening relationship portends an effect of environmental factors on the political tolerance of whites.

The last section of Table 8.10 considers the effects of the endogenous predictors on threat perceptions. The table reports all coefficients greater

---

22 These variables are influential despite the fact that they are themselves relatively unstable over time. This suggests that the cause of the instability is not simply random measurement error.

than .05, even though we continue to treat .10 as the minimum threshold for confirming a hypothesized relationship. Four endogenous variables are hypothesized to contribute to threat perceptions in 1997, and two in 1996.

Among Africans, none of the hypotheses is supported in 1997, and essentially none is supported in 1996 (the .07 coefficient for closedmindedness is too small to treat as substantively significant). For Africans, threat perceptions appear to be exogenous, at least in the conventional tolerance model.

Once more, the findings among whites are quite different. Threat perceptions in both 1996 and 1997 depend upon levels of closedmindedness. These relationships are substantively significant, even if they are not particularly strong. This finding is important since many have long suspected this association but no prior analysis has demonstrated it empirically. Indeed, the volatility of this relationship can be seen in the total lack of support for the connection among Africans, and the wrongly signed (but trivial) relationships among Coloured people and those of Asian origin in 1997. In general, support for the hypothesized connection between closedmindedness and threat perceptions is found only among whites.

The influence of democratic values on threat perceptions among Coloured South Africans is also quite interesting because earlier research has failed to detect such a relationship. In both 1996 and 1997, those more supportive of democracy were *less* threatened by the political group they oppose, just as hypothesized. Within no other racial group is this hypothesis supported (and some of the trivial coefficients are wrongly signed). For most South Africans, attitudes toward democracy do not innoculate against perceptions that one's political enemies are highly threatening.

Thus, this analysis supports nearly all of the conventional hypotheses about the origins of intolerance, including the difficulty of predicting who feels threatened by their political enemies. It remains to consider whether the model can explain attitude change.

The analysis to this point has not considered the influence of the exogenous variables. Table 8.11 reports the coefficients necessary to test the central hypotheses accounting for the dynamics of change in tolerance in South Africa. To reiterate, Figure 8.4 specifies the hypotheses under consideration in this table. Note that most of the hypothesized influence of these environmental perceptions on tolerance is indirect, mediated through support for democratic institutions and processes and/or perceptions of threat. And finally, these coefficients describe the effects of the exogenous variables on *change* in attitudes in 1997, since in every instance the attitudes in 1996 are included in the set of equations.

Table 8.11. *The Effects of Exogenous Variables on Change in Tolerance, 1996–7*

Hypotheses and Variables	Race of Respondent			
	African	White	Coloured	Asian Origin
Satisfaction with Democracy →				
Democratic Values$_{1997}$	.16	.13	.05	.17
Threat Perceptions$_{1997}$	−.07			−.05
Tolerance$_{1997}$			.05	
Perceptions of Change in Crime →				
Democratic Values$_{1997}$	.06	−.35		.11
Threat Perceptions$_{1997}$		.16		
Tolerance$_{1997}$			−.06	.09
Quality of Life Under Apartheid →				
Democratic Values$_{1997}$		−.24	−.09	.06
Threat Perceptions$_{1997}$		.08	−.23	−.13
Democratic Values$_{1996}$	−.06		−.06	.05
Threat Perceptions$_{1996}$	−.07		.10	
Tolerance$_{1996}$	−.05	−.11	.06	.06

Note: Only coefficients greater than or equal to .05 are reported.

Consider first the relationships in 1997. Satisfaction with the performance of democracy in South Africa contributes to increasing support for democratic institutions and processes among all groups except Coloured people (among whom the relationship is correctly signed, but trivial). This may well reflect the process of converting so-called specific support into diffuse support for democracy. Democratic legitimacy (diffuse support) depends upon the slow accretion of satisfaction, resulting in the transformation of that satisfaction into more obdurate attitudes toward the regime itself. This process requires far more than the eighteen months between the two interviews, so the effects we observe in Table 8.11 are not particularly strong. They are, nonetheless, compatible with the hypothesis.

A second important finding from the coefficients in this table concerns the impact of perceptions of crime, particularly among whites. White South Africans who perceive crime to have gotten worse are much less supportive of democratic institutions and processes, as well as more threatened by their political enemies. These relationships speak to the political implications of crime in South Africa, and the ability of fear of social disorder to undermine democracy, at least among whites.

However, crime perceptions have little systematic impact on Africans, Coloured people, and South Africans of Asian origin. Even the .11 coefficient between crime perceptions and democratic values among those of Asian origin is in the wrong direction (as is the .09 coefficient for the direct effect of crime perceptions on political tolerance).[23]

Generally, perceptions of crime most affect those who held a secure and privileged position under apartheid – whites. With the demise of apartheid, whites have come to experience social reality in ways similar to the less privileged portion of South African society, and they are not happy about it. Whites apparently blame politics for crime, which is quite natural. But some seem to blame democracy as well, an ominous finding from the point of view of the consolidation of democracy.

Finally, Table 8.11 also reports the effects of the exogenous variable "quality of life under apartheid" on attitudes in 1996. Since prior attitudes are not controlled in these equations, the 1996 dependent variables should not be understood as change but are instead levels of the attitude as they existed in 1996.

The impact of perceived changes in the quality of life since apartheid ended is most strongly felt among whites and Coloured people, although by pathways that differ in important ways. Among Coloured South Africans, perceptions of their lives under apartheid influence tolerance primarily through threat perceptions. Those who believed in 1996 that their lives had improved were slightly *more* likely to be threatened in 1996, but considerably *less* likely to be threatened in 1997. This may reflect the gradual improvement of the conditions of Coloured South Africans, accompanied by a growing perception of their political power and security.

Among whites, however, perceptions of an improving quality of life were slightly related to being *less* tolerant in 1996, although these whites were also slightly less threatened as well. But the most curious finding is that those who judged themselves to be better off in 1996 were substantially *less* likely to support democratic institutions and processes in 1997. This finding may reflect an interactive effect between the perceived quality of life in 1996 and the perceived quality of life *in 1997* (which was not measured in the 1997 survey). Perhaps the effect of changes in the quality of life between 1996 and 1997 is greatest among those with the highest quality of life in 1996 – those with the most to lose. Among those who had already experienced and perceived a diminution in the quality of their lives in 1996, little further change was possible between

23 This finding is *not* due to racial differences in perceptions of crime. Though whites judge crime to have worsened the most, their average response is only slightly higher than the mean among Coloured people and among South Africans of Asian origin. Only African South Africans differ significantly in their judgments that crime has not changed radically since the end of apartheid.

1996 and 1997. The effect of change would therefore be concentrated among those whose lives had not deteriorated by 1996. If so, this would account for the negative coefficient.

Discussion

The statistical results from the full model of change are certainly not simple, in part because the findings vary substantially across the four racial groups. It is therefore perhaps useful to take a step away from the data – and become a bit more speculative – and to try to provide some overall perspective about how and why changes in political tolerance differ across the various groups. In doing so, we are trying to understand how attitudes change in response to the actions of the South African political and economic systems.

Among the African majority, only a single coefficient for the environmental perceptions variables exceeds .10 – those who were more satisfied with the performance of democracy in South Africa tended to become more committed to democratic institutions and processes. Neither perceptions of crime nor perceptions of the quality of life have much impact on any of the attitudes. The attitudes of Africans are not particularly stable, but nor are they very sensitive to perceived changes in South African political or social life.

Instead, among Africans, the story of intolerance is mainly a story of threat perceptions. The connections between the two variables are strong and both are relatively insensitive to environmental influences. Nor are tolerance attitudes closely connected with more general attitudes toward democracy. Those supportive of democratic institutions and processes are neither more nor less likely to be politically tolerant.

Perhaps the threat perceptions of Africans reflect historical factors more than contemporary politics. That is, for Africans, it is their history of oppression under apartheid that defines the threats they perceive (as least in 1996 and 1997). Perceived threats are stable – Africans know who their enemies are – and therefore threat perceptions require little contemporaneous updating.

Another aspect of this story is that democratic values may not be well developed among Africans. Consequently, perhaps not many Africans have learned the virtue of democratic forbearance: When a threat is perceived, it readily translates into intolerance; it is not blocked by some larger consideration of the value of democracy in South Africa. Without the cushion of democratic legitimacy, Africans simply translate their historical understanding of the threat to them into political intolerance.

What is the source of change in tolerance among Africans? The diagram in the first panel of Figure 8.5 (extracted from Tables 8.10 and

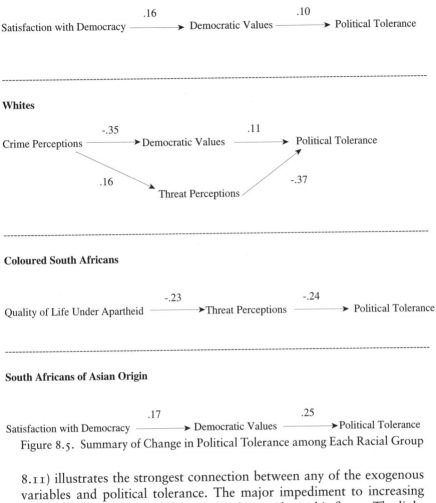

Africans

Satisfaction with Democracy —.16→ Democratic Values —.10→ Political Tolerance

Whites

Crime Perceptions —-.35→ Democratic Values —.11→ Political Tolerance

.16 ↘ Threat Perceptions -.37 ↗

Coloured South Africans

Quality of Life Under Apartheid —-.23→ Threat Perceptions —-.24→ Political Tolerance

South Africans of Asian Origin

Satisfaction with Democracy —.17→ Democratic Values —.25→ Political Tolerance

Figure 8.5. Summary of Change in Political Tolerance among Each Racial Group

8.11) illustrates the strongest connection between any of the exogenous variables and political tolerance. The major impediment to increasing levels of tolerance among Africans is obvious from this figure: The linkages between these variables are quite weak, meaning that satisfaction must increase enormously to have much impact on tolerance. It is doubtful that satisfaction with democracy in South Africa can grow to the extent required to produce widespread political tolerance among black South Africans. Still, according to this model, that is the only pathway available for increasing political tolerance among Africans.

The story for whites is surely one of change in their status and security within South African society. It is often difficult for outsiders to appreciate how privileged the life of white South Africans was under apartheid. Much of this has changed – especially whites' perceptions of their vulnerability to crime – and these changes have a powerful influence on the political attitudes of whites.

On the basis of the coefficients in Tables 8.10 and 8.11, the diagram in the second panel of Figure 8.5 represents the most powerful linkages between environmental factors and political tolerance among whites. The single most important perceptual variable is judgments of the change in crime in South Africa, and such perceptions influence both democratic values and threat perceptions. This makes crime a particularly important influence on whites since crime perceptions directly affect two of the strongest causes of intolerance. Thus, whites are quite sensitive to changes in their environment and such changes conspire to reduce political tolerance within the white community.

Among Coloured South Africans, perhaps the most important determinant of tolerance is the change in threat perceptions brought about by the changing status of Coloured people in the post-apartheid regime. Among Coloured people who have fared well in the New South Africa, perceptions of political threat have declined, leading to an increase in political tolerance. A simple summary of the findings can be found in the third panel of Figure 8.5. Of course, not all Coloured people have improved their lot, but the effects of such changes are stronger among Coloured people than among others who were oppressed under apartheid.

Other changes may have also contributed to declining perceptions of threat among Coloured people. In particular, as Coloured South Africans have come to embrace democratic institutions and processes, they may have become less threatened. Perhaps this is also related to the majority status of Coloured people in the Western Cape. In that province, Coloured people have clearly profited from democratic politics since the fall of apartheid, perhaps rendering their democratic commitments more crystallized and more consequential. This combination of being able to compete in the democratic political arena and of being freed from the restrictions of apartheid means that Coloured people no longer have to be afraid in their own country. Such beliefs contribute to political tolerance.

The commitments of Asians to democratic institutions and processes are the most stable of any group in the survey. Moreover, we observe the strongest impact of democratic values on tolerance among Asians. Perhaps this is an indication of how well integrated democratic attitudes are among South Africans of Asian origin. This may reflect the relatively high level of education of Asians, as well as their orientations toward India, often hailed as the world's largest democracy, and often regarded as a source of pride among South Africans of Asian origin.

Commitment to democratic institutions and processes are fueled as well by satisfaction with the performance of democracy in South Africa. Indeed, the model of change characterizing those of Asian origin is not unlike the model describing black South Africans (see the last panel in Figure 8.5). An important difference between Asian and black South Africans is the strength of the connection between democratic values and political tolerance, but among both groups, growing satisfaction with democracy contributes to greater political tolerance.

If these various speculations are indeed accurate, then we conclude that the dominant characteristics of tolerance among the various groups are:

- Africans – the lack of crystallization of a democratic belief system that includes and integrates political tolerance
- Whites – the declining status of whites, and the concomitant increase in insecurity
- Coloureds – the increasing political security brought about by the emancipation from apartheid, including the ability to compete in majoritarian politics (at least at the provincial level)
- Asians – the strength of commitments to democratic institutions and processes and the incorporation of tolerance into their democratic belief systems

CONCLUSIONS AND DISCUSSION

This chapter has covered a great deal of territory, making simple conclusions about change in political intolerance impossible. Nonetheless, some important lessons have been learned:

- Despite the appearance of stability produced by aggregate data, there is a considerable amount of change in political tolerance among South Africans. Indeed, tolerance is among the less stable attitudes, especially as compared with quite stable perceptions of group threat. From these analyses, it does not appear that tolerance is an obdurate attitude, initiated at birth and solidified through childhood socialization. Instead, tolerance is malleable.
- Change in political tolerance is complicated, however, because several different processes influence tolerance. Among some (perhaps most), tolerance is not anchored in a democratic belief system, so it is free to change with relatively few constraints. Among others, tolerance flows directly from threat perceptions, and as these perceptions change, so too do tolerance attitudes. Among a relatively few, tolerance is embedded in a broader system of beliefs, making it resistant to change unless these more basic attitudes toward democratic institutions and processes themselves change (as they do

among some groups in South Africa). Thus, no single process can account for changes in political tolerance.

- Threat perceptions are generally fairly stable – indeed, among some, threat seems to reflect historical patterns of oppression – but even perceptions of threat can change. Threat may be diminished by changes in the distribution of power in South Africa, and by eliminating the stigma imposed by apartheid. Though we see little evidence of it, a breakdown of historical animosities – or perhaps the replacement of old patterns of group conflict by new ones – can ameliorate threat as well. Anything that contributes to group security is likely to contribute to political tolerance, by reducing the level of perceived threat.

- Thus, this analysis contributes to our understanding of the etiology of threat perceptions. We have shown that at least under some circumstances, threat perceptions can change in response to environmental factors. Our analysis of perceived threat has been most successful among white South Africans – especially in the finding that threat perceptions are both environmentally influenced and determined as well by levels of closedmindedness. Still, the puzzle of threat deepens in the sense that we have little understanding of why some groups are influenced by these factors but others are not.

- In this and other senses, this analysis has confirmed much of the conventional wisdom of Western-based research on political tolerance. Perhaps we have not emphasized these findings as strongly as we should. That the core tolerance model works as well among various racial groups in South Africa as it does among Americans is perhaps a finding worthy of more attention. The principal conclusions of decades of research on political tolerance seem not to be confined to advanced, industrialized democracies.

- Some stress should be given to our *null* findings as well. Perhaps most significant is the trivial role played by perceptions of the performance of the economy. Those desirous of predicting the future of South African commitments to democratic reform must of course pay attention to the economy. But *politics is about more than economics*. Crime has political implications in South Africa (as well might the other policy shortcomings of the political leadership). And perhaps most important, South African commitments to democratic institutions and processes, while not impervious to influences from the sociopolitical environment, are not terribly dependent upon the economic performance of the incumbents. South African political culture may slowly evolve in a more democratic direction even despite the failure of its leaders to create a more successful and equitable economic system.

- Whether one tolerates one's political enemies is a dynamic process, and research on political tolerance must therefore focus more on processes of change. We will have more to say about this in the concluding chapter of this book, but it is clear that static, crosssectional analyses of tolerance are limited in what they can teach us. This study has been confined to two surveys, conducted roughly eighteen months apart. Future research would profit from employing longitudinal methods to study the ebb and flow of tolerance. It is remarkable how little we know about changes in tolerance over the relative long term – how and why, for instance, the intolerance toward Communists in the United States became dissipated. A long-term study of whether political tolerance can get a foothold in a transitional country such as South Africa would contribute immensely to our understanding of the dynamics of tolerance and intolerance.

- Any study of change must confront the complexities associated with the least-liked measurement strategy. We sidestepped that issue to some extent by conducting a "constant group" analysis in this chapter, a strategy defensible for a study of short-term change. But any research concerned with the dynamics of intolerance must simultaneously consider (a) change in the targets of intolerance, (b) change in the threat posed by the targets, and (c) change in willingness to tolerate the targets. This is not an intractable task, but is one that requires more sophisticated data than we generated in this two-wave panel study.

- A more dynamic analysis of tolerance would surely investigate more carefully the process through which satisfaction with short-term political outputs is converted into commitment to the fundamental institutions and processes of a democratic polity. In many areas of political science, we share the intuition that legitimacy – a reservoir of good will – is essential to effective democratic governance. But we have little idea about exactly how this conversion takes place. Diamond (1999) and others have referred to the consolidation of democracy as the belief that democracy is "the only game in town." How loyalty to democratic institutions gets created is an issue of utmost importance for those attempting to understand and explain democratic transformations.

9

Conclusions: Experimenting with Tolerance in the New South Africa

We entitled this chapter "Experimenting with Tolerance" as a means of calling attention both to South Africa's experiment with political tolerance at the societal level, as well as to our experiments at the individual level with manipulating attitudes and preferences. This double entendre reflects our interest in both the macro- and micropolitics of South Africa. Thus, in this final chapter, we draw conclusions about both aspects of the South African experiment.

EXPERIMENTS IN CREATING TOLERANT SOUTH AFRICANS

Our analysis has been concerned with both the nature of South African political culture and its possibilities for change – what it is, and what it might become. Consequently, the first portion of this book was devoted to a careful examination of the structure of South African intolerance, based on an unusually powerful, randomly selected sample of three thousand ordinary people. We discovered that political intolerance is fairly widespread in South Africa – although not as common as it is in Russia – and that South African intolerance has many pernicious characteristics. For instance, intolerance is not relegated to the fringes of the active political spectrum in South Africa, but is instead centered on one of the country's major political parties. Nor is intolerance dispersed "pluralistically"; one of the innovations of the methodology we employ here is that it allows us to determine whether in fact majorities form around one or more unpopular political minorities. Our conclusions from this portion of our analysis are discouraging for those who favor open political competition among all political ideas.

An important enigma emerged from this analysis: The degree of power that a group is perceived to hold has little to do with perceptions of the threat posed by the group. Nor is political intolerance a function of perceptions of group strength. This is not the first time this finding has been reported, but it remains a puzzle. Logically, as a group grows in power, it should become more threatening to its enemies, perhaps resulting in a demand that "something be done" about the group. This process does not seem to characterize South African political culture.

Further, and surely related, *sociotropic* threat is a more powerful predictor of intolerance than *egocentric* threat. It seems that intolerance is based more on the *ideas* of the group than on the likelihood that the ideas will become powerful and influential. Some groups seem to represent an affront to the community (as each individual defines it), and it matters little whether the individual feels directly threatened or whether the country seems immediately endangered by the strength of a group. These findings surely provide insight into the nature of political intolerance, and future research must consider those implications with some care. That people do not discount threats by the improbability of implementation also seems to strike at the heart of rational-choice assumptions about the nature of political attitudes.

One of the most important contributions of this research lies in the discovery of the etiology of threat perceptions. We have long known that perceptions of threat produce intolerance, and our empirical analysis confirms that conclusion for South Africa. Yet extant research has been unable to account for differences in perceptions of threat. Earlier research has not taught us why some people come to see their enemies as more threatening while others see them as less threatening. This is an issue of considerable theoretical and empirical importance and urgency.

Our analysis sheds some light on this question; threat perceptions, at least in South Africa, are bound up with group identities. It is not identity *per se* that causes perceptions of threat – and this is a significant corrective to the conventional literature on social identities – but it is rather the attitudes and values that sometimes flow from strong group identifications. Groups encouraging an ideology of solidarity often produce political intolerance as their by-product. Thus, we are reminded once again that politics is about more than lone individuals – how people fit or do not fit into groups has powerful political consequences. We confess that the causal structure of these relationships is neither well established nor well understood in our research, and we believe that this should be one of the most important areas for future inquiry.

Tolerance research can be rightly criticized for being too abstract and too insensitive to the role of contextual factors in tolerance judgments. Thus, rather than devoting all of our attention to the conventional "least-liked" approach to measuring political tolerance, we also employed an experimental vignette in an effort to assess the importance of contextual factors for South African intolerance. This experiment holds many advantages over the traditional measurement approach, not the least of which is that it presents to the survey respondent a highly realistic scenario and calls for a nuanced judgment about whether to tolerate political activity by a hated enemy. This experiment makes a great deal of substantive sense in South Africa, in that conflicts over efforts of groups to exercise their civil liberties are commonplace (even today, but especially at the time of the survey). The experiment, in addition to having the virtue of verisimilitude, also has strong internal and external validity. That is, the findings are readily generalizable to the population as a whole, and the causal inferences are uncommonly strong. Thus, we believe we have shown that experimental research can contribute to an understanding of intolerance beyond that provided by the conventional measurement approaches.

Our analysis of the contextual factors influencing tolerance judgments suggests that context matters, but not exactly in the direct way we originally hypothesized. As it turns out, the specific elements of the civil liberties dispute have little to do with whether a group will be tolerated. Groups can make promises, leaders can try to persuade people, local authorities may get involved, but, in the end, none of these factors makes much difference. Instead, perceptions of the context are overwhelmingly determined by threat perceptions, and it is threat perceptions, not contextual perceptions, that influence tolerance. We argue that these findings most likely reflect the South African *context* and, in particular, the realism and immediacy of intergroup conflict in the country. It is one thing to ask an undergraduate student at a prestigious U.S. university whether a hypothetical group should be allowed to exercise civil liberties, and quite another to ask a black ANC supporter whether the IFP should be allowed to give a speech in her community, a speech that has a high likelihood of being associated with insult, disruption, and violence. Civil liberties conflicts in South Africa are real and intense; because this is so, the specific elements of a dispute are not of much importance to the formation of opinions.

Our analysis of context is an effort to incorporate some dynamism into the study of political tolerance. After all, people do not form judgments about real political events by simply deducing specific conclusions from abstract principles. Civil liberties disputes unfold; they are dynamic. Frames of understanding change as various elites attempt to dominate the ways in which disputes are seen (and hence judged). Our vignette does not capture a great deal of this dynamism, but it does encapsulate some of it.

We presented more direct evidence of the dynamic nature of intolerance in the last part of the book. In this portion of our analysis, we were less concerned with "what is" and more concerned with "what might be." That is, we know that the opening "bids" of most South Africans are intolerant; but opening bids are not necessarily the same thing as final bids, and much intervenes between the beginning and the ending of disputes. Thus, the last three substantive chapters of the book have addressed change, in one manner or another.

Persuasion is one form of change, and persuasion is crucial to politics. In politics, people talk to one another and try to convince each other to alter their views. We have attempted to capture something of this process in our "persuasibility experiment." Like the vignettes, this methodology has many attributes that commend it. Our view is that its main strength lies in its ability to address the social context of politics, and the fact that people do not form and hold their views in splendid isolation from others. Arguments are important in politics, so we have tried to incorporate them into our analysis.

We enjoyed considerable success in getting South Africans to change their opinions through substantive argumentation, a finding that vindicates our central hypothesis. However, unfortunately, we were more successful at producing intolerance than tolerance. This asymmetry in pliability has earlier been observed in other contexts; South Africans seem to respond to arguments in much the same ways as Americans and Russians. But the unfortunate fact (from the point of view of protecting civil liberties) is that tolerance is relatively malleable; intolerance is relatively obdurate. This may be a function of the particular arguments we used in the experiment, but we doubt it, since these findings fit so well with earlier research (and since we had such strong incentives to concoct the most pro-tolerance arguments we could imagine).

Responses to persuasive argumentation are not random; indeed, we have had some success in explaining why some respond to arguments while others do not. The complexity of belief systems has something to do with this, as does dogmatism. It seems that democratic beliefs contain the seeds of their own destruction. Democratic values are associated with other values that can be used to "trump" tolerance. Democrats often want, for instance, people to be free from insult, but freedom from insult frequently can be achieved only through the suspension of the civil liberties of those whose views are insulting. We had little success at finding effective appeals to those not generally supportive of democratic institutions and processes that would convert them to political tolerance. Thus, from the point of view of political psychology, this experiment was a success; from the point of view of democratic consolidation in South Africa, it was a failure.

Another form of persuasion has to do with the intervention of political institutions. Civil liberties disputes often wind up involving courts and other political institutions, and these institutions represent a type of persuasion quite different from interpersonal discussions, but no less important. We have tried to capture some of the dynamics of this process in our acquiescence experiment. Reasoning that it is not always necessary to get citizens to change their views, we asked whether the intervention of a court can defuse opposition to the efforts of an unpopular political minority to exercise its civil liberties. This section of our work does not consider actual political behavior (except insofar as doing nothing is a behavior), but it does investigate the behavioral intentions flowing from tolerance attitudes.

Our findings here are again discouraging, from the perspective of enhancing democratic freedom in South Africa. The intervention of a tolerant court certainly contributes to more widespread acceptance of a tolerant outcome to the dispute. But an *intolerant* court is even more effective at creating *intolerance*. Should the judiciary in South Africa (specifically, the Constitutional Court) decide in favor of expanding civil liberties, its decision would certainly be persuasive with many. Unfortunately, however, it would be least persuasive with the African majority, which is not much predisposed to tolerate in the first place. We have been unable to explore the impact on elites in South Africa; presumably they would be more willing to accept a tolerant court decision. But should the court decide in favor of intolerance, the mass public would be essentially consensual, making it difficult for elites, however committed to tolerance, to carry the day.

Our final set of empirical conclusions has to do with short-term change in political tolerance and intolerance. Unlike many cultural theorists, we hypothesize that attitudes such as these can change over the short term in response to environmental stimuli. Many are concerned in South Africa that the spiraling crime rate, the growing racial animosity, and the failure to ameliorate the conditions of the vast South African poor all conspire to increase political intolerance. Though we find evidence that tolerance attitudes change in the short term, our data do not support the hypothesis that intolerance is growing in South Africa. We do find that tolerance is responsive to environmental events – especially through the linkage to threat perceptions – although many of our findings are specific to each racial group. For instance, we have discovered that white fear of crime has important political implications since it contributes to white intolerance. Our most general finding is that tolerance does indeed change, largely due to changes in threat perceptions, and we suggest that these are changes that are grounded in the nature of intergroup conflict and political security in the New South Africa.

If we take a few steps away from the structured empirical analysis, several additional conclusions are warranted. First, we are impressed with the dominant role of threat perceptions in virtually all of our analyses. Our finding that threat contributes to intolerance is not surprising;

this is one of the strongest conventional wisdoms in research on political psychology. But the influence of threat perceptions is far broader than we originally expected, affecting, for instance, reactions to persuasive appeals by others, overwhelming judgments of the local circumstances of civil liberties disputes, and rendering intolerance more obdurate and resistant to change. Threat is a powerful variable, structuring nearly all aspects of political intolerance.

We have argued that our research is among the first to provide even a slight theoretical *and* statistical accounting of the origins of threat perceptions. But frankly, our account is far more pleasing from the theory perspective than it is from the data perspective (and we are uncertain how our findings might apply to cultures in which group identifications are neither strong nor salient). Political psychologists still do not know much about why some become highly threatened by their enemies while others do not. Our analysis – our findings concerning the pervasive influence of threat perceptions – should reinforce the urgency of investigations into the etiology of threat perceptions. If we could discover ways to ameliorate and control threat, then we could vastly improve the possibilities for creating political tolerance.

Second, we earlier argued that South Africa constitutes a theoretically useful research site since political tolerance is such a central and salient part of contemporary politics. The analysis in this book vindicates that claim in some, but not all, ways. We are struck, for instance, by the degree to which the core findings of the tolerance literature can be reproduced in South Africa. At the most elemental level, the forces producing intolerance are much the same in the highly democratized countries of the West and the transitional polity in South Africa. We are encouraged that such important theory does not seem to be context-specific.

On the other hand, perhaps the dominating role of threat perceptions in our analysis is related to the South African context. In South Africa, political threats are neither abstract nor hypothetical. As a consequence, it is perhaps not surprising that so many of the processes we have studied are heavily dependent upon the degree to which South Africans feel threatened by their political enemies.

This returns us to our earlier point about the importance of threat, and reinforces the need to understand threat at both the micro and the macro levels. Perhaps one of the most important differences across political systems is in the nature of the perceived threats of opponents. How some systems have come to develop the idea of a "loyal opposition" – rather than traitors and infidels – is not well understood. How do the boundaries of legitimate political competition get established? What causes those boundaries to broaden or shrink over time? How do groups come to be seen as either inside the boundary or outside it? What strategies are useful for legitimizing and delegitimizing groups? The politics of legitimate opposition are little understood; only studies that include variability on this key variable can contribute to our understanding of the definition of legitimate opposition.

Third, one cannot help but be impressed – and perhaps depressed – by the powerful role of race in this analysis. Race is not the simple black versus white distinction perceived by many in the West – Coloured people, for instance, often share more with whites than they do with blacks. But race plays a dominant role in virtually all of our analyses.

The story of race in South Africa is a tale of inequality. The economic inequality of the races in the country is obvious and requires little further comment. The inequality that is so important and unmistakable to us is a deeper, cultural inequality, borne out of colonial racism, ripened and matured by apartheid, and exacerbated by the years of struggle against the old regime. This history contributes to an enormous "democracy deficit" in the hearts of the South African majority – an elemental failure to understand and appreciate the essential components of democratic governance. We have reported the racial differences in perceptions of threat, levels of intolerance, responsiveness to intolerant appeals, and so forth. In most instances, it is black South Africans who are least likely to accept democratic values and appeals. This is a profoundly disturbing finding.

These differences did not occur "naturally." The apartheid system put up enormous barriers to the development of a democratic culture among the African majority. We cannot resist making the comparison to the effects of Soviet-style Communism. The evidence on the Communist legacy is essentially positive from the point of view of democratic reform. The Communists did not enslave and exclude the majority. Instead, Communism contributed to universal literacy, modernization, the development of bureaucracy and the concomitant empowerment of bureaucrats, and even to respect for the concept of "democracy," however it might have been maligned in practice. Consequently, when the time became propitious, the people in Communist systems largely embraced democracy – through a dialectical process, Communism had prepared people for self-government.[1] Whatever the problems of the transitions in Central and Eastern Europe, the difficulties of democratic reform cannot be ascribed to lack of support for democracy among ordinary people. To that extent, the political culture is democratic, and a return to authoritarianism is unlikely.

---

1 Rohrschneider (1999) has provided persuasive evidence that the political culture of East Germany changed prior to the institutional changes merging East and West Germany. A variety of research on the former Soviet Union reaches the same conclusion (e.g., Gibson 1995).

Not so in South Africa. The cultural infrastructure was destroyed by apartheid, not built and sustained. Even the struggle against the old regime produced an enormous, enduring deficit for the current regime, as in for instance the legacy of the schools being a major battleground in the struggle over apartheid. School protests and boycotts were common in the last twenty years,[2] and many South Africans refer to the "lost generation" created by the struggle (Orr 2000). Today, this "lost generation" of freedom fighters and school boycotters struggles with myriad political and social problems. All political systems undergoing radical political transformations suffer generational losses to some degree, but the legacy of the apartheid system continues to undermine democracy in South Africa to an uncommon extent.

The democratic election of 1994 ended apartheid, an evil political system based on a repugnant ideology. But like the East Germans who still have "a wall in their heads," South Africans are finding that the legacy of apartheid persists and continues to undermine the democratic transition. Apartheid denied the benefits of modernization to the vast majority of South Africans, scarring the political culture. If a democratic political culture can be built in South Africa, it must be built from scratch, from the ground up.

Speaking of modernization, it is important to try to understand how these findings – and South Africa – fit within broader theories of democratic transitions. Is South Africa unique? Do these empirical results have implications for other attempts at the consolidation of democratic change?

South Africa may be extreme but it is not unique. That is, on the key continuum representing the degree to which the political culture is supportive of democratic institutions and processes, South Africa can be placed – it is not *sui generis*. But its location on this continuum is surely toward the least democratic position on the scale. The general theory that asserts that democratic cultures contribute to the consolidation of democracy applies with full force to South Africa; the relative lack of such attributes as political tolerance predicts that the future of South Africa's democracy may be rocky. Recovering from the damage caused by apartheid will be no quick or easy task for South Africa. It is in this respect that South Africa differs so much from the experiences of transitional regimes in Central and Eastern Europe and the former Soviet Union.

How can the damage done by apartheid be repaired? A full answer to this question is beyond the scope of this analysis, but some speculative

---

2 For instance, "1980 was a year in which almost no black education happened at all" (Davenport and Saunders 2000, 489). See also pp. 449–54.

replies are readily apparent. The democratization of South African culture will most likely require a "top down" rather than "bottom up" approach. If Russia is an example of cultural change preceding institutional change, then South Africa may become an instance of cultural change responding to institutional reform. The South African political culture was not essentially democratic at the beginning of the transformation process – unlike Russia and parts of Central and Eastern Germany – and therefore its citizens will need to acquire democratic orientations as politics unfolds. This will surely be a slow process, one without much certainty of ultimate success. Learning to tolerate in the context of intense political struggles exacerbated by widespread poverty and economic decline is a difficult task indeed. In light of the empirical findings of this book, avoiding the temptations of unrestrained majoritarianism will be one of the most formidable challenges for new South Africa.

THE EXPERIMENT WITH DEMOCRATIC TOLERANCE IN SOUTH AFRICA

We have repeatedly asserted that our analysis is about what "could be" in South Africa. It is time to address this question head on.

As we noted in the opening chapter of this book, the odds are heavily against South Africa successfully completing its democratic transition. South Africa is too poor, its wealth distributed too unequally, its culture too heterogenous. Now we add widespread intolerance to its list of traits undermining democracy. With these factors in mind, how could any but the most pessimistic conclusion emerge from this analysis?

Perhaps our most optimistic conclusion is that intolerance is not entirely obdurate. That is, intolerance can be influenced, even if it is less pliable than tolerance. Those who are intolerant are not entirely unresponsive to arguments to tolerate, nor would they ignore a tolerant ruling from their Constitutional Court. The asymmetry in the pliability of tolerance and intolerance has led us to pessimistic conclusions at several points in this book, but to be entirely pessimistic is to ignore the fact that some our strategies for creating tolerance have been at least somewhat successful.

One could imagine an entirely different result. If intolerance were a "natural" state of affairs – or even if it were a state that could be overcome only with extensive education (which has been absent to date) – then South Africa would face a more difficult future. That is not what we have found, and we therefore note that the possibilities for tolerance are not entirely foreclosed.

A tolerant future for South Africa thus may rely heavily upon the role of elites. As the most obvious example, such an outcome relies upon a tolerant Constitutional Court. But our conclusion also necessitates someone making an argument in favor of tolerance; without an argument, no deliberation takes place, and therefore there can be no persuasion. We know little about the tolerance of South African elites – especially the sort of local elites whom we model in some aspects of this research. A crucial next step in understanding South African tolerance would be to place the questions addressed in this book before a data set based on local elites.

In the end, no one can be sure how the South African experiment will turn out. Our analysis is confined to only a single variable – the South African mass political culture – within a larger matrix of causes of success and failure in consolidating democratic reform. It is possible that elites will be able to guide the South African political system to a democratic conclusion. At some point, however, the lack of political tolerance among the mass public will surely have to be addressed if South Africa is not to go the way of so many failed African democracies.

Appendix A

Research Design and Methodology

Survey research is not a novel technology in South Africa, since both academic and commercial interests employ surveys on a regular basis. For instance, South Africa has been included in each of the waves of the World Values Surveys (although as with many of the surveys in that series, the representativeness of especially the earlier samples is extremely limited).[1] Nonetheless, survey researchers in South Africa face some formidable obstacles. In this chapter, we discuss the ways in which we have overcome these obstacles.

Our objectives in the survey upon which we rely in this book were (a) to use our survey data to draw inferences about the attributes (univariate and multivariate) of the entire South African population; (b) to be able to analyze differences across the major racial/ethnic/linguistic groups in South Africa with some degree of precision; and (c) to assess change in South African political culture, even if over a fairly short period of time. With these goals in mind, this chapter presents the details of our research design. In addition, we address a variety of threats to the validity and reliability of the data we collected in the survey.

THE SURVEY FIRM

The fieldwork for this project was conducted by Decision Surveys International (DSI), a prominent South African survey firm with

---

1 For instance, in the 1981 survey in South Africa, the sample was a quota sample of people sixteen years old or older. Four distinct subsamples were employed: "600 Whites . . . living in urban and rural areas throughout South Africa"; "600 Blacks . . . living in the following metropolitan areas: Johannesburg, Reef, Pretoria, Durban and East London"; "200 Coloureds . . . living in Cape Town"; and "200 Asians . . . living in Durban" (Markinor 1982, 5). Such a sample can hardly be considered representative of the entire population of South Africa. This survey turns

headquarters in Johannesburg. The project was managed by Carrol Moore, and the logistics of the survey were supervised by Danny Manuel. DSI has had vast experience in survey research in South Africa. However, we selected the firm not only on the basis of its experience, but also on its willingness to adopt certain specific methodological practices that are more common to academic surveys than to commercial surveys. Moreover, DSI was willing to allow us direct participation in virtually all of the aspects of the survey. These procedures give us an uncommonly high level of confidence in the quality of the survey effort.

SAMPLING AND FIELDWORK

Our objectives in sampling were to select a representative sample of the entire South African mass public, with representative subsamples of each of the major racial/ethnic/linguistic groups in society.[2] Consequently, we selected a *primary* sample of South Africans, and then supplemented it with a *boost* sample to ensure sufficient numbers of respondents for analysis within each of the country's major racial groups.

Because of the enormous racial/ethnic/linguistic differences within South African society – and in light of our desire to analyze these differences as part of our inquiry – we employed a stratified (rather than simple) random sampling strategy. The mass public sample was stratified according to province, race, and community size, with the strata defined according to population estimates from the Demographic Information Bureau. Table A.1 reports data on the racial make-up of the South African population. The primary sample for each group was proportionate to the size of the group in the population. To ensure a reasonable number of respondents from the major racial/ethnic/linguistic groups (minimum N = 250), we oversampled within some strata.

The South African sample is composed of 2,557 respondents in the primary sample and 477 respondents in the various boost samples. The relationships between these two samples are somewhat complicated and require further discussion.

The supplementary samples were drawn so as to boost the number of respondents in several racial/linguistic categories to a minimum of

---

out to be especially important since it is the basis of Ellmann's (1995) analysis of trust in law and police institutions in South Africa.

2 Groups within South African politics are not defined entirely by race, and, in any event, race is a very complicated variable itself. Our sampling strategy involves the respondent's race, ethnicity, and language, and therefore the proper way to refer to the groups is as "racial/ethnic/linguistic" groups. This is an awkward phrase, however, and we therefore generally refer to these as "racial" groups.

Table A.1. *South African Population Attributes*

Province	Population[a]	Racial Composition[b]				
		Black	White	Coloured	Asian Origin	Total
Western Cape	9.8	17.2	27.4	54.6	.8	100.0
Northern Cape	2.0	31.6	19.3	48.9	.3	100.1
Free State	7.4	82.0	15.5	2.5	0.0	100.0
Eastern Cape	14.5	84.1	8.1	7.6	.3	100.1
KwaZulu-Natal	19.8	78.1	9.6	1.5	10.8	100.0
Mpumalanga	6.7	85.4	13.5	.6	.4	99.9
Northern Province	9.9	95.4	4.3	.2	.1	100.0
Gauteng	21.5	63.6	31.1	3.4	1.9	100.0
North West	8.4	88.8	9.8	1.1	.3	100.0
South Africa	100.0	72.3	16.1	8.8	2.8	100.0

Notes:
[a] This is the percentage of the total South African population eighteen years or older (approximately 25 million people) residing in the province.
[b] This is the distribution of the provincial population according to the four main racial/ethnic/linguistic groups. The entries are percentages, which total to 100 percent, except for rounding errors.

250 respondents. Oversamples (with the number of oversampled respondents) were drawn for the following groups: Tswana-speaking Africans (N = 28), North Sotho-speaking Africans (N = 19), South Sotho-speaking Africans (N = 26), Afrikaans-speaking whites (N = 52), English-speaking whites (N = 89), Coloured South Africans (N = 64), and South Africans of Asian origin (N = 194). (The remainder are Africans speaking other languages.) Whenever we conduct analysis *within* a group, we merge the respondents in the primary and supplementary samples and analyze the data without weights. The smallest group in this sort of analysis is the amalgam "Africans speaking other languages" (N = 209).

For many purposes, however, we wish to generalize to the South African population as a whole. Without weights, it would be entirely inappropriate to collapse the primary and supplementary samples since this would result in the smaller groups (e.g., whites) contributing disproportionately to the overall population estimate. We could simply discard the supplementary samples when conducting this type of analysis, but have chosen not to do so in order to take full advantage of the within-group diversity resulting from the merged primary and supplementary samples.

The oversamples were not drawn from the nation as a whole; instead, we targeted specific areas of the country for selecting the oversample for each group. To have done otherwise would have been enormously and prohibitively expensive. For instance, very few Tswana-speaking Africans live in KwaZulu-Natal, so efforts to oversample in that province would be fruitless. Practical limitations required us to sample particular groups in areas where these groups are known to live.[3]

This should not be taken, however, to imply excessive concentration of respondents. The numbers of provinces in which respondents of each oversampled group were found in the oversample and in the primary sample are as follows: Tswana-speaking Africans, four provinces represented in the boost sample of six provinces in the primary sample; North Sotho-speaking Africans, three of five; South Sotho-speaking Africans, two of eight; Afrikaans-speaking whites, seven of nine; English-speaking whites, five of seven; Coloured South Africans, two of five; and South Africans of Asian origin, two of three. Thus, we struck a balance between the inefficiency of looking for a needle in a haystack (e.g., an Asian South African in the Northern Province) and excessive geographical concentration (e.g., drawing all Asian South Africans from KwaZulu-Natal).

Our weighting scheme is structured around this sampling strategy. Specifically, we weight within ethnic/racial/linguistic group and within province, weighting both the primary and supplementary respondents so as to maintain the actual number of respondents in the primary sample (which is important to avoid creating any bias in tests of statistical significance). For instance, there are 112 Coloured people in the primary sample in the Western Cape and 50 in the supplementary sample. Each respondent is weighted by the fraction $(112/(112 + 50)) = .691$. This strategy has the advantage of maintaining the proportionate size of each group, while taking advantage of the entire range of variability in the combined primary and supplementary samples, and without artificially inflating the number of completed interviews.

Ours is an area-probability sample, with dwelling units selected using a map grid technique.[4] Eligible respondents were adult South Africans

---

3 Samplers face this same problem in the United States when trying to draw an oversample of African Americans. One strategy (used in part in the black oversample in the 1982 General Social Survey in the United States) is to draw the oversample from areas of the country where blacks are known to live. An alternative strategy is to draw a national sample, contact each household, determine whether it contains a black person, then discard the white households. The 1987 General Social Survey uses this strategy. For a comparison of these alternative sampling approaches, see Tourangeau and Smith 1985 (see also Smith 1987). This latter strategy is difficult and expensive to implement in South Africa (as it is in the United States). As Table A.1 makes plain, it is fruitless to attempt to draw a sample of South Africans of Asian origin anywhere except KwaZulu-Natal and Gauteng.

4 As in most research in South Africa, we specifically excluded residents of hostels from our design. Hostels are essentially dormitories (with communal toilets). There

(eighteen years old and older, the voting age in South Africa). Individual respondents were selected using random procedures.[5] Because of the high levels of homogeneity within some communities (especially in the rural areas), no more than two interviews were conducted at any given sampling point. Unlike most surveys in South Africa, our study did not allow replacement of respondents who could not be interviewed.[6] The initial sample size for the primary mass public sample was 2,780; 2,557 interviews were completed. A maximum of four call-backs was employed prior to abandoning a respondent (with at least one of the calls being in the evening or over a weekend). Detailed records were kept of the results of each attempted contact with the respondents. The survey was in the field from 1 April 1996, through 14 June 1996.

Interviewing in rural areas and small towns was done by traveling teams of interviewers working out of DSI's main offices. All respondents were interviewed in their home language (or preferred language).[7] DSI interviewers are highly trained in the use of visual aids and the interviewing of illiterate and poorly educated respondents. Extensive monitoring, back-checking, and quality control procedures were carried out during the fieldwork.

DSI made several efforts to ensure the quality of the fieldwork. For instance, interviewing commenced in areas close to the DSI regional offices. During the early days of the fieldwork, all interviewers were required to return all completed questionnaires to the firm on a daily basis, thus allowing the checking clerks to check and monitor the quality of interviewing of every interviewer continuously. Once it was

are two types of hostels in South Africa: those run by companies (including the mining companies) and those organized by political parties for itinerant workers and the poorest of the poor. It is difficult for survey researchers to get access to the former (since the hostels are located on company property), and interviewing in either would be extremely dangerous, especially since violence escalated during the transition period (on violence in the hostels, see Morris and Hindson 1992). In South Africa, survey researchers routinely exclude hostel residents from their populations. We did, however, include people living in informal housing such as squatter camps and backyard shacks. To exclude respondents living in this type of housing would be to produce a seriously unrepresentative sample.

5 Specifically, we used a politz grid selection methodology.

6 For instance, the World Values surveys conducted by Markinor allowed the replacement of respondents. See Markinor 1991.

7 Language is a highly controversial political issue in South Africa. But according to estimates reported by the South African Institute of Race Relations (1997, 24–5), the most common home language in South Africa is Zulu, spoken by 22 percent of the population. English is the home language of about 10 percent of the population, while Afrikaans is spoken at home by 15 percent of South Africans. (Xhosa is the second most common language, spoken by 18 percent of South Africans.)

determined that no consistent interviewer errors were being made, the interviewers were sent on field trips to non-urban and rural areas. To ensure that the same quality standards were enforced, a DSI field supervisor traveled with each fieldwork team. The field supervisors reported to DSI every other day on the teams' progress and any problems encountered. The supervisor also manually monitored and checked that all questionnaires were correctly and fully completed.

Validation of completed interviews was done both by telephone and in-person visits. During the validation, certain questions were re-asked, and the respondents were queried about the amount of time taken to complete the interview. The respondents were also asked to comment on the interviewer's conduct and behavior while conducting the interview. A minimum of 15 percent of the interviews was validated on each interviewer's work.

The Interviewers

The interviewers were trained by DSI staff and Amanda Gouws. After an initial training session, all interviewers were required to conduct test/role interviews with one another in an attempt to identify any problems regarding the manner in which the questions were to be asked. All interviewers were then required to attend a second training session, during which all problems were discussed and rectified. To ensure that the quality of training was uniform for all DSI regional offices, we required the managers of all DSI regional offices to attend an initial training session in Johannesburg. The audiotapes of the two training sessions were also sent to all DSI regional offices.

Response Rate

In the primary sample, 2,780 interviews were attempted and 2,557 were fully completed, resulting in a response rate of 92.0 percent. Of the 223 unsuccessful interviews, 78 were started but then broken off at some point by the respondent,[8] 188 were direct refusals by the respondent, and the remainder were instances in which no contact was ever made with a member of the designated dwelling unit. By the standards of contemporary survey research, this is a very high response rate, and any fears about the unrepresentativeness of the sample due to nonresponse can be laid to rest.

---

8 Of course, were we to count these as completed interviews, our response rate would increase.

A total of 477 supplementary interviews were conducted as part of the oversampling of various racial/ethnic/linguistic groups. Combining the two samples, interviews were completed with 2,006 black South Africans, 502 whites, 256 Coloured South Africans, and 270 South Africans of Asian origin. A total of 53.5 percent of the sample is female, which slightly overrepresents women (as virtually all surveys do). We have no doubt that the sample systematically underrepresents the lumpen-proletariat in South Africa, just as do all samples drawn in the West.[9]

The Panel Reinterview

In late 1997, an attempt was made to reinterview the respondents in the 1996 survey.[10] The response rate for the panel reinterviews was 53 percent. This is certainly lower than the first-wave response rate, but the percentage nonetheless compares favorably with panels conducted in other parts of the world. For instance, the highly influential Political Action Panel reported response rates ranging from 65 percent in the Netherlands to 40 percent in West Germany (Jennings, van Deth, et al. 1989, Table A.1, 376). Gibson (1996a, 1996b) reports analysis of Russian and Ukrainian panel data based on a response rate of 52 percent, and Gibson and Caldeira (1996, 1998) analyze panel data with rates between 30 and 76 percent across the countries of the European Union.

THE QUESTIONNAIRE

Several principles guided the construction of the questionnaire:

- *Multiple indicators of concepts.* In light of the enormous difficulty of fielding a survey in seven languages, we felt it essential to use multiple indicators of most of the major concepts included in our study. In practice, we employed a general rule that concepts should be measured by no fewer than three or four items. Important exceptions exist, as with concepts easily measured (e.g., gender) and concepts with alternative conventional approaches (e.g., confidence in leaders and institutions).
- *Acceptance of "don't know" responses.* Many researchers do everything possible to discourage respondents from giving "don't know"

9 For the consequences of such underrepresentation, see Brehm 1993.
10 The interviews were conducted between 4 October 1997, and 28 November 1997. The average length of the interview was 71 minutes (standard deviation = 16 minutes).

or "uncertain" replies, under the assumption that respondents often try to disguise views they think unpopular by giving "don't know" responses. We took exactly the opposite tack, encouraging and legitimizing "don't know" as a response alternative. This strategy is based on the assumption that many South Africans do not hold opinions on a variety of issues, and that to encourage them to fabricate views would do little more than generate random measurement error. Thus, in general, the interviewers were instructed to accept "don't know" responses. Furthermore, the showcard with the possible answers for items based on a Likert response set explicitly included an "uncertain" response.

- *Translation/back-translation.* The respondents were interviewed in their language of choice. The original survey instrument was created in English and then translated into Afrikaans, Zulu, Xhosa, Tswana, North Sotho, and South Sotho by employees of the survey firm.[11] The instrument was then back-translated into English completely independently by another person (i.e., using the "double-blind technique" – see Brislin 1970; Sperber, Devellis, and Boehlecke 1994). Reconciliation of the back-translations took place in a large (and quite lengthy) meeting involving the translators, back-translators, representatives of the firm, and the principal investigators. This process produced an instrument in each language,[12] which was then pretested in February 1996, with sixty-five respondents, mostly from Soweto, but all from Gauteng.[13] The pretest interviews were conducted in seven languages. While the substantive content of the interview itself posed few difficulties for the respondents, the instrument was proven to be much too long.[14] Extensive revisions took place as a consequence of the pretest (especially in the length of the instrument). The final printed version of all questionnaires, irrespective of primary language, also included the English version of each question.

---

11 The principal investigators are fluent in Afrikaans and English. The survey firm naturally employs people fluent in each of the languages.

12 Prior to the pretest, the survey firm conducted a handful of interviews in English, Afrikaans, Zulu, and Xhosa, at the firm's office (using two-way mirrors). Several changes were made as a result of this testing.

13 According to the evaluations of the interviewers, 22 percent were upper- or upper-middle class, 32 percent middle class, non-manual workers, 35 percent were skilled or semiskilled manual workers, and 11 percent were unskilled manual workers or were unemployed.

14 The interviewers judged 52 percent of the respondents to be friendly and interested, 80 percent to have understood the questions well (75 percent seemed to use the showcards without any apparent difficulty), and 72 percent to be about as honest and open as most respondents.

Translation is an arduous and error-prone process, and we often experienced difficulty in finding correct words and phrases in the vernacular of the African languages. We are certain that the imprecision of the translations introduced considerable measurement error, as in all crossnational projects. Consequently, our research relies heavily on multiple-item indicators. We know of no process we could have used to reduce measurement error further.

THE QUALITY OF THE RESPONSES

The interviews were fairly lengthy, with the average interview consuming 74 minutes (median = 70), although there was considerable variability (standard deviation = 23 minutes). Only 2.3 percent of the interviews were completed in under 45 minutes, and a similar proportion required over two hours to finish. The length of the interview varied insignificantly according to the race of the respondent, although, on average, interviews with Coloured respondents required slightly less time.

We can get some indication of how well the interviews were received and understood by the respondents from the judgments of the interviewers. These data must be used with some caution, of course, since the interviewers were likely bringing all of their preconceptions and other attitudes to bear in evaluating the respondents. Nonetheless, these data, as reported in Table A.2, yield some insight into the quality of the interview.

As is typically the case in survey research, most respondents were perceived as friendly and interested in the survey. Even most of those who were not particularly interested (no doubt because of the political content of the survey) were generally cooperative. Only a tiny fraction of the respondents seemed openly hostile toward the interview, and less than one in ten were judged impatient and restless. Crossracial differences are small.

Even if most respondents were interested in the interview, our questions were difficult for many to understand. Fortunately, only a small proportion of the sample was judged to understand the questions "poorly," but, still, only one-half of the African respondents and about three-fifths of the Coloured respondents were thought to understand the questions "well." The vignette proved even more difficult for the respondents. The lack of understanding is no doubt at least partly a function of low levels of literacy.[15] Less than one-half of the African respondents

15 The adult illiteracy rate in South Africa is estimated at 29 percent (South African Institute of Race Relations 1997, 152). Those with less than a standard five level of education are deemed to be illiterate.

Table A.2. *Perceived Attributes of the Respondents, as Reported by the Interviewers*

Respondent Attribute	All South Africans	Race of Respondent			
		African	White	Coloured	Asian Origin
Interest in the Interview[a]					
Friendly & interested	63.9	62.6	67.5	69.5	70.7
Cooperative, not					
interested	24.5	25.3	23.9	18.0	22.2
Impatient & restless	10.0	10.3	8.2	9.8	6.7
Hostile	1.7	1.8	.4	2.7	.4
Understanding of Questions[b]					
Well	57.8	51.1	88.4	60.5	76.3
Not very well	32.2	37.0	11.2	27.7	21.1
Poor	10.0	11.8	.4	11.7	2.6
Able to Read Showcards[c]					
Without difficulty	52.7	42.9	91.8	65.2	83.7
Some difficulty	27.8	33.2	6.6	22.3	12.6
Great difficulty	8.6	10.5	1.2	5.1	2.6
Unable	10.9	13.5	.4	7.4	1.1
Understanding of Vignette[d]					
Better than most	31.0	29.3	37.2	35.1	35.2
As well as most	53.5	52.7	59.8	50.0	58.8
Worse than most	15.4	18.0	3.1	14.9	6.0
Quick-Wittedness[e]					
A great deal more than					
most	5.3	4.9	7.2	4.3	8.1
Somewhat more than					
most	12.8	13.8	11.0	6.6	11.5
About the same as most	36.4	30.3	64.5	40.6	51.1
Not as quick-witted as					
most	45.5	51.1	17.4	48.4	29.3
Honesty & Openness[f]					
A great deal more than					
most	6.4	6.8	4.4	3.9	8.5
Somewhat more than					
most	11.5	12.5	11.2	3.5	8.9
About the same as most	59.9	55.7	74.3	72.3	72.6
Not as honest & open					
as most	22.2	25.0	10.2	20.3	10.0

Note: The entries are percentages, within each race, for each question, and they total to 100 percent, except for rounding errors. For instance, 62.6 percent of the African respondents were judged to have been friendly and interested in the interview.
Crossracial Differences:
[a] $\eta = .07$; $p = .002$.   [b] $\eta = .29$; $p < .000$.   [c] $\eta = .36$; $p < .000$.
[d] $\eta = .14$; $p < .000$.   [e] $\eta = .17$; $p < .000$.   [f] $\eta = .08$; $p < .000$.
[g] $\eta = .08$; $p < .000$.

seemed to have no difficulty reading the showcards we presented, and about a third of the Coloured respondents had at least some difficulty. According to the interviewers, many of the respondents were simply not very quick-witted, especially the African and Coloured respondents. There should be little doubt that our interview severely taxed a considerable number of respondents, and this consequently injected some measure of unreliability into the data.

The problems we encountered with respondents unable to answer our questions probably stemmed more from lack of experience in thinking about issues of democratic politics than from a desire to conceal their true opinions. Most respondents were judged to be relatively open and honest in their responses, although about one-quarter of the African respondents and one-fifth of the Coloured respondents were judged to be not as honest and open as most people. Generally, large percentages of each racial group were judged to have been frank in expressing their views. These are subjective assessments, of course. Fortunately, there is another means of assessing whether the respondents were being truthful in their responses.

At one point during the interview, the respondents were presented with a series of questions about their affective attitudes toward various groups. These questions were asked as a prelude to other questions on political tolerance. We explicitly told the respondents to indicate when they in fact had no attitude toward a group. For one group about which we asked – "Mishlenti" – it was impossible for the respondents to have an opinion; "Mishlenti" is an entirely *fictitious* group.[16]

Large majorities of the respondents in each racial group offered no substantive opinion toward the fictitious group, just as they should have (see Table A.3). For instance, 70 percent or more of each group claimed to have no opinion toward "Mishlenti." However, a significant proportion of respondents did express a view toward "Mishlenti," and, unfortunately, there are some racial differences in the propensity to fabricate an opinion. South Africans of Asian origin were the least likely to fabricate a view; Africans were the most likely. And for all groups except Africans, the overwhelming valence among those with an opinion is negative (by huge margins). Thus, Africans are more likely to express a view

---

16 We gave very careful consideration to any connotations that might be associated with the name of the fictitious group. "Mishlenti" was a figment of the imagination of Gennady Denisovsky, one of our Russian colleagues, and derives from the names of several of the stops on the route Gennady typically takes on the Moscow subway. "Mishlenti" has no particular connotations in any of the South African languages, and it is also a word that does not sound jarring in any of the languages.

Table A.3. *Attitudes toward a Fictitious Group – "Mishlenti"*

Racial Group	Percentages (Total to 100%, Except for Rounding Errors)			N
	No Opinion	Dislike	Like	
All South Africans	72.0	20.7	7.3	2,516
African	69.6	20.9	9.5	1,973
White	77.0	22.2	.8	492
Coloured	80.5	18.7	.8	251
Asian	83.4	14.3	2.3	265

Note: Cross race differences: $\eta = .11$; $p < .000$.

Table A.4. *Opinionation toward a Fictitious Group and Level of Education*

Level of Education	Respondent's Race			
	African	White	Coloured	Asian Origin
No Formal Schooling	37.9	n/a	n/a	n/a
Sub A or B	33.1	n/a	n/a	n/a
Standard 1–5	27.0	n/a	11.1	14.3
Standard 6–10	32.2	26.0	20.4	17.2
Standard 1–9 Plus	17.4	19.0	n/a	n/a
Standard 10 & Diploma	18.0	22.0	31.6	16.7
College Education	16.7	14.1	n/a	22.7

Note: Entries are the percentages of South Africans in the cell giving a substantive response to "Mishlenti." For instance, 37.9 percent of the African respondents with no formal schooling expressed an opinion (positive or negative) toward "Mishlenti."
n/a = not applicable; cell size ≤ 10 respondents.

toward the group and, though most disliked the group, they are more likely than others to view it positively.[17]

To what degree is opinion fabrication a function of the respondent's level of education? Table A.4 offers some evidence on this score.

Within each racial group, there is some tendency for opinionation to be related to level of education. However, among Africans and whites,

17 Schuman and Presser (1981) report an earlier experiment on a fictitious issue. They confirm that explicitly allowing the respondents a "don't know" answer significantly reduces the fabrication of opinions. Not unexpectedly, level of education is a strong (negative) predictor of opinion fabrication. They also note that the favor-to-oppose ratio on their fictitious issue was nearly 2:1 (1981, 152), so people are clearly not simply flipping an unbiased coin in their minds. "Respondents make an educated (though often wrong) guess as to what the obscure [stimuli] represent, then answer reasonably in their own terms about the constructed object" (1981, 159).

opinionation decreases with level of education; among Coloured and Asian South Africans, opinionation increases with level of education. Though none of these relationships is very strong (the largest correlation coefficient is .10, among Coloured respondents), these are puzzling findings indeed.

The modal level of education for each racial group is the "standard 6–10" category. Controlling for this level of education, African respondents are still slightly more likely to express a view than non-black South Africans. The differences are not great, but nor are they entirely trivial.

Finally, the "Mishlenti" experiment was repeated in the second-wave interview, conducted roughly eighteen months after the initial interview. Only a very weak relationship exists between opinionation in 1996 and opinionation in 1997. Of those expressing an opinion in 1996, 68.9 percent did *not* express an opinion in 1997 (compared to 78.4 percent of those who gave no view in 1996). That a large majority of those fabricating a view in 1996 did not in 1997 suggests that this process should be understood mainly as one of randomly distributed error.

The principal conclusion from this analysis is that measurement error is most likely more common among the African respondents in our survey, a conclusion that should surprise no one. The consequence of measurement error is to attenuate relationships. We will be mindful of this throughout the analysis that follows.

CONCLUSIONS

Generally, the design of this survey is as rigorous and systematic as any survey ever conducted in South Africa. The sample represents nearly all relevant segments of the South African population, and includes representative subsamples of at least 250 respondents of most major racial/ethnic/linguistic groups. Great care was taken in preparing the survey instrument and ensuring comparability in the questions across the different languages included in the survey. The evidence suggests that most respondents were cooperative and willing to answer our questions openly and honestly.

However, our survey certainly taxed a portion of the sample, in part due to illiteracy. As a result, our variables reflect a certain amount of random error (and perhaps some systematic error). To the extent that the error is randomly distributed, its effect is to attenuate correlation coefficients. Since the amount of random error surely varies by race, we must adjust our standards for judging the magnitude of the coefficients that we consider, especially among the African majority.

References

Abelson, Robert P., Elliot Aronson, William J. McGuire, Theodore M. Newcomb, Milton J. Rosenberg, and Percy H. Tannenbaum. 1968. *Theories of Cognitive Consistency: A Sourcebook*. Chicago: Rand McNally.

Adamany, David W. 1973. "Legitimacy, Realigning Elections, and the Supreme Court." *Wisconsin Law Review* 3: 790–846.

Alexander, Neville. 1985. *Sow the Wind*. Johannesburg: Skotaville Publishers.

Allen, Richard L., Michael C. Dawson, and Ronald E. Brown. 1989. "A Schema-Based Approach to Modeling an African-American Racial Belief System." *American Political Science Review* 83 (June): 421–41.

Almond, Gabriel A., and Sidney Verba. 1963. *The Civic Culture: Political Attitudes and Democracy in Five Nations*. Princeton: Princeton University Press.

Almond, Gabriel A., and Sidney Verba (eds.) 1980. *The Civic Culture Revisited*. Boston: Little Brown.

Anderson, Christopher J., and Christine A. Guillory. 1997. "Political Institutions and Satisfaction with Democracy: A Cross-National Analysis of Consensus and Majoritarian Systems." *American Political Science Review* 91 (#1, March): 66–81.

Babad, Elisha Y., Max Birnbaum, and Kenneth D. Benne. 1983. *The Social Self Group Influences on Personal Identity*. Beverly Hills: Sage Publications.

Bahry, Donna, Cynthia Boaz, and Stacy Burnett Gordon. 1997. "Tolerance, Transition, and Support for Civil Liberties in Russia." *Comparative Political Studies* 30 (#4, August): 484–510.

Barnum, David G. 1982. "Decision-Making in a Constitutional Democracy: Policy Formation in the Skokie Free Speech Controversy." *Journal of Politics* 44 (#2, May): 480–508.

Barnum, David G., and John L. Sullivan. 1989. "Attitudinal Tolerance and Political Freedom in Britain." *British Journal of Political Science* 19 (Part 1, January): 136–46.

Bar-Tal, Daniel, and Ervin Staub (eds.). 1997. *Patriotism in the Lives of Individuals and Nations*. Chicago: Nelson-Hall Publishers.

Berry, J. W. 1984. "Multicultural Policy in Canada: A Social Psychological Analysis." *Canadian Journal of Behavioral Science* 16 (October): 353–70.

Billig, Michael. 1978. *Fascists: A Social Psychological View of the National Front*. London: Academic Press.

Bobo, Lawrence, and Franklin D. Gilliam, Jr. 1990. "Race, Sociopolitical Participation, and Black Empowerment." *American Political Science Review* 84: 377–93.

References

Bobo, Lawrence, and Frederick C. Licari. 1989. "Education and Political Tolerance: Testing the Effects of Cognitive Sophistication and Target Group Affect." *Public Opinion Quarterly* 53 (#3, Autumn): 285–308.

Bollen, Kenneth A., and Robert W. Jackman. 1985. "Economic and Non-economic Determinants of Political Democracy in the 1960s." *Research in Political Sociology* 1 (September): 27–48.

Booysen, Susan. 1993. "Cohesion, Dissension and Contradiction in the Political World of South Africa's White Student Youth: A Comparative Study of White University Students," in IDASA. *Worlds of Difference – The Political Attitudes of White Students in South Africa.* Pp. 35–62.

Booysen, Susan, and J. Fleetwood. 1994. "Political Events as Agent of Political Socialization: A Case Study of Change in Racial Attitudes in South Africa." *South African Journal of Sociology* 25 (3): 95–103.

Booysen, Susan, and Hennie Kotze. 1985. "The Political Socialization of Isolation: A Case Study of the Afrikaner Student Youth." *Politikon: South African Journal of Political Studies* 12 (2): 23–46.

Brehm, John. 1993. *The Phantom Respondents: Opinion Surveys and Political Representation.* Ann Arbor: University of Michigan Press.

Brewer, Marilynn B., and Roderick M. Kramer. 1985. "The Psychology of Intergroup Attitudes and Behavior." *Annual Review of Psychology* 36: 219–43.

Brislin, Richard W. 1970. "Back-Translation for Cross-Cultural Research." *Journal of Cross-Cultural Psychology* 1 (#3, September): 185–216.

Brookes, Edgar H. 1968. *Apartheid – A Documentary Study of Modern South Africa.* London: Routledge and Kegan Paul.

Brown, Nathan J. 1998. "Judicial Review and the Arab World." *Journal of Democracy* 9 (#4): 85–99.

Bundy, Colin. 2000. "A Rich and Tangled Skein: Strategy and Ideology in Anti-Apartheid Struggles." In *Beyond Racism: Embracing an Interdependent Future.* Atlanta, GA: Southern Education Foundation. Pp. 60–71.

Caldeira, Gregory A., and James L. Gibson. 1992. "The Etiology of Public Support for the Supreme Court." *American Journal of Political Science* 36 (#3, August): 635–64.

1995. "The Legitimacy of the Court of Justice in the European Union: Models of Institutional Support." *American Political Science Review* 89 (#2, June): 356–76.

Campbell, Donald T., and Julian T. Stanley. 1963. *Experimental and Quasi-Experimental Designs for Research.* Chicago: Rand McNally.

Carleton, Don E. 1985. *Red Scare! Right-Wing Hysteria, Fifties Fanaticism, and Their Legacy in Texas.* Austin, TX: Texas Monthly Press.

Carmines, Edward G., and James H. Kuklinski. 1990. "Incentives, Opportunities, and the Logic of Public Opinion in American Political Representation." In *Information and Democratic Processes,* eds. John A. Ferejohn and James H. Kuklinski. Chicago: University of Illinois Press.

Carmines, Edward G., and James Stimson. 1980. "The Two Faces of Issue Voting." *American Political Science Review* 74: 78–91.

1989. *Issue Evolution: Race and the Transformation of American Politics.* Princeton: Princeton University Press.

Carnaghan, Ellen, and Donna Bahry. 1990. "Political Attitudes and the Gender Gap in the USSR." *Comparative Politics* 22: 379–99.

References

Caspi, D., and M. A. Seligson. 1983. "Toward an Empirical Theory of Tolerance: Radical Groups in Israel and Costa Rica." *Comparative Political Studies* 15 (#4, September): 385–404.

Chanley, Virginia. 1994. "Commitment to Political Tolerance: Situational and Activity-Based Differences." *Political Behavior* 16 (#3, September): 343–63.

Cobb, Michael D., and James H. Kuklinski. 1997. "Changing Minds: Political Arguments and Political Persuasion." *American Journal of Political Science* 41 (January): 88–121.

Cobbett, Willliam, and Robin Cohen (eds.). 1988. *Popular Struggles in South Africa*. Trenton, NJ: Africa World Press.

Converse, Philip E. 1964. "The Nature of Belief Systems in Mass Publics." In *Ideology and Discontent*, ed. David Apter New York: Free Press.

　1970. "Attitudes and Non-Attitudes: Continuation of a Dialogue." In *The Quantitative Analysis of Social Problems*, ed. Edward Tufte. Reading, MA: Addison-Wesley. Pp. 165–89.

Cook, Thomas D., and Donald T. Campbell. 1979. *Quasi-Experimentation: Design and Analysis Issues for Field Settings*. Chicago: Rand McNally.

Cooper, Joel. 1976. "Deception and Role-Playing: On Telling the Good Guys from the Bad Guys." *American Psychologist* 31 (#8, August): 605–10.

Crawford, Beverly, and Arend Lijphart. 1995. "Explaining Political and Economic Change in Post-Communist Eastern Europe: Old Legacies, New Institutions, Hegemonic Norms, and International Pressures." *Comparative Political Studies* 28 (#2, July): 171–99.

Dahl, Robert A. 1957. "Decision Making in a Democracy: The Supreme Court as a National Policy Maker." *Journal of Public Law* 6: 279–95.

　1971. *Polyarchy: Participation and Opposition*. New Haven: Yale University Press.

　1989. *Democracy and Its Critics*. New Haven: Yale University Press.

Davenport, T. R. H., and Christopher Saunders. 2000. *South Africa: A Modern History*, Fifth Edition. New York: St. Martin's Press, Inc.

Davis, James A. 1975. "Communism, Conformity, Cohorts, and Categories: American Tolerance in 1954 and 1972–73." *American Journal of Sociology* 81 (#3, November): 491–513.

de Kock, Eugene. 1998. *A Long Night's Damage: Working for the Apartheid State*. Saxonwold, South Africa: Contra Press.

de Lange, Johnny. 2000. "The Historical Context, Legal Origins and Philosophical Foundation of the South African Trust and Reconciliation Commission." In *Looking Back Reaching Forward: Reflections on the Truth and Reconciliation Commission of South Africa*, eds. Charles Villa-Vicencio and Wilhelm Verwoerd. Cape Town: University of Cape Town Press. Pp. 14–31.

Diamond, Larry 1996. "Democracy in Latin America: Degrees, Illusions, and Directions for Consolidation." In *Beyond Sovereignty: Collectively Defending Democracy in the Americas*, ed. Tom Farer. Baltimore: Johns Hopkins University Press.

　1999. *Developing Democracy: Toward Consolidation*. Baltimore: Johns Hopkins University Press.

Diamond Larry, and Juan J. Linz. 1989. "Introduction: Politics, Society, and Democracy in Latin America." In *Democracy in Developing Countries: Latin America* (Vol. 4), eds. Larry Diamond, Juan J. Linz, and Seymour M. Lipset. Boulder: Lynne Rienner. Pp. 1–58.

References

Dollard, J., L. Doob, N. E. Miller, O. Mowrer, and R. Sears. 1939. *Frustration and Aggression.* New Haven: Yale University Press.

Donovan, Robert J., and Susan Leivers. 1993. "Using Paid Advertising to Modify Racial Stereotype Beliefs." *Public Opinion Quarterly* 57: 205–28.

Doty, Richard M., Bill E. Peterson, and David G. Winter. 1991. "Threat and Authoritarianism in the United States, 1978–1987." *Journal of Personality and Social Psychology* 61 (#4, October): 629–40.

Douglas, Tom. 1995. *Scapegoats: Transferring Blame.* New York: Routledge.

Downs, Donald Alexander. 1985. *Nazis in Skokie: Freedom, Community and the First Amendment.* Notre Dame: University of Notre Dame Press.

Duch, Raymond. 1999. "Information Pre-Requisites to Economic Voting in Post-Communist Democracies." Paper presented at the workshop on "Political Institutions: Intermediaries Between Economics and Politics" at the European Consortium of Political Research 1999 Meetings, Mannheim, Germany.

Duch, Raymond M., and James L. Gibson. 1992. " 'Putting Up with' Fascists in Western Europe: A Comparative, Cross-Level Analysis of Political Tolerance." *Western Political Quarterly* 45 (#1, March): 237–73.

Duckitt, John. 1989. "Authoritarianism and Group Identification: A New View of an Old Construct." *Political Psychology* 10 (1): 63–84.

Ellmann, Stephen. 1995. "Law and Legitimacy in South Africa." *Law and Social Inquiry.* 20 (Spring): 407–79.

Esterhuyse, Willie. 2000. "Truth as a Trigger for Transformation: From Apartheid Injustice to Transformational Justice." In *Looking Back Reaching Forward: Reflections on the Truth and Reconciliation Commission of South Africa*, eds. Charles Villa-Vicencio and Wilhelm Verwoerd. Cape Town: University of Cape Town Press. Pp. 144–54.

Evans, Geoffrey, and Stephen Whitefield. 1995. "The Politics and Economics of Democratic Commitment: Support for Democracy in Transition Societies." *British Journal of Political Science* 25 (#4, October): 485–514.

Fearon, James D., and David D. Laitin. 1996. "Explaining Interethnic Cooperation." *American Political Science Review* 90 (December): 715–35.

Feldman, Stanley, and Karen Stenner. 1997. "Perceived Threat and Authoritarianism." *Political Psychology* 18 (#4, December): 741–70.

Feshbach, Seymour, and Noboru Sakano. 1997. "The Structure and Correlates of Attitudes toward One's Nation in Samples of United States and Japanese College Students: A Comparative Study." In *Patriotism in the Lives of Individuals and Nations*, eds. Daniel Bar-Tal and Ervin Staub. Chicago: Nelson-Hall Publishers.

Fiske, Susan T. 1980. "Attention and Weight in Person Perception: The Impact of Negative and Extreme Behavior." *Journal of Personality and Social Psychology* 38: 889–906.

Fletcher, Joseph F. 1989. "Mass and Elite Attitudes about Wiretapping in Canada: Implications for Democratic Theory and Politics." *Public Opinion Quarterly* 53 (#2, Summer): 225–45.

1990. "Participation and Attitudes toward Civil Liberties: Is There an 'Educative Effect'?" *International Political Science Review* 11: 439–59.

Forward, John, Rachelle Canter, and Ned Kirsch. 1976. "Role-Enactment and Deception Methodologies: Alternative Paradigms?" *American Psychologist* 31 (#8, August): 595–604.

References

Franklin, Charles, and Liane C. Kosaki. 1989. "Republican Schoolmaster: The U.S. Supreme Court, Public Opinion, and Abortion." *American Political Science Review* 83 (September): 751–71.

Friedman, Steven, and Louise Stack. 1994. "The Magic Moment – The 1994 Election." In *The Small Miracle – South Africa's Negotiated Settlement*, eds. Steven Friedman and Doreen Atkinson. *South African Review* 7. Johannesburg: Ravan Press. Pp. 310–30.

Frost, Mervyn. 1996. "Preparing for Democracy in an Authoritarian State." In *Launching Democracy in South Africa*, eds. R. W. Johnson and Lawrence Schlemmer. New Haven: Yale University Press. Pp. 16–34.

Gibson, James L. 1985. "Pluralistic Intolerance in America: A Reconsideration." *American Politics Quarterly* 14: (#4, October): 267–93.

———. 1987. "Homosexuals and the Ku Klux Klan: A Contextual Analysis of Political Intolerance" *Western Political Quarterly* 40 (#3, September): 427–48.

———. 1988. "Political Intolerance and Political Repression during the McCarthy Red Scare." *American Political Science Review* 82 (#2, June): 511–29.

———. 1989a. "The Policy Consequences of Political Intolerance: Political Repression during the Vietnam War Era." *Journal of Politics* 51 (#1, February): 13–35.

———. 1989b. "The Structure of Attitudinal Tolerance in the United States." *British Journal of Political Science* 19 (1989): 562–70.

———. 1989c. "Understandings of Justice: Institutional Legitimacy, Procedural Justice, and Political Tolerance." *Law & Society Review* 23 (1989): 469–96.

———. 1990. "Pluralism, Federalism, and the Protection of Civil Liberties." *Western Political Quarterly* 43 (September): 511–33.

———. 1992a. "Alternative Measures of Political Tolerance: Must Tolerance Be 'Least-Liked'?" *American Journal of Political Science* 36 (#2, May): 560–77.

———. 1992b. "The Political Consequences of Intolerance: Cultural Conformity and Political Freedom." *American Political Science Review* 86 (#2, June): 338–56.

———. 1995. "The Resilience of Mass Support for Democratic Institutions and Processes in the Nascent Russian and Ukrainian Democracies." In *Political Culture and Civil Society in Russia and the New States of Eurasia*, ed. Vladimir Tismaneanu. Armonk, NY: M. E. Sharp, 1995. Pp. 53–111.

———. 1996a. "'A Mile Wide, But an Inch Deep' (?): The Structure of Democratic Commitments in the Former USSR." *American Journal of Political Science* 40 (#2, May): 396–420.

———. 1996b. "Political and Economic Markets: Changes in the Connections between Attitudes toward Political Democracy and a Market Economy within the Mass Culture of Russia and Ukraine." *Journal of Politics* 58 (#4, November): 954–84.

———. 1996c. "'Putting Up with' Fellow Russians: An Analysis of Political Tolerance in the Fledgling Russian Democracy." Conference on "Civic Culture in Post-Communist Societies," Center for European Studies, Nuffield College, Oxford University, Oxford, UK., 8–9 March.

———. 1996d. "The Paradoxes of Political Tolerance in Processes of Democratization." *Politikon: South African Journal of Political Studies* 23 (#2, December): 5–21.

———. 1997a. "The Political Significance of Mass Political Intolerance: A Cross-National Inquiry." Paper delivered at the conference on "Comparative Human Rights and Repression: Theory, Explanatory Variables, and

References

Persisting Paradoxes," Boulder, Colorado, University of Colorado at Boulder, 19–22 June.

1997b. "The Struggle between Order and Liberty in Contemporary Russian Political Culture." *Australian Journal of Political Science* 32 (#2, July): 271–90.

1997c. "Mass Opposition to the Soviet Putsch of August 1991: Collective Action, Rational Choice, and Democratic Values in the Former Soviet Union." *American Political Science Review* 91 (#3, September): 671–84.

1998a. "A Sober Second Thought: An Experiment in Persuading Russians to Tolerate." *American Journal of Political Science* 42 (#3, July): 819–50.

1998b. "Putting Up with Fellow Russians: An Analysis of Political Tolerance in the Fledgling Russian Democracy." *Political Research Quarterly* 51 (March): 37–68.

2002. "Becoming Tolerant? Short-Term Changes in Russian Political Culture." *British Journal of Political Science* 32 (April): 309–34.

Gibson, James L., and Richard D. Bingham. 1982. "On the Conceptualization and Measurement of Political Tolerance." *American Political Science Review* 76 (#3, September): 603–20.

1985. *Civil Liberties and Nazis: The Skokie Free Speech Controversy.* New York: Praeger.

Gibson, James L., and Gregory A. Caldeira. 1995. "The Legitimacy of Transnational Legal Institutions: Compliance, Support, and the European Court of Justice." *American Journal of Political Science* 39 (#2, May): 459–89.

1996. "The Legal Cultures of Europe." *Law and Society Review* 30 (#1, April): 55–85.

1998. "Changes in the Legitimacy of the European Court of Justice: A Post-Maastricht Analysis." *British Journal of Political Science* 28 (#1, January): 63–91.

2000. "The Emerging Legitimacy of the South African Constitutional Court." Paper presented at the 2000 Annual Meeting of the American Political Science Association, Marriott Wardman Park, 31 August–3 September 2000.

Gibson, James L., Gregory A. Caldeira, and Vanessa Baird. 1998. "On the Legitimacy of National High Courts." *American Political Science Review* 92 (#2, June): 343–58.

Gibson, James L., and Raymond M. Duch. 1991. "Elitist Theory and Political Tolerance in Western Europe." *Political Behavior* 13 (#3, September): 191–212.

1993a. "Political Intolerance in the USSR: The Distribution and Etiology of Mass Opinion." *Comparative Political Studies* 26 (#3, October): 286–329.

1993b. "Emerging Democratic Values in Soviet Political Culture." In *Public Opinion and Regime Change: The New Politics of Post-Soviet Societies*, eds. Arthur H. Miller, William M. Reisinger, and Vicki L. Hesli. Boulder, CO: Westview Press, 1993. Pp. 69–94.

Gibson, James L., Raymond M. Duch, and Kent L. Tedin. 1992. "Democratic Values and the Transformation of the Soviet Union." *Journal of Politics* 54 (#2, May): 329–71.

Gibson, James L., and Amanda Gouws. 1997a. "Political Tolerance in the Emerging South African Democracy." Paper delivered at the 1997 Annual Meeting of the American Political Science Association, Washington Sheraton Hotel, Washington, DC, and 27–31 August.

1997b. "Support for the Rule of Law in the Emerging South African Democracy." *International Social Science Journal* 152 (June): 173–91.

1999. "Truth and Reconciliation in South Africa: Attributions of Blame and the Struggle over Apartheid." *American Political Science Review* 93 (#3, September): 501–17.

2000. "Social Identities and Political Intolerance: Linkages within the South African Mass Public." *American Journal of Political Science* 44 (#2, April): 278–92.

Gibson, James L., and Kent L. Tedin. 1988. "The Etiology of Intolerance of Homosexual Politics." *Social Science Quarterly* 69 (#3, September): 587–604.

Giliomee, Hermann. 1995. "Democratization in South Africa." *Political Science Quarterly* 110 (#1, Spring): 83–104.

Giliomee, Hermann, and Lawrence Schlemmer. 1994. "Overview: Can a South African Democracy Become Consolidated?" In *The Bold Experiment*, eds. Hermann Giliomee, Lawrence Schlemmer (with Sarita Hauptfleisch). Johannesburg: Southern. Pp. 168–202.

Giliomee, Hermann, and Lawrence Schlemmer (with Sarita Hauptfleisch). 1994. *The Bold Experiment: South Africa's New Democracy*. Johannesburg: Southern.

Glaser, Daryl. 1998. "Changing Discourses of Democracy and Socialism in South Africa." In *South Africa in Transition – New Theoretical Perspectives*, eds. David R. Howarth and Aletta J. Norval. London: Macmillan Press. Pp. 31–48.

Gouws, Amanda. 1992. "A Study of Political Tolerance in the Context of South Africa." Unpublished Ph.D. thesis. Champaign-Urbana: University of Illinois.

1993. "Political Tolerance and Civil Society: The Case of South Africa." *Politikon: South African Journal of Political Studies* 20 (#1, July): 15–31.

1996. "Intolerance in KwaZulu-Natal: Illustrating the Complexity of Tolerance Attitudes." *Politikon: South African Journal of Political Studies* 23 (2): 22–35.

Graubard, Stephen R. 2001. "Preface to the Issue 'Why South Africa Matters.'" *Daedalus* 130 (#1, Winter): v–viii.

Grey, Robert D., William L. Miller, Stephen White, and Paul Heywood. 1995. "The Structure of Russian Public Opinion." *Co-existence* 32 (#2, September): 183–215.

Gurin, Patricia, Arthur H. Miller, and Gerald Gurin. 1980. "Stratum Identification and Consciousness." *Social Psychology Quarterly* 43 (March): 30–47.

Guth, James L., and John C. Green. 1991. "An Ideology of Rights: Support for Civil Liberties among Political Activists." *Political Behavior* 13: 321–44.

Habib, Adam. 1997. "South Africa – The Rainbow Nation and Prospects for Consolidating Democracy." *African Journal of Political Science* 2 (#2): 15–37.

Haggard, Stephan and Robert R. Kaufman. 1995. *The Political Economy of Democratic Transitions*. Princeton: Princeton University Press.

Hand, Learned. 1952. "The Spirit of Liberty." In *The Spirit of Liberty: Papers and Addresses of Learned Hand*, collected, and with an introduction and notes, by Irving Dilliard. New York: Alfred A. Knopf.

Hart, H. L. A. 1968. *Punishment and Responsibility*. New York: Oxford University Press.

References

Hibbing, John R., and Elizabeth Theiss-Morse. 1995. *Congress as Public Enemy: Public Attitudes toward American Political Institutions.* Cambridge: Cambridge University Press.

Hinkle, Steve, and Rupert Brown. 1990. "Intergroup Comparisons and Social Identity: Some Links and Lacunae." In *Social Identity Theory: Constructive and Critical Advances,* eds. Dominic Abrams and Michael A. Hogg. New York: Springer-Verlag. Pp. 48–70.

Hinkle, Steve, and J. Schopler. 1986. "Bias in the Evaluation of Ingroup and Outgroup Performance." In *Psychology of Intergroup Relations,* eds. S. Worchel and W. F. Austin. Chicago: Nelson Hall.

Hoekstra, Valerie J. 1995. "The Supreme Court and Opinion Change: An Experimental Study of the Court's Ability to Change Opinion." *American Politics Quarterly* 23 (January): 109–29.

2000. "The Supreme Court and Local Public Opinion." *American Political Science Review* 94 (#1, March): 89–100.

Hoekstra, Valerie J., and Jeffrey A. Segal. 1996. "The Shepherding of Local Public Opinion: The Supreme Court and *Lamb's Chapel.*" *The Journal of Politics* 58 (#4, November): 1079–102.

Horowitz, Donald. 1985. *Ethnic Groups in Conflict.* Berkeley: University of California Press.

Horowitz, Donald L. 1991. *A Democratic South Africa? Constitutional Engineering in a Divided Society.* Berkeley: University of California Press.

Horrel, Muriel. 1982. *Race Relations as Regulated by Law in South Africa 1948–1979.* Johannesburg: South African Institute of Race Relations.

Hovland, Carl H., and Robert S. Sears. 1940. "Minor Studies of Aggression VI. Correlation of Lynchings with Economic Indices." *Journal of Psychology* 9 (April): 301–10.

Huntington, Samuel P. 1991. *The Third Wave: Democratization in the Late Twentieth Century.* Norman: University of Oklahoma Press.

Hurwitz, Jon, and Jeffery J. Mondak. 2002. "Democratic Principles, Discrimination and Political Intolerance." *British Journal of Political Science* 32 (#1, January): 93–118.

Inglehart, Ronald. 1997. *Modernization and Postmodernization: Cultural, Economic and Political Change in 41 Societies.* Princeton: Princeton University Press.

Iyengar, Shanto. 1991. *Is Anyone Responsible? How Television Frames Political Issues.* Chicago: University of Chicago Press.

Iyengar, Shanto, and Donald R. Kinder. 1987. *News That Matters: Television and American Opinion.* Chicago: University of Chicago Press.

James, Wilmot, and Jeffrey Lever. 2000. "South Africa – The Second Republic: Race, Inequality and Democracy in South Africa." In *Beyond Racism: Embracing an Interdependent Future.* Atlanta, GA: Southern Education Foundation. Pp. 42–59.

Jennings, M. Kent. 1989. "The Crystallization of Orientations." In *Continuities in Political Action: A Longitudinal Study of Political Orientations in Three Western Democracies,* eds. M. Kent Jennings, Jan W. van Deth, et al. Berlin: Walter de Gruyter. Pp. 313–48.

Jennings, M. Kent, Jan W. van Deth, Samuel H. Barnes, Dieter Fuchs, Felix J. Heunks, Ronald Inglehart, Max Kaase, Hans-Dieter Klingemann, and Jacques J. A. Thomassen. 1989. *Continuities in Political Action: A*

References

Longitudinal Study of Political Orientations in Three Western Democracies.
New York and Berlin: Walter de Gruyter.

Johnson, Charles A., and Bradley C. Canon. 1984. *Judicial Policies: Implementation and Impact.* Washington: Congressional Quarterly Press.

Johnson, R. W., and Lawrence Schlemmer. 1996. "Introduction: The Transition to Democracy." In *Launching Democracy in South Africa*, eds. R. W. Johnson and Lawrence Schlemmer. New Haven: Yale University Press. Pp. 1–15.

Johnson, R. W., and Paulus Zulu. 1996. "Public Opinion in KwaZulu-Natal." In *Launching Democracy in South Africa: The First Open Election, April 1994*, eds. R. W. Johnson and Lawrence Schlemmer. New Haven: Yale University Press. Pp. 189–211.

Jordan, Donald L. 1993. "Newspaper Effects on Policy Preferences." *Public Opinion Quarterly* 57 (#2, Summer): 191–204.

Jordan, Pallo. 1988. "Why Won't Afrikaners Rely on Democracy?" *Die Suid-Afrikaan.* (February): 24–5, 29.

Jöreskog, Karl G. 1993. "Testing Structural Equation Models." In *Testing Structural Equation Models*, eds. Kenneth A. Bollen and J. Scott Long. Newbury Park, CA: Sage Publications. Pp. 294–316.

Jung, Courtney, and Ian Shapiro. 1995. "South Africa's Negotiated Transition: Democracy, Opposition, and the New Constitutional Order." *Politics & Society* 23 (September): 269–308.

Kane-Berman, John. 1993. *Political Violence in South Africa.* Johannesburg: SAIRR.

Kaplan, Cynthia S. 1995. "Political Culture in Estonia: The Impact of Two Traditions on Political Development." In *Political Culture and Civil Society in Russia and the New States of Eurasia*, ed. Vladimir Tismaneanu. Armonk, NY: M. E. Sharpe. Pp. 27–267.

Karatnycky, Adrian. 1999. "The Decline of Illiberal Democracy." *Journal of Democracy* 10 (#1): 112–25.

Karpov, Vyacheslav. 1999. "Political Tolerance in Poland and the United States." *Social Forces* 77 (#4, June): 1525–49.

Kelly, Caroline. 1988. "Intergroup Differentiation in a Political Context." *British Journal of Social Psychology* 27 (December): 319–32.

Kinder, Donald R., and Thomas R. Palfrey (eds.) 1993. *Experimental Foundations of Political Science.* Ann Arbor: University of Michigan Press.

Kinder, Donald R., and David Sears. 1981. "Prejudice and Politics: Symbolic Racism versus Racial Threat to the Good Life." *Journal of Personality and Social Psychology* 40: 414–31.

Kliamkin, I. M. 1994. "What Kind of Authoritarian Regime Is Possible in Russia Today?" *Russian Politics and Law* 32 (#6, November–December): 33–41.

Klug, Heinz. 2000. *Constituting Democracy: Law, Globalism and South Africa's Political Reconstruction.* Cambridge: Cambridge University Press.

Koelble, Thomas, and Andrew Reynolds. 1996. "Power-Sharing Democracy in the New South Africa." *Politics & Society* 24 (September): 221–36.

Kotze, Hennie. 1989. "Aspect of the Public Policy Process in South Africa." In *The South African Government and Politics*, ed. Albert Venter. Johannesburg: Southern. Pp. 170–200.

Kotze, Hennie, Johann Mouton, Anneke Greyling, Heide Hackmann, and Amanda Gouws. 1994. "The Sociopolitical Beliefs and Attitudes of South

African Matriculants." In *Youth in the New South Africa*, eds. F. van Zyl, Slabbert, C. Malan, H. Marais, J. Olivier, and R. Riordan. Pretoria: Human Sciences Research Council. Pp. 325–34.

Kraus, Stephen J. 1995. "Attitudes and the Prediction of Behavior: A Meta-Analysis of the Empirical Literature." *Personality and Social Psychology Bulletin* 21: 58–75.

Kuklinski, James H., and Norman L. Hurley. 1996. "It's a Matter of Interpretation." In *Political Persuasion*, eds. Diana C. Mutz, Paul M. Sniderman, and Richard A. Brody. Ann Arbor: University of Michigan Press. Pp. 125–44.

Kuklinski, James H., Ellen Riggle, Victor Ottati, Norbert Schwarz, and Robert S. Wyer, Jr. 1991. "The Cognitive and Affective Bases of Political Tolerance Judgments." *American Journal of Political Science* 35 (#1, February): 1–27.

1993. "Thinking about Political Tolerance, More or Less, with More or Less Information." In *Reconsidering the Democratic Public*, eds. G. E. Marcus and R. L. Hanson. University Park, PA: Pennsylvania State University Press. Pp. 225–47.

Lau, Richard R. 1985. "Two Explanations for Negativity Effects in Political Behavior." *American Journal of Political Science* 29: 119–38.

Lauderdale, Pat L., Phil Smith-Cunnien, Jerry Parker, and James I. Inverarity. 1984. "External Threat and the Definition of Deviance." *Journal of Personality and Social Psychology* 46 (May): 1058–68.

Lawrence, David G. 1976. "Procedural Norms and Tolerance: A Reassessment." *American Political Science Review* 70: 80–100.

Lawrence, Ralph. 1994. "From Soweto to Codesa." In *The Small Miracle – South Africa's Negotiated Settlement*, eds. Steven Friedman and Doreen Atkinson. *South African Review* 7. Johannesburg: Ravan Press.

Lazarus, Richard S. 1982. "Thoughts on the Relations between Emotion and Cognition." *American Psychologist* 37: 1019–24.

Leatt, James, Theo Kneifel, and Klaus Nurnberger. 1986. *Contending Ideologies in South Africa*. Cape Town: David Philip. Pp. 105–19.

Lee, Lynn, and Colleen Ward. 1998. "Ethnicity, Idiocentrism – Allocentrism, and Intergroup Attitudes." *Journal of Applied Social Psychology* 28 (January): 109–23.

Levin, Jack., and William C. Levin. 1982. *The Functions of Discrimination and Prejudice*. New York: Harper and Row.

LeVine, Robert A., and Donald T. Campbell. 1971. *Ethnocentrism: Theories of Conflict, Ethnic Attitudes, and Group Behavior*. New York: John Wiley & Sons.

Lijphart, Arend. 1977. *Democracy in Plural Societies: A Comparative Exploration*. New Haven: Yale University Press.

1985. *Power-Sharing in South Africa*. Berkeley: University of California Institute of International Studies.

Lipset, Seymour Martin. 1994. "The Social Requisites of Democracy Revisited." *American Sociological Review* 59 (February): 1–22.

Lipset, Seymour Martin, Kyoung-Ryung Seong, and John C. Torres. 1993. "A Comparative Analysis of the Social Requisites of Democracy." *International Social Science Journal* 136: 155–75.

Lodge, Milton G., and Charles Taber. 2000. "Three Steps toward a Theory of Motivated Reasoning." In *Elements of Reason: Cognition, Choice, and the*

Bounds of Rationality, eds. Arthur Lupia, Mathew D. McCubbins, and Samuel L. Popkin. New York: Cambridge University Press.

Lodge, Tom. 1991. "Rebellion: The Turning of the Tide." In *All Here and Now: Black Politics in South Africa in the 1980s*, eds. Tom Lodge and Bill Nasson. Cape Town: David Philip. Pp 23–204.

Lodge, Tom, and Bill Nasson. 1991. *All, Here, and Now: Black Politics in South Africa in the 1980's*. Cape Town: David Philip.

Lupia, Arthur. 1995. "Who Can Persuade?: A Formal Theory, A Survey and Implications for Democracy." Paper delivered at the Annual Meeting of the Midwest Political Science Association, Chicago, Illinois, 6–8 April.

Marcus, Georges E., John L. Sullivan, Elizabeth Theiss-Morse, and Sandra L. Wood. 1995. *With Malice toward Some: How People Make Civil Liberties Judgments*. New York: Cambridge University Press.

Mare, Gerhard. 1993. *Ethnicity and Politics in South Africa*. London: Zed Books.

Markinor. 1982. *The Markinor South African Social Value Study – In Association with Gallup International – March 1982*.

——— 1991. *The World Social Value Study – South Africa – Urban Written Report*.

Marks, Monique. 2001. *Young Warriors: Youth Politics, Identity and Violence in South Africa*. Johannesburg: Witwatersrand University Press.

Marshall, Thomas. 1989. *Public Opinion and the Supreme Court*. New York: Longman.

Marx, Anthony W. 1997. "Apartheid's End: South Africa's Transition from Racial Domination." *Ethnic and Racial Studies* 20 (#3, July): 474–96.

Mattes, Robert. 1999. "Do Diverse Social Identities Inhibit Democracy? Initial Evidence from South Africa. In *National Identity and Democracy in Africa*, ed. Mai Palmberg. Uppsala: Nordic Africa Institute/Cape Town: Mayibuye Centre at the University of the Western Cape/Pretoria, HSRC. Pp. 261–86.

Mattes, Robert, and Hermann Thiel. 1998. "Consolidation and Public Opinion in South Africa." *Journal of Democracy* 9 (#1, January): 95–110.

McCaul, Colleen. 1988. "The Wild Card: Inkatha and Contemporary Black Politics." In *State Resistance and Change in South Africa*, eds. Philip Frankel, Noam Pines, and Mark Swilling. Johannesburg: Southern Book Publishers.

McClosky, Herbert. 1964. "Consensus and Ideology in American Politics." *American Political Science Review* 58: 361–82.

McClosky, Herbert, and Alida Brill. 1983. *Dimensions of Tolerance: What Americans Think about Civil Liberties*. New York: Russell Sage Foundation.

McGraw, Kathleen M. 1991. "Managing Blame: An Experimental Test of the Effects of Political Accounts." *American Political Science Review* 85 (December): 1133–57.

——— 1996. "Political Methodology: Research Design and Experimental Methods." In *A New Handbook of Political Science*, eds. Robert E. Goodin and Hans-Dieter Klingemann. New York: Oxford University Press. Pp. 769–86.

Meer, Fatima. 1994. "The Myth of Black on Black Violence." In *Critical Choices for South Africa*, eds. Nic Rhoodie and Ian Liebenberg. Pretoria: HSRC. Pp. 365–75.

Messick, David M., and Diane M. Mackie. 1989. "Intergroup Relations." *Annual Review of Psychology* 40: 45–81.

References

Miller, Arthur H., Patricia Gurin, Gerald Gurin, and Oksana Malanchuk. 1981. "Group Consciousness and Political Participation." *American Journal of Political Science* 25 (August): 494–511.

Miller, Arthur H., Vicki L. Hesli, and William M. Reisinger. 1993. "Group Identification and Support for Economic and Political Reform in the Former Soviet Union." Paper delivered at the 51st Annual Meeting of the Midwest Political Science Association, Chicago, Illinois, 15–17 April.

1997. "Conceptions of Democracy among Mass and Elite in Post-Soviet Societies." *British Journal of Political Science* 27 (#2, April): 157–91.

Mishler, William, and Richard Rose. 2001. "What Are the Origins of Political Threat? Testing Institutional and Cultural Theories in Post-Communist Societies." *Comparative Political Studies* 34 (#1, February): 30–62.

Mondak, Jeffrey J. 1991. "Substantive and Procedural Aspects of Supreme Court Decisions as Determinants of Approval." *American Politics Quarterly* 19 (April): 174–88.

1992. "Institutional Legitimacy, Policy Legitimacy, and the Supreme Court." *American Politics Quarterly* 20 (October): 457–77.

1993. "Source Cues and Policy Approval." *American Journal of Political Science* 37: 186–212.

1994. "Policy Legitimacy and the Supreme Court: The Sources and Contexts of Legitimation." *Political Research Quarterly* 47: 675–92.

Morris, Mike, and Doug Hindson. 1992. "The Disintegration of Apartheid – From Violence to Reconstruction." In *South African Review 6 – From "Red Friday" to CODESA*, eds. Glenn Moss and Ingrid Obery. Johannesburg: Ravan. Pp. 152–70.

Muller, Edward N. 1979. *Aggressive Political Participation*. Princeton: Princeton University Press.

Muller, Edward N., and Mitchell A. Seligson. 1994. "Civic Culture and Democracy: The Question of Causal Relationships." *American Political Science Review* 88 (#3, September): 635–52.

Murphy, Walter F., and Joseph Tanenhaus. 1968. "Public Opinion and the United States Supreme Court: A Preliminary Mapping of Some Prerequisites for Court Legitimation of Regime Change." *Law and Society Review* 2 (May): 357–82.

1990. "Publicity, Public Opinion, and the Court." *Northwestern University Law Review* 84: 985–1023.

Mutz, Diana C. 1998. *Impersonal Influence: How Perceptions of Mass Collectives Affect Political Attitudes*. New York: Cambridge University Press.

Mutz, Diana C., Paul M. Sniderman, and Richard A. Brody. 1996a. *Political Persuasion*. Ann Arbor: University of Michigan Press.

1996b. "Political Persuasion: The Birth of a Field of Study." In *Political Persuasion*, eds. Diana C. Mutz, Paul M. Sniderman, and Richard A. Brody. Ann Arbor: University of Michigan Press.

Nagin, Daniel S., and Raymond Paternoster. 1993. "Enduring Individual Differences and Rational Choice Theories of Crime." *Law and Society Review* 27: 467–96.

Nelson, Thomas E., Rosalee A. Clawson, and Zoe M. Oxley. 1997. "Media Framing of a Civil Liberties Conflict and Its Effect on Tolerance." *American Political Science Review* 91 (#3, September): 567–83.

Nkomo, M. 1990. "Post-Apartheid Education: Preliminary Reflections." In *Pedagogy of Domination*, ed. M. Nkomo. New Jersey: Africa World Press.

References

Nunn, Clyde Z., Harry J. Crockett, Jr., and J. Allen Williams, Jr. 1978. *Tolerance for Nonconformity*. San Francisco: Jossey-Bass Publishers.

Obolonsky, A. V. 1995. "Russian Politics in the Time of Troubles: Some Basic Antinomies." In *Russia in Search of its Future*, eds. Amin Saikal and William Maley. New York: Cambridge University Press. Pp. 13–27.

Olson, J. M., and M. P. Zanna. 1993. "Attitudes and Attitude Change." *Annual Review of Psychology* 44: 117–54.

Orr, Wendy. 2000. *From Biko to Basson: Wendy Orr's Search for the Soul of South Africa as a Commissioner of the TRC*. Saxonwold: Contra Press.

Peffley, Mark, and Lee Sigelman. 1989. "Intolerance of Communists during the McCarthy Era: A General Model." *Western Political Quarterly* 43: 93–111.

Pityana, N. Barney, Mamphela Ramphele, Malusi Mpumlwana, and Linday Wilson (eds). 1991. *The Bounds of Possibility*. Cape Town: David Philip. Pp. 130–6.

Przeworski, Adam, Adam Alvarez, Jose Antonio Cheibub, and Fernando Limongi. 1996. "What Makes Democracies Endure." *Journal of Democracy* 7 (#1, January): 39–55.

Przeworski, Adam, Michael E. Alvarez, José Antonio Cheibub, and Fernando Limongi. 2000. *Democracy and Development: Political Institutions and Well-Being in the World, 1950–1990*. New York: Cambridge University Press.

Prothro, James W., and Charles M. Grigg. 1960. "Fundamental Principles of Democracy: Bases of Agreement and Disagreement." *Journal of Politics* 22: 276–94.

Putnam, Robert D., Robert Leonardi, and Raffaella Y. Nanetti. 1993. *Making Democracy Work*. Princeton: Princeton University Press.

Remmer, Karen L. 1991." The Political Impact of Economic Crisis in Latin America in the 1980s." *American Political Science Review* 85 (#3, September): 777–800.

Rohrschneider, Robert. 1996. "Institutional Learning versus Value Diffusion: The Evolution of Democratic Values among Parliamentarians in Eastern and Western Germany." *Journal of Politics* 58 (#2, May): 422–46.

1999. *Learning Democracy: Democratic and Economic Values in Unified Germany*. New York: Oxford University Press.

Rosenberg, Gerald N. 1991. *The Hollow Hope: Can Courts Bring about Social Change*. Chicago: University of Chicago Press.

Rossi, Peter H., and Andy B. Anderson. 1982. "The Factorial Survey Approach: An Introduction." In *Measuring Social Judgments: The Factorial Survey Approach*, eds. Peter H. Rossi, and Steven L. Nock. Beverly Hills: Sage. Pp. 15–67.

Rossi, Peter H., and Steven L. Nock. 1982. *Measuring Social Judgments: The Factorial Survey Approach*. Beverly Hills: Sage.

Sales, Stephen M. 1973. "Threat as a Factor in Authoritarianism: An Analysis of Archival Data." *Journal of Personality and Social Psychology* 28 (#1, October): 44–57.

Schuman, Howard, and Stanley Presser. 1981. *Questions and Answers in Attitude Surveys: Experiments on Question Form, Wording, and Content*. Orlando, FL: Academic Press.

Schwarz, Norbert, and Gerald L. Clore. 1988. "How Do I Feel about It? The Informative Function of Affective States." In *Affect, Cognition, and Social Behavior*, eds. K. Fiedler and J. Forgas. Toronto: Hogrefe. Pp. 44–62.

References

Seekings, Jeremy. 2000. *The UDF – A History of the United Democratic Front in South Africa, 1983–1991*. Cape Town: David Philip.

Shamir, Michal. 1991. "Political Intolerance among Masses and Elites in Israel: A Reevaluation of the Elitist Theory of Democracy." *Journal of Politics* 53 (November): 1018–43.

Shamir, Michal, and John Sullivan. 1983. "The Political Context of Tolerance: The United States and Israel." *American Political Science Review* 77: 911–28.

Shapiro, Ian, and Courtney Jung. 1996. " South African Democracy Revisited: A Reply to Koelble and Reynolds." *Politics and Society* 24 (September): 237–47.

Shaw, Mark. 1994. "The Bloody Backdrop – Negotiating the Violence." In *The Small Miracle – South Africa's Negotiated Settlement*, eds. Steven Friedman and Doreen Atkinson. *South African Review* 7. Johannesburg: Ravan Press.

Sibisi C. D. T. 1991. "The Psychology of Liberation." In *Bounds of Possibility: The Legacy of Steve Biko and Black Consciousness*, eds. N. Barney Pityana, Mamphela Ramphele, Malusi Mpumlwana, and Lindy Wilson. Cape Town: David Philip. Pp. 130–6.

Sidanius, Jim. 1993. "The Psychology of Group Conflict and the Dynamics of Oppression: A Social Dominance Perspective." In *Explorations in Political Psychology*, eds. Shanto Iyengar and William McGuire. Durham: Duke University Press.

Sidanius, Jim, and Felicia Pratto. 1999. *Social Dominance: An Intergroup Theory of Social Hierarchy and Oppression*. New York: Cambridge University Press.

Sidanius, Jim, Felicia Pratto, and Joshua L. Rabinowitz. 1994. "Gender, Ethnic Status, and Ideological Asymmetry: A Social Dominance Interpretation." *Journal of Cross-Cultural Psychology* 25 (June): 194–216.

Skowronski, John J., and Donald E. Carlston. 1987. "Social Judgment and Social Memory: The Role of Cue Diagnosticity in Negativity, Positivity, and Extremity Biases." *Journal of Personality and Social Psychology* 52 (#4, Summer): 689–99.

Smith, A. Wade. 1987. "Problems and Progress in the Measurement of Black Public Opinion." *American Behavioral Scientist* 30 (March/April): 441–55.

Smooha, Sammy, and Theodor Hanf. 1992. "The Diverse Modes of Conflict-Regulation in Deeply Divided Societies." *International Journal of Comparative Sociology* 33 (1–2): 26–47.

Sniderman, Paul M. 1975. *Personality and Democratic Politics*. Berkeley: University of California Press.

Sniderman, Paul M. 1993. "The New Look in Public Opinion Research." In *Political Science: The State of the Discipline II*, ed. Ada W. Finifter. Washington: American Political Science Association. Pp. 219–45.

Sniderman, Paul M., Richard A. Brody, and Philip E. Tetlock. 1991. *Reasoning and Choice: Explorations in Political Psychology*. New York: Cambridge University Press.

Sniderman, Paul M., Joseph F. Fletcher, Peter H. Russell, and Philip E. Tetlock. 1996. *The Clash of Rights: Liberty, Equality, and Legitimacy in Pluralist Democracy*. New Haven: Yale University Press.

Sniderman, Paul M., Joseph F. Fletcher, Peter H. Russell, Philip E. Tetlock, and Brian J. Gaines. 1991. "The Fallacy of Democratic Elitism: Elite

References

Competition and Commitment to Civil Liberties." *British Journal of Political Science* 21: 349–70.

Sniderman, Paul M., and Douglas B. Grob. 1996. "Innovation in Experimental Design in Attitude Surveys." *Annual Review of Sociology* 22: 377–99.

Sniderman, Paul M., Philip E. Tetlock, James M. Glaser, Donald Philip Green, and Michael Hout. 1989. "Principled Tolerance and the American Mass Public." *British Journal of Political Science* 19 (#1, January): 25–45.

Sperber, Ami D., Robert F. Devellis, and Brian Boehlecke. 1994. "Cross-Cultural Translation: Methodology and Validation." *Journal of Cross-Cultural Psychology* 25: 501–24.

Stouffer, Samuel C. 1955. *Communism, Conformity and Civil Liberties.* New York: Doubleday.

Strauss, A. C. P. 1995. "Die Goldstone-Kommissie." *Journal for Contemporary History* 20 (2): 155–79.

Strum, Philippa. 1999. *When the Nazis Came to Skokie: Freedom for Speech We Hate.* Lawrence, KS: University Press of Kansas.

Sullivan, John L., James E. Piereson, and George E. Marcus. 1979. "An Alternative Conceptualization of Political Tolerance – Illusionary Increases 1950s–1970s." *American Political Science Review* 73: 233–49.

———. 1982. *Political Tolerance and American Democracy.* Chicago: University of Chicago Press.

Sullivan, John L., Michal Shamir, Patrick Walsh, and Nigel S. Roberts. 1985. *Political Tolerance in Context: Support for Unpopular Minorities in Israel, New Zealand, and the United States.* Boulder, CO: Westview Press.

Sullivan, John L., Patrick Walsh, Michal Shamir, David G. Barnum, and James L. Gibson. 1993. "Why Are Politicians More Tolerant? Selective Recruitment and Socialization among Political Elites in New Zealand, Israel, Britain, and the United States." *British Journal of Political Science* 23 (January): 51–76.

Swilling, Mark, and Mark Phillips. 1989. "The Emergency State: Its Structure, Power and Limits." In *South African Review 5*, eds. Glenn Moss and Ingrid Obery. Johannesburg: Ravan. Pp. 68–90.

Tajfel, Henri. 1978. "Social Categorization, Social Identity and Social Comparison." In *Differentiation between Social Groups. Studies in the Social Psychology of Intergroup Relations*, ed. Henri Tajfel. New York: Academic Press. Pp. 61–76.

———. 1981. *Human Groups and Social Categories.* New York: Cambridge University Press.

Tajfel, Henri, and J. C. Turner. 1979. "An Integrative Theory of Intergroup Conflict." In *The Social Psychology of Intergroup Relations*, eds. S. Worchel and W. G. Austin. Monterey, CA: Brooks Cole.

Tate, Katherine. 1993. *From Protest to Politics. The New Black Voters in American Elections.* New York: Russell Sage.

Taylor, Donald M., and Fathah M. Moghaddam. 1994. *Theories of Intergroup Relations: International Social Psychological Perspectives.* Westport, CT: Praeger.

Thompson, Leonard, and Andrew Prior. 1982. *South African Politics.* Cape Town: David Philip.

Tourangeau, Roger, and A. Wade Smith. 1985. "Finding Subgroups for Surveys." *Public Opinion Quarterly* 49 (Fall): 351–65.

References

Truth and Reconciliation Commission. 1998. *Truth and Reconciliation Commission of South Africa Report*. Cape Town: Juta.

Tyler, Tom R., and Gregory Mitchell. 1994. "Legitimacy and the Empowerment of Discretionary Legal Authority: The United States Supreme Court and Abortion Rights." *Duke Law Journal* 43: 703–815.

Weingast, Barry R. 1997. "The Political Foundations of Democracy and the Rule of Law." *American Political Science Review* 91 (June): 245–63.

Weissberg, Robert. 1998. *Political Tolerance: Balancing Community and Diversity*. Thousand Oaks, CA: Sage Publications.

Whitefield, Stephen, and Geoffrey Evans. 1994. "The Russian Election of 1993: Public Opinion and the Transition Experience." *Post-Soviet Affairs* 10 (January/March): 38–60.

Willhoite, Fred H., Jr. 1977. "Evolution and Collective Intolerance." *Journal of Politics* 39: 667–84.

Winer, Jonathan M. 1997. "International Crime in the New Geopolitics: A Core Threat to Democracy." In *Crime and Law Enforcement in the Global Village*, ed. William F. McDonald. Cincinnati, OH: Anderson Publishing Company. Pp. 41–64.

Wyman, Matthew. 1994. "Russian Political Culture: Evidence from Public Opinion Surveys." *Journal of Communist Studies and Transition Politics* 10 (March): 25–54.

Zakaria, Fareed. 1997. "The Rise of Illiberal Democracy." *Foreign Affairs* (November/December 1997): 22–43.

Zaller, John R. 1992. *The Nature and Origins of Mass Opinion*. Cambridge: Cambridge University Press.

Zaller, John, and Stanley Feldman. 1992. "A Simple Theory of the Survey Response: Answering Questions versus Revealing Preferences." *American Journal of Political Science* 36 (#3, August): 579–616.

Books in the series